T0301605

Transforming Industrial Policy for the
Digital Age

Transforming Industrial Policy for the Digital Age

Production, Territories and Structural Change

Edited by

Patrizio Bianchi

Department of Economics and Management, University of Ferrara, Italy

Clemente Ruiz Durán

Faculty of Economics, National Autonomous University of Mexico

Sandrine Labory

Department of Economics and Management, University of Ferrara, Italy

Cheltenham, UK • Northampton, MA, USA

Published by
Edward Elgar Publishing Limited
The Lypiatts
15 Lansdown Road
Cheltenham
Glos GL50 2JA
UK

Edward Elgar Publishing, Inc.
William Pratt House
9 Dewey Court
Northampton
Massachusetts 01060
USA

A catalogue record for this book
is available from the British Library

Library of Congress Control Number: 2019938897

This book is available electronically in the **Elgar**online
Economics subject collection
DOI 10.4337/9781788976152

ISBN 978 1 78897 614 5 (cased)
ISBN 978 1 78897 615 2 (eBook)

Typeset by Servis Filmsetting Ltd, Stockport, Cheshire
Printed and bound in Great Britain by TJ International Ltd, Padstow, Cornwall

Contents

v

Contributors

Elisa Barbieri is Associate Professor at the University Cà Foscari in Venice, Italy and Member of c.MET05 (National Centre for Applied Economic Studies).

Marco Bellandi is Professor at the Department of Economics and Management, University of Florence, and Fondazione per la Ricerca e l'Innovazione, Italy.

Patrizio Bianchi is Professor of Applied Industrial Economics at the Department of Economics and Management, University of Ferrara, Italy.

Lukas Brun is a Faculty Fellow at the World Food Policy Center, Sanford School of Public Policy at Duke University, USA.

Ha-Joon Chang is Director of the Centre of Development Studies at the University of Cambridge, UK.

Lisa De Propris is Professor at the Birmingham Business School, University of Birmingham, UK.

Marco R. Di Tommaso is Professor of Applied Industrial Economics at the Department of Economics and Management, University of Ferrara, Italy, and Member of c.MET05 (National Centre for Applied Economic Studies) and EmiliaLab (The Universities of Emilia-Romagna Network of Economic Studies Departments).

Andrea Ferrannini is a PhD student at the Department of Economics and Management, University of Ferrara, Italy, and Member of c.MET05 (National Centre for Applied Economic Studies).

Gary Gereffi is Emeritus Professor of Sociology at Duke University, USA.

Jostein Hauge is a Research Associate at the Institute for Manufacturing at the University of Cambridge, UK.

Sandrine Labory is Associate Professor of Applied Industrial Economics at the Department of Economics and Management, University of Ferrara, Italy.

Jongho Lee is professor at the Department of Economics, Seoul National University, Seoul, Korea.

Keun Lee is Professor at the Department of Economics, Seoul National University, Seoul, Korea.

Jorge Máttar is ECLAC Consultant, Former Chief, Latin American and the Caribbean Institute of Economic and Social Planning, ECLAC.

Michael J. Piore is Emeritus Professor of Political Economy in the Department of Economics, Massachusetts Institute of Technology, USA.

Chiara Pollio is a Researcher at the Department of Economics and Management, University of Ferrara, Italy and Member of c.MET05 (National Centre for Applied Economic Studies) and of the EmiliaLab (The Universities of Emilia-Romagna Network of Economic Studies Departments).

Lauretta Rubini is Associate Professor of Applied Industrial Economics at the Department of Economics and Management, University of Ferrara, Italy, and Member of c.MET05 (National Centre for Applied Economic Studies).

Clemente Ruiz Durán is Professor at the School of Economy of the Universidad Nacional Autònoma de México, Mexico.

Enrica Santini is a Researcher at the Department of Economics and Management, University of Florence, and Fondazione per la Ricerca e l'Innovazione, Italy.

David W. Skinner is Professor of Political Economy in the Department of Economics, Massachusetts Institute of Technology, USA.

Mattia Tassinari is a Lecturer at the Department of Economics and Management, University of Ferrara, Italy, and Member of c.MET05 (National Centre for Applied Economic Studies).

James Zhan is Director of the Investment and Enterprise Division and the lead author of the UN *World Investment Report*, United Nations Conference on Trade and Development (UNCTAD).

Introduction

Patrizio Bianchi, Sandrine Labory and Clemente Ruiz Durán

The beginning of the twenty-first century is turning out to be full of disruptions and challenges for economies and societies. Climate change, world population growth, migratory pressures, are pressing challenges; the financial crisis has had a dramatic effect and many economies have had difficulties in recovering their pre-crisis development level.

Meanwhile, innovation and technological changes are accelerating, in various fields including genomics, nanotechnologies, information and communication technologies (ICTs) and big data, robotics and artificial intelligence, new materials, and others. ICTs, with the Internet of Things (IoT), the Cloud, big data, are allowing hyper-connection of people and objects and digitisation of production processes. The change induced is so disruptive that there is quite wide consensus that we are experiencing an industrial revolution, the fourth one. New means of production and new products are appearing and will continue doing so, changing individuals' life in important aspects, namely economic, social and cultural.

Globalisation has continued not so much in terms of volumes of goods and services traded, but in terms of volumes of data globally traded and exchanged. This 'digital globalisation' is having important socio-economic impact on countries and territories, through its effects on industries.

Many companies are investing in the new technologies to develop new processes and new products. Regarding the former, 'smart manufacturing' is diffusing, characterised by factories organised as systems of machines and robots, that are connected together and with the products, but also with the consumer who can send requests on product characteristics to the system, which adapts in real time to produce it. This new production system allows both large economies of scale and high economies of scope, so that it has been called 'mass customisation' (Bianchi and Labory, 2018a).

New market intermediaries have also emerged, namely online platforms that are expanding their businesses to all sorts of goods and services. Amazon is a primary player, which has become a global marketplace selling goods to people all over the world, except China where specific national platforms prevail. In 2000, a tiny fraction of the world population used the Internet, while almost half did so in 2015; most people use the Internet to access information on goods and services, and most use online marketplaces.

As argued by Bianchi and Labory (2018a), online platforms have had important implications for firms existing in industries, primarily by putting pressure on prices. Consumers can confront prices more easily and also get more information on products. In addition, small firms have been able to enter markets by selling their products on platforms and getting a share of the market of established firms. For instance, Yoox is a business created by an Italian entrepreneur in 2000, selling luxury clothing online; Uber has disrupted the taxi industry; Airbnb is challenging hotels; and online ticket booking is disrupting established physical travel and cultural ticket agencies. These companies were created very recently: Uber in 2009 and Airbnb in 2012.

The main advantage of online platforms is their ability to match users of the different sides by means of personal and business data they collect, exploiting economies of scope in large data sets. Thanks to these big data analytics and the development of algorithms, these companies can target ads, which are their main revenue source, but also suggest products according to preferences.

As a consequence, companies have to adopt new business models, creating their own platforms in order to directly interact with consumers, or using other platforms such as Amazon. The online market makes it easier for small companies to access the global market, since they can interact with consumers all over the world with an online platform; but it also makes them more vulnerable to the big platforms, which have the resources to accumulate and analyse the big data that small businesses do not develop so easily.

Big data are the strategic assets of companies: in the online community they collect data on consumers, on their preferences, past choices and purchases, which become even richer if these data can be matched with data on other choices made by these consumers, in their travels, leisure activities, purchase of other products. The companies that collect such rich sets of big data, such as Google or Amazon – namely, pure platform businesses – have large market power, and have become key market intermediaries, selling an ever-increasing range of products on their online platform.

As outlined by Brun et al. in Chapter 2 of this book, companies become 'light': the key asset is not the physical capital but the data, the big data that can be exchanged, accumulated and analysed.

In other words, market competition is changing. Products are more varied, more differentiated, and the marketplace is global and primarily digital, although physical shops have not disappeared.

Global value chains (GVCs) also transform (Bianchi and Labory, 2018a, 2018b). Existing GVCs reshape, taking advantage of the new technologies to reorganise production of existing products or launching new ones. One tendency that seems to be emerging is reshoring: many companies that have invested in smart manufacturing have reshored production in their home country or in advanced countries. When factories are organised as networks of machines and robots, less labour is needed, and the labour which is hired in the factory is highly skilled, able to identify and solve problems in the machines and robots, and reprogramme them when necessary. Smart manufacturing requires territories where highly skilled labour is available and where infrastructure is sufficiently developed, particularly connection infrastructure. New GVCs are also emerging as a result of the development of new products and processes generated from innovation and technological change.

Besides reshoring, another trend in production reorganisation that can be outlined is company focus on high phases of the production process, namely pre- and post-manufacturing. Manufacturing is increasingly performed by robots in smart factories, that can be located anywhere, provided there is access to energy, high-capacity Internet and materials. The key assets for a firm become its knowledge base, its technologies, its experiences, together with its capacity to identify market trends and consumers' tastes, and its capacity to innovate, to renew products and services.

However, beyond global trends it is still too early to outline systematic tendencies and evolution, or characteristics that would be valid for all firms across sectors. More research is needed on how production is transforming in the various sectors. This is important to provide answers to another important question which has been debated recently: the impact of the fourth industrial revolution on skills and jobs.

A characteristic that has been repeatedly mentioned regarding this fourth industrial revolution is its speed: smartphones appeared about a decade ago, yet they now represent a global product that almost all human beings on the planet own. Billions of people are connected through this product, exchanging data, getting information, and buying other products and services, since this product has become both a new market intermediary (buying goods through the various apps), a means of payment (no need to have a credit card in your pocket if it is registered on the smartphone), and a repository of all individual information (such as name, age, tastes and preferences, contacts, and so on).

The transformations implied by the industrial revolution are complex and deep. Structural change is multidimensional. It means adoption of new technologies, new production systems, which imply new skills in the labour force. Hence the adaptability of the labour force – namely, its capability to learn new skills – is an essential factor for structural changes. New knowledge and competencies may be required, implying the need for vocational training and also adaptation of the education system so that young people might get the preparation for new types of jobs. New sectors might emerge, implying the reform of institutions that provide new regulations (product standards, protection of intellectual property rights, contract law, and so on). Structural changes generally require institutional changes. This process might create systemic failures, in that institutions and productive sectors change at different speeds. One particular problem is the large amount of time needed to adapt skills provided in the educational systems. The latter might be changed, but it takes a generation to take full effect: only pupils having performed their whole schooling in the new system will have full preparation for the new skills. In addition, teachers have to be trained to be able to transmit new knowledge and skills to their students.

Structural changes arising in specific industries might have effects on other industries (due to complementarities) and on the whole economic system. Industrial policy must therefore be based on an analysis of productive processes, but also on analyses of the interactions between different productive processes. Favouring structural changes in one sector may have positive or negative impacts on other sectors; it may also impact upon the labour market, changing the skill required in the labour force, as well as wages. The analysis of trajectories of structural change must therefore be performed to choose specific trajectories and a mix of measures to favour the evolution of the economy towards these trajectories. Industrial policy has always been implemented in times of important structural changes for industries. Governments at various levels are concerned that the industries in the territory will be able to adapt, as well as develop in new ways.

So many questions are raised: can some trends be outlined in productive transformations? Are services more important than manufacturing? How should action be articulated at national and regional, but also supranational levels?

This book originates from a conference organized by the Emilia-Romagna Region of Italy in October 2017, aiming at reflecting on these crucial matters by creating a network of academics, economists from international organization, institutional and business stakeholders, as well as representatives of the civil society.

The book is not aimed at a review of industrial policy. The literature is now wide and there is consensus that it is useful and that it aims at favouring structural changes in industries (Rodrik, 2004, 2008; Chang, 1994, 2010; O'Sullivan et al., 2013; Bianchi and Labory, 2011, 2018a; Bailey et al., 2015; Noman and Stiglitz, 2016). The above-mentioned changes are structural and require industrial policy: the institutional framework has to adapt (think, for instance, of the new regulation needed for artificial intelligence, particularly for traffic with self-driving cars, but also for new medical treatments based on nanorobots introduced into the body to directly cure infected cells), and innovation, education and social policies respectively have to provide appropriate infrastructure and favour the development of adequate capabilities.

Bianchi and Labory (2018a, 2018b) analyse what industrial policy is needed today. They argue that in order to favour structural changes one has to look at the mechanisms of productive transformation. Structural changes imply developing new productive capabilities, which are necessary to reshape global value chains and favour the emergence of new ones. For this purpose, coordinated action is needed in the multilevel governance process: actions at regional, national and supranational levels must be coordinated and coherently implemented. They also argue that action at regional level is particularly important in order to prepare for the industrial revolution.

In this context, this book aims at realising a reflection on market trends, structural changes, and how much industrial policy currently implemented in countries really promotes structural changes and orientates industrial development towards specific and preferred paths.

The conference was intended as the first in a series of reflections on these very complex issues. It started from an analysis of the state of the art, hence industrial policies at national level, highlighting the different approaches and implemented actions. An analysis of current market trends – namely, globalisation and the disruptive impact of the fourth industrial revolution – was performed to outline the new issues that are raised in terms of industrial policy in this context. Finally, the conference concluded by outlining the role of territories. Briefly, territories have a role to play in mobilising tangible and intangible resources to build the capabilities necessary to make them hubs in the digital and globalised world. There are many examples of effective regional industrial policies, implemented coherently in a multi-level governance framework, which have contributed to making the regional territory attractive to businesses and oriented towards favourable industrial development paths. The Emilia-Romagna region is one case illustrated in Bianchi and Labory (2018a, 2018b). Innovation and high-tech is important, but industrial development concerns all sectors, so that even lagging regions can define and implement industrial policy that are appropriate to their local conditions. This is very important to induce a balanced industrial development and growth, which should be a primary aim of policy, as shown by current events such as Brexit and the rise of populism in many areas, as outlined by Michael Piore and David Skinner in the concluding Chapter 9 of this book. The chapter regards the United States of America (US), but its analysis applies to any place.

The book is organised as follows. In Chapter 1, Jostein Hauge and Ha-Joon Chang discuss the importance of manufacturing in economic development. They examine the various arguments that have been put forward for and against, and they show that it is indeed essential, and industrialisation remains a necessary phase of development. More precisely, the authors conclude that while both the potential for contribution to productivity growth and the tradability of services have increased, manufacturing remains the backbone of productivity growth and economic development. Economic development has hardly ever happened without industrialisation; manufacturing has a larger multiplier effect in the economy than services; the falling share of the manufacturing sector in gross domestic product (GDP) in many countries is somewhat of an illusion; manufactured goods remain far more tradable than services; and the supposed risk of automation of manufacturing jobs in developing countries is mostly hype without evidence.

Chapter 2 by Lukas Brun, Gary Gereffi and James Zhan analyses recent evolutionary trends in GVCs, with a particular focus on the implications of the adoption of the new technologies of the fourth industrial revolution (Industry 4.0). They argue that recent dynamics in GVCs include: rationalisation, in that lead firms have tended to reduce the number of suppliers; regionalisation, namely a concentration of production in broad regions, mainly North America, Europe and Asia; and resiliency and digitisation, which means the use of advanced data analytical tools and physical technologies to improve the digital connectivity and technological capabilities of supply chains. The authors outline three major effects of Industry 4.0 on GVCs and derive three possible scenarios of future evolution according to whether digital multinational organisations (MNEs) will develop in a complementary manner to existing firms (complementary scenario), will disrupt existing firms (displacement scenario), or whether existing firms will be able to adapt and develop alongside digital MNEs (adaptation scenario).

Chapter 3 by Keun Lee and Jongho Lee examines to what extent are countries prepared for the fourth industrial revolution, by looking at several dimensions of their National Innovation Systems (NISs). The focus is on five countries, namely South Korea, Germany, France, Italy and the United Kingdom (UK). Using patent data in the last decade, the authors compare five indicators: originality, cycle time of technologies, knowledge localisation, technological diversification, and inventor-level concentration of innovation activities. They conclude that the UK and Germany appear to be well prepared for the fourth industrial revolution, France has medium preparation, Italy exhibits low preparation, and the Korean NIS has good indicators but is still low in terms of originality.

These first chapters in Part I provide useful insights on the productive transformations occurring as a result of digital globalisation, namely the fourth industrial revolution, as well as its policy implications. Industrial policy aims at favouring structural changes in industries, so it is the main policy that has to be mobilised in order to favour the transition. As shown by Bianchi and Labory (2018a, 2018b), industrial policy in times of deep structural transformation such as an industrial revolution has to be designed and implemented jointly and coherently with other policies, particularly education and training, social and labour, infrastructure, trade, antitrust and regulation policies.

Part II of the book therefore looks at the lessons that can be drawn from past experiences of national industrial policies. To begin with, Chapter 4 by Marco Di Tommaso, Mattia Tassinari and Andrea Ferrarinni looks at the US industrial policy in the long run. The authors show that the US government has continuously promoted structural changes in its industries, through various means and actions that are analysed in the chapter.

In Chapter 5, Marco Di Tommaso, Chiara Pollio, Elisa Barbieri and Lauretta Rubini examine and show the essential role of industrial policy in the industrialisation process of China. An interesting focus of the chapter is on the 'specialized towns' programme, which reflects attention of the Chinese government to places, since it has favoured the agglomeration of industrial activities in some Chinese provinces. The programme has been successful in spurring industrial development in these areas; however, it has produced uneven development in the country, since other areas have been left behind.

In fact, Bianchi and Labory (2018a) outline that the risk of uneven development is generally high in times of industrial revolution. Previous industrial revolutions, from the first to the third, have tended to favour some places or regions at the expense of others. Consequently, unless governments intervened to rebalance development, disparities were created. The evidence of Industry 4.0 is that this risk also exists nowadays, implying a role for regional industrial policy (Bianchi and Labory, 2018b).

Chapter 6 by Jorge Máttar looks at industrial policy in Latin America and the Caribbean. He shows that past industrial policies have not been effective, because they missed actions to prepare industries to structural changes. For instance, many countries based their development on exports of raw materials and encountered problems when their prices fell. Industrial policy favouring upgrading – and particularly, in this case, the transformation of raw materials – could have helped to mitigate the negative effects of price reductions. Jorge Máttar therefore argues that the fourth industrial revolution could be taken as an occasion to adopt appropriate industrial policies, namely policies aimed at preparing the national industrial systems for the deep structural changes taking place and expected to take place in the future. The author delineates some principles and elements that these industrial policies should adopt. He stresses in particular the necessity for participative governance processes, where governments and stakeholders dialogue and interact in order to identify possible development paths and choose actions in favour of the chosen path.

Chapter 7 by Clemente Ruiz Durán shows the complexity of the challenges of today's global society and argues that industrial policy has a role to play in resolving these challenges. One particular issue which is outlined is that current structural changes require institutional adaptation, which is usually a slow process, while technologies and businesses change fast.

These chapters highlight that industrial development is an engine of social and cultural development. Industrial revolutions have profound impacts not only on economic, but also on social and cultural life. Industrial adaptation and industrial policy therefore have to take these socio-cultural implications into account in order to ensure an even development of the territory. The last two chapters of the book, in Part III, outline the risks of uneven development and the necessity of this comprehensive view in which the design and implementation of industrial policy should be considered.

Marco Bellandi, Lisa de Propris and Enrica Santini highlight in Chapter 8 that industrial policy has to pay attention to local specificities, and has to be comprehensive in the sense of taking all dimensions of development (not only economic, but also social) into account. This is important especially for the adaptation of small and medium-sized enterprise (SME) systems. They therefore delineate place-based industrial policies at the intersection between technological change and territories.

In Chapter 9, Michael Piore and David Skinner show that the risks of uneven development are reflected in the boom of reactionary populism in the US; due, according to the authors, to the implementation of wrong policies. The chapter argues that past policy paradigms such as the 'Washington consensus' or the 'Silicon Valley consensus' have failed, mainly because the structural adjustment processes vary across territories and countries, with different speeds and different characteristics. Each territory should design coherent policies favouring structural changes in an inclusive manner, starting from a dialogue with stakeholders. In particular, the authors stress the importance of the dialogue between businesses and schools so that appropriate skills are trained in workers.

More generally, they argue that the Keynesian paradigm should be referred to today; not to implement it straight away, but as a reference for a reflection on what type of policies are desirable today. This, they say, 'seems particularly important at the current moment, which in so many ways resembles the inter-war period where public policy was caught by surprise, unprepared and ill-equipped to respond to the political reaction against globalization'.

A political economy approach to industry analysis and industrial policy design and implementation thus seems highly relevant in these times of deep structural transformations (Bianchi and Labory, 2018c). There is indeed a real risk of not having the right tools for a full understanding of the changes in social and political relations that structure economic actions. We need to gain an understanding of complex social phenomena, using all the tools of interdisciplinary dialogue at our disposal, in order to avoid the reactions against globalization turning into a wave of anti-democratic closed-mindedness.

This book therefore aims at contributing to this need for a better comprehension of the ongoing structural transformations, by highlighting their structuring elements, namely innovation, territory, people's rights and institutions. The democratic development of our world will depend on how these elements are balanced in the near future.

REFERENCES

Bailey, D., Cowling, K. and Tomlinson, P. (eds) (2015), *New Perspectives on Industrial Policy for a Modern Britain*, Oxford University Press, Oxford.

Bianchi, P. and Labory, S. (2011), *Industrial Policy after the Crisis: Seizing the Future*, Edward Elgar Publishing, Cheltenham, UK and Northampton, MA, USA.

Bianchi, P. and Labory, S. (2018a), *Industrial Policy for the Manufacturing Revolution: Perspectives on Digital Globalisation*, Edward Elgar Publishing, Cheltenham, UK and Northampton, MA, USA.

Bianchi, P. and Labory, S. (2018b), 'What policies, initiatives or programmes can support attracting, embedding and reshaping GVCs in regions?', OECD and European Commission Project: Broadening Innovation Policy: New Insights for Regions and Cities, OECD, Paris.

Bianchi, P. and Labory, S. (2018c), 'The political economy of industry', in I. Cardinale and R. Scazzieri (eds), *The Palgrave Handbook of Political Economy* (Chapter 13), Palgrave Macmillan, Basingstoke.

Chang, H-J. (1994), *The Political Economy of Industrial Policy*, Macmillan, London.

Chang, H-J. (2010), 'Industrial policy: can we go beyond an unproductive confrontation?', Turkish Economic Association, Working Paper no. 2010/1, Ankara.

Noman, A. and Stiglitz, J.E. (2016), *Efficiency, Finance and Varieties of Industrial*

Policies, Initiative for Policy Dialogue at Columbia: Challenges in Development and Globalization, Columbia University Press, New York.

O'Sullivan, E., Andreoni, A., Lopez-Gomez, C. and Gregory, M. (2013), 'What is new in the new industrial policy? A manufacturing systems perspective', *Oxford Review of Economic Policy*, 29(2), 432–462.

Rodrik, D. (2004), 'Industrial policy for the 21st century', Working Paper, http://www.ksg.harvard.edu/rodrik/.

Rodrik, D. (2008), 'Normalizing industrial policy', Commission on Growth and Development, Working Paper no. 3, Washington, DC.

PART I

Impact of Industry 4.0 on manufacturing

1. The role of manufacturing versus services in economic development

Jostein Hauge and Ha-Joon Chang

INTRODUCTION

Throughout the history of capitalism, practically all countries that have transformed their economies from low to high income have done so through a process of industrialisation. In the field of development economics, the theories recognising the strong relationship between industrialisation and economic development (or the lack of industrialisation and no economic development) that we consider most seminal today started emerging in the 1950s and 1960s, and most importantly include contributions by Hollis Chenery, Alexander Gercschenkron, Albert Hirschman, Nicholas Kaldor, Simon Kuznets, Arthur Lewis, Gunnar Myrdal, Ragnar Nurkse and Raul Prebisch.[1]

However, not long after the publication of 'pro-industrialisation' theories by these scholars, the traditional view of the manufacturing sector as the engine of economic growth and development came to be challenged. It arguably started with Daniel Bell's 1976 book, *The Coming of Post-Industrial Society*. In the book, Bell argued that the wealth of future societies would rely less on the production of goods and more on the provision of services and the spread of a 'knowledge class' (Bell, 1976).[2] It seems as though Bell's prediction turned out to be correct. The services sector has come to dominate the economic structure of many economies in the latter half of the twentieth century and even more so in the twenty-first century,

---

[1] See Chenery (1960), Gerschenkron (1962), Hirschman (1958), Kaldor (1966), Kuznets (1966), Lewis (1954), Myrdal (1957), Nurkse (1961) and Prebisch (1950).

[2] However, Bell was not the first to argue that the services sector would come to play a more prominent role in the economy. Chenery (1960), Clark (1940), Fisher (1935) and Kuznets (1966) all theorised that the services sector as a share of total economic output would rise at the expense of the industrial sector, following a period of industrialisation. But they were not proponents of the post-industrial society discourse, as Bell was.

in terms of both output and employment. This trend is especially apparent in high-income countries, where the manufacturing sector is shrinking as share of gross domestic product (GDP) at the expense of a growing services sector.

A number of arguments have since emerged, claiming that in this 'post-industrial age', economies that want to grow and raise their productivity need to put more effort into developing their services sector (e.g., Baer and Samuelson, 1981; Bhagwati, 1984, 2010; Ghani, 2010; Ghani and O'Connel, 2014; Haskel and Westlake, 2017; Romer, 2012). In an interview with *Manufacturing and Technology News*, Michael Porter, one of the most well-known advocates of this post-industrial society discourse, has argued that services are where the high value is today:

> We used to think of services as flipping hamburgers, now we have to think of services as rocket science. Services are where the high value is today, not in manufacturing. Manufacturing stuff per se is relatively low value. That is why it is being done in China or Thailand. (McCormack, 2006, p. 1)

While the post-industrial society discourse is debated most fiercely in the context of high-income countries, it is also discussed in the context of developing countries. Like high-income countries, many developing countries are seeing the share of the manufacturing sector in their economies declining (see Figure 1.1[3]) – a development Palma (2005) has called 'premature de-industrialisation'.

Understanding the driving forces behind premature de-industrialisation, and more generally the industrialisation struggle that today's developing countries are facing, is beyond the scope of this chapter to tackle in detail.[4]

---

[3]   China is excluded from East and Southeast Asia because its inclusion would significantly affect the aggregate figures for that region. Like other world regions, manufacturing value-added as a share of GDP in China has decreased, from 39.9% in 1980 to 29.4% in 2016 (WDI, 2018). However, in China's case, we should be careful in interpreting this as de-industrialisation. First, the country's GDP has grown more than 30-fold since 1980 (at constant prices), meaning that manufacturing value-added would have to grow at an unimaginably high rate in order not decrease its share of GDP. Second, China's current figure for manufacturing value-added as share of GDP (29.4%) is a high figure by any standard.

[4]   Premature de-industrialisation is partly caused by decreasing relative prices of manufactured goods, especially those exported by developing countries. We will discuss this trend in greater detail in the section 'Argument 3: the smile on the smile curve has grown'. Additionally, the development literature highlights the 1980s policy shift towards neoliberalism – and thus the rejection of industrial policy – as a major cause of premature de-industrialisation. For example, UNCTAD (2016a) states, 'Unilateral trade opening, financial deregulation, regressive income redistribution and the retreat of the developmental state led to premature deindustrialisation in several countries, notably in Latin America'.

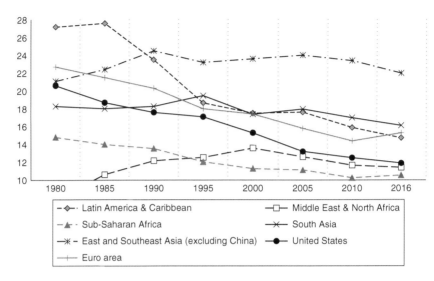

Sources: Calculations based on WDI database and UNCTAD statistics database.

Figure 1.1   Manufacturing value-added as percentage of GDP in world regions, 1980–2016

However, it is important to note that this phenomenon is partly driving the belief of the post-industrial society in developing countries. For example, in its recent World Economic Outlook, the International Monetary Fund states that 'a shift in employment from manufacturing to services need not hinder economy-wide productivity growth and the prospects for developing economies to gain ground toward advanced-economy income levels' (IMF, 2018, p. 129).

In this chapter, we will summarise and analyse the arguments on both sides of the debate on development strategies of developing countries: those that are pro-services and those that are pro-manufacturing. The chapter first presents the pro-services arguments. It then presents the pro-manufacturing arguments in a way that critically engages with the narrative and the evidence of the pro-services arguments.

We acknowledge that there are reasons for developing countries to take the post-industrial society discourse seriously. Some services are characterised by higher tradability and more productivity growth potential than before, and it seems that developing countries will have a hard time breaking the 'middle-income trap' without specialising in at least some high-value services. But we conclude that, unless you are a small and unusual economy that can specialise in one or two activities,[5] you will not achieve sustained economic development without developing an internationally competitive manufacturing sector.

THE POST-INDUSTRIAL SOCIETY DISCOURSE: PRO-SERVICES ARGUMENTS

Argument 1: Services Contribute More to Productivity Growth and Technological Development than They Used To

Developments in information and communication technology (ICT) and massive increases in the size of firms mean that scale economies are more easily achieved in a range of services (Hallward-Driemeier and Nayyar, 2018), and that it is more profitable to procure some services from specialist providers rather than produce them within a manufacturing firm (the latter largely having been the case in the past) (Nayyar, 2013).

Most importantly, we are seeing increasing incidences of scale economies in services that use digital technology and/or are highly digitalised. In some digitalised services, the marginal cost of providing an additional unit of service has actually come close to zero. Think about data centres and search engines, whose characteristics are not too different from how economists are taught to think about manufacturing operations: fixed assets are costly (for example, server farms, cooling systems, secure sites, and so on) but costs rapidly decrease with scale. These features are also true for media streaming services. For example, Netflix and Spotify can deliver their services around the globe in a flash. By the end of 2017, Netflix had 118 million paying subscribers, while Spotify had 65 million. Only seven years before that, both services had barely any subscribers (Statista, 2018).

Services have also become more closely linked to innovation. A common way to measure an economy's rate of innovation and technological development has been to look at how much research and development (R&D) is being carried out; and there is clear evidence that R&D is focusing more on services. On a global scale, R&D expenditure in services increased from an annual average of 6.7% of total business R&D during 1990–1995 to 17% during 2005–2010[6] (WTO, 2013).

---

5   For example, a small economy that is rich in natural resources (for example, Brunei, Kuwait, Oman, Qatar), or that specialises in being a financial haven (for example, Monaco, Lichtenstein), or specialises in tourism (for example, Malta).

6   However, some of this increase in services' share of R&D is most likely attributable to outsourcing of R&D to specialised laboratories that are now being reclassified from

Companies providing the high-tech digitalised services mentioned above, like Netflix and Spotify, are mostly based in high-income countries. But there is also evidence that services in developing countries are showing productivity-enhancing characteristics. A study conducted by Cruz and Nayyar (2017) on six low- and middle-income countries – Brazil, China, Egypt, India, Nigeria and Russia – found that ICT service activities in these countries are as technology-intensive (as measured by a range of learning-by-doing and innovation metrics) as the manufacture of electronics. ICT services have had a particularly positive impact in India, where the growth of such services is closely associated with the increase in economic growth since the late 1990s (McMillan et al., 2017).

Also in Africa, the increase in economic growth since the late 1990s has been associated with an expansion of services. While Africa has experienced almost no structural change in the traditional sense, from agriculture to manufacturing, it has experienced some structural change from agriculture to services (McMillan et al., 2017). According to UNECA's *Economic Report on Africa* in 2015, Africa's services sector grew at an annual rate of 5.8% in 2000–2012, higher than the world average growth rate of services. The report stresses that growth of services and the growth of the continent's GDP are highly correlated, although it is more careful about claiming a causal link in any direction. The growth has been strongest in ICT services, transport services (mostly airlines) and tourism (UNECA, 2015). Many of these services earn foreign exchange, contributing to easing severe balance of payments constraints in many African countries.

Argument 2: Services Have Become More Tradable

Traditionally, manufacturing has been viewed as a stronger driver of economic development than services because all manufacturing products can in theory be exported. Exports not only ease a country's balance of payments constraints, but they also make economies of scale more easily achieved through specialisation. Most services, on the other hand, cannot be traded. This is because they require proximity between the consumer and producer. Think about eating in a restaurant, getting a haircut, having a medical check-up or getting your house cleaned.

However, technological developments – particularly the decline in the cost of phone calls and use of the Internet – and the reduction of regulatory trade barriers have made more services tradable (Bhagwati, 1984;

---

manufacturing to services, and better measurement of R&D in services (Hallward-Driemeier and Nayyar, 2018). We will discuss this further in the next section.

Ghani and Kharas, 2010). These, most importantly, include information, communication, banking, insurance and business-related services. The poster child of services-based trade success is the United Kingdom (UK), where trade in services now accounts for 19.4% of GDP – roughly 50% higher than the world average (WDI, 2018) – thanks to growth in trade of mainly financial and business services.

India is another country that has achieved success through exporting services. In fact, it has become the world's largest exporter of 'Telecommunications, computer, and information services', with an export value in this category of $74 billion in 2014 (Loungani et al., 2017, p. 30). According to Bosworth and Collins (2008), this increase in exports is due not only to more services being 'produced', but also to increasing productivity of India's services. The country's total factor productivity in services grew by 2.4% between 1980 and 2006, twice the level of total factor productivity growth in both industry and agriculture. Hyderabad, the capital of Telangana, is hailed as the prime example of services-led growth in India. Experiencing a 45-fold increase in services exports between 1998 and 2008 (Ghani and Kharas, 2010), it has become India's hub for ICT-related services, thus earning the nickname 'Cyberabad'.

A third example is Rwanda, a country that in the last few years has increased its foreign exchange earnings considerably through the expansion of tourism services, such as gorilla viewing. In fact Rwanda, and many other African countries such as Uganda, Tanzania and Tunisia, report that tourism is the top single earner of foreign exchange for their respective countries (Chang et al., 2016).

Argument 3: The Smile on the Smile Curve has Grown

The smile curve – coined by Stan Shih, Acer's[7] chief executive oficer in the early 1990s – is an illustration of the value-adding potentials at different stages of a value chain. It suggests that services such as R&D, product design (the left side of the smile), branding, advertising and retail (the right side of the smile) constitute a larger share of value-added than the manufacturing and assembly process (the bottom part of the smile). For example, Ali-Yrkko et al. (2011) found that only one-third of the value of a Nokia N95 phone comes from manufacturing: making the parts (33%) – processors, memory chips, integrated circuits, displays and cameras – and assembling the phone (2%). Two-thirds of the value comes from services, such as support services (30%), licences (4%), distribution (4%), retailing

---

[7]   The Taiwanese electronics company.

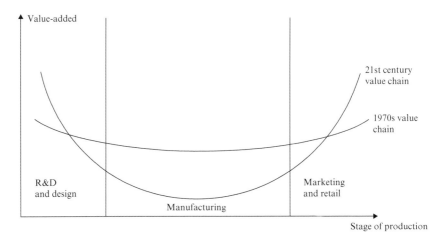

Figure 1.2   The growing smile of value chains

(11%) and operating profit (16%). Since the 1970s, the smile on the smile curve has grown (WIPO, 2017), suggesting that manufacturing is becoming less profitable and services are becoming more profitable; at least, those services that are part of a 'production' value chain (Figure 1.2).[8]

Kaplinsky (2005) confirms this trend: after sustained growth in the prices of globally traded manufactures until the early 1980s, we have witnessed an aggregate relative decline in these prices, most significantly for those exported by developing countries. Using more recent data, Milberg and Winkler (2013) find a similar result by looking at the price manufactured imports from developing countries into the United States (US). They find that clothing, footwear, textiles, furniture and toys have all experienced a 40% import price decline relative to US consumer prices from 1986 to 2006.

The growth of the smile curve is a result of many factors. First, as value chains have become global, several transnational corporations based in the West that derive profits from 'intangible' parts of the value chains have expanded their global reach and power. Since the early 2000s, a

---

[8]   The smile curve as an illustration of value capture in a value chain has shortcomings, though. First, some manufacturing activities are high value and do therefore not fit into this typology (examples being the manufacture of machine tools, lasers, medical imaging systems and aircraft propulsion systems). Thus, the smile curve is more fitting to describe manufacturing value capture in developing countries rather than advanced economies. Second, it is debatable whether services that depend on engineering know-how, such as R&D and industrial design, should be counted as separate from manufacturing. This point will be discussed further in the 'Pro-Manufacturing' section.

handful of firms have accounted for 50% or more of the market share in practically every global industry (Chang et al., 2016). In essence, a small number of actors are appropriating increasing shares of profits over a larger market, accruing these from technological dominance (fortified by strong protection of intellectual property rights), brand name recognition, and privileged access to low-cost capital.

In particular, branding is becoming a key strategy by which these corporations make profits. We are seeing this most prominently in industries where production technology is now standardised, such as apparel, footwear, consumer electronics and, to some extent, automobiles. The profits of the manufacturing and assembly stages of these global value chains – activities that are often outsourced to companies in developing countries – are being squeezed by the sheer power that these transnational companies have. In the words of Ford Chairman William Clay Ford Jr, 'It's easy to build a car. It's harder to build a brand' (Davis, 2009, p. 200). Some brand power is associated with considerable technological design content (such as Apple), but the maintenance of brand loyalty is usually the main source of rent generation (think about the marketing and advertising efforts by Nike).

Second, the profits of the manufacturing and assembly stages of global value chains are shrinking because of increased competition among developing countries. With greater participation of China and other Southeast Asian countries in the global economy, the developing-country share of low-tech manufacturing exports has almost tripled since 1980, and the global pool of unskilled labour has doubled since 1990 (Hauge, 2018). Alongside untapped capacity in the Asian production system, the number of people looking for unskilled work in the manufacturing sector in Africa is also rapidly increasing. All of the above means that developing countries have to find a way to develop capabilities in the services segments of global value chains. If not, they will end up capturing decreasing value at the bottom of the smile curve.

Argument 4: New Technological Developments Will Make Manufacturing Jobs in Developing Countries Redundant

With the advent of the so-called fourth industrial revolution – technological breakthroughs associated with things such as artificial intelligence, robotics, the Internet of Things, autonomous vehicles, and three-dimensional (3D) printing – there is a growing fear that manufacturing will become less reliant on labour. International development organisations are therefore suggesting that developing countries should start looking for alternative ways to absorb surplus labour (e.g., UNCTAD, 2016b; World Bank, 2016).

A study by Manyika et al. (2017) shows that, with currently demonstrable technologies, 60% of all occupations in the world contain at least 30% technically automatable activities. These technically automatable activities represent 1.2 billion jobs. In a breakdown of economic sectors by activity type, the study reveals that manufacturing is in the top three among automatable activities, where 60% of jobs can potentially be automated.

Developing countries typically specialise in manufacturing that is highly labour-intensive, raising the 'automation alarm' to even higher levels in the developing-country context. The World Bank's 2016 World Development Report estimates that two-thirds of all jobs in developing countries are susceptible to automation (World Bank, 2016). In particular, assembly manufacturing stands at risk of automation. For example, sewing machine operators are currently 100% automatable (Manyika et. al., 2017). China stands out as the developing country most rapidly automating production. The stock of industrial robots in China increased from 25 000 in 1995 to 206 000 in 2015. By 2018, this number was expected to reach 400 000, which will give China the highest stock of industrial robots in the world (Hallward-Driemeier and Nayyar, 2018).

Africa is another region where people are worrying about the potential negative impact of automation. The impact of automation in Africa is understudied, but if we assume that labour-intensive manufacturing will become drastically less labour-intensive, this will have dire consequences for industrialisation in most African countries. Most importantly because Africa's population is growing at an alarming rate: by 2030, the continent is expected to have 1.6 billion people. With the current youth bulge in Africa, an estimated 800 million of these are expected to be eligible for work in 2030, compared to 460 million in 2010 (Fengler and Rowden, 2013).

MANUFACTURING MATTERS: PRO-MANUFACTURING ARGUMENTS

Counter-Argument 1: Economic Growth and Development has Very Rarely Happened Without Industrialisation

The arguments supporting the manufacturing sector as the main driver of economic development are rooted in the clear observation that, throughout the history of capitalism (in both the near and the distant past), practically all countries that have transformed their economies from low- to high-income have done so through a process of industrialisation.

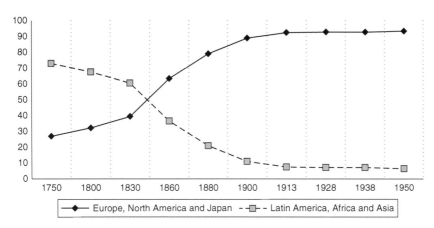

Source: Bairoch (1982).

Figure 1.3   Distribution of global manufacturing output (%)

Between 1750 and 1950, the West's gradual establishment as the world economic hegemon – starting with the industrial revolution in Britain in the late eighteenth century – was also a process of establishing itself as the world's manufacturing hegemon (Figure 1.3). In 1750, Europe, North America and Japan constituted only 27% of manufacturing production in the world.[9] But by 1900, those regions made up 90% of world manufacturing production (Bairoch, 1982). Unsurprisingly, economic growth rates between the West and 'the rest' started diverging as well. Between 1820 and 1950, per capita GDP in the West grew at an average annual rate of 1.08% per year, compared to only 0.29% per year in the rest of the world.[10] By the early twentieth century, the world was clearly divided into two groups of economies: one was rich and industrialised, the other was poor and dependent on agriculture and natural resources. Industrialisation came to be seen as the main driver of economic development.

After World War II, the world's manufacturing landscape started to change. As developing countries were given more autonomy in steering policies towards their own development objectives, they implemented policies to promote industrialisation. As a result, a significant share of the world's manufacturing production has relocated to these countries,

---

[9]   In the seventeenth and first half of the eighteenth century, global manufacturing was dominated by China (porcelain and silks) and India (cotton textiles) (Nayyar, 2013).
[10]   The West includes Western Europe, Western Offshoots, Eastern Europe, the former USSR and Japan. The rest of the world includes Asia, Africa and Latin America. Calculations are made from the Maddison Online Database with 1996 Geary-Khamis dollars.

particularly to East Asia. The star performers include Hong Kong, Singapore, South Korea and Taiwan, whose pace of industrialisation and economic growth between roughly 1960 and 1990 was unprecedented in history, and still is. Since then, they have been followed by countries including China, Indonesia, Malaysia, Thailand and Vietnam.

According to a study of 'growth miracles' by the World Bank in 2008, only 13 countries in the world have been able to sustain an annual growth rate of 7% or higher since 1950. Only two countries, both with small populations and highly idiosyncratic economic structures – Botswana and Oman[11] – are among the group of 13 that have not grown on the basis of industrialisation (World Bank, 2008). A similar study has been carried out by Ocampo et al. (2009). They constructed a sample of 57 developing and transition economies grouped into 12 regions, and looked at the relationship between the production structure of the economy and economic growth between 1970 and 2007. They found that GDP growth rates were positively correlated with an increase in industry's share of GDP in all regions that went through sustained periods of growth.

The relationship between growth of the manufacturing sector and sustained economic growth has in fact been documented as robust by many more scholars (e.g., McMillan and Rodrik, 2011; Nayyar, 2013; Rodrik, 2007; Szirmai, 2009; Szirmai and Verspagen, 2011). Thus, it is not surprising that no country, except a few states exceptionally rich in oil (for example, Brunei, Kuwait, Qatar) or very small financial havens (for example, Monaco, Lichtenstein), has achieved high and sustainable standards of living without developing its manufacturing sector.[12] This is why the terms 'industrialised country' and 'developed country' are often used interchangeably.

If we look in greater detail at the countries that have experienced de-industrialisation, or premature de-industrialisation, we see a clear trend of decelerating economic growth, as the manufacturing sector shrank and the service sector expanded. For example, Organisation for Economic Co-operation and Development (OECD) countries have on aggregate experienced a growth slowdown since the 1980s (WDI, 2018). In the United States, it is no coincidence that the 2016 presidential campaign saw the emergence of two candidates, at opposite ends of the political spectrum (Bernie Sanders and Donald Trump), campaigning for a manufacturing renaissance. In Latin America – the region that most notably experienced

---

[11]   Botswana has amassed its wealth from precious stones (diamonds), while Oman has done so through oil.

[12]   Neither Botswana nor Oman are mentioned, as their current level of GDP per capita arguably does not qualify for having achieved 'high and sustainable standards of living'.

premature de-industrialisation – the decline in manufacturing as share of GDP also caused a growth slowdown (Palma, 2005, 2014). In Africa, premature de-industrialisation caused a decline in economic growth.[13]

In summary, economic development has never happened without industrialisation, apart from in a few countries with highly idiosyncratic structures. Moreover, countries and regions that have de-industrialised or prematurely de-industrialised have experienced a slowdown in economic growth or, at worst, declining economic growth.

Counter-Argument 2: Manufacturing Still Remains the Driver of Productivity Growth and Technological Development

As highlighted earlier in this chapter, it is important to acknowledge that some services have increased their potential for productivity growth and technological development. But the manufacturing sector still remains the driver of productivity growth and technological development. Part of the reason for this can be found in Nicholas Kaldor's three growth laws, which are perhaps the most classic endorsements of manufacturing as the engine of economic growth.

The three laws postulate the following. First, the growth of GDP is positively correlated with the growth of the manufacturing sector, in part explained by the absorption of surplus labour from agriculture to industry. Second, the productivity of the manufacturing sector is positively correlated with output growth of the manufacturing sector (also known as Verdoorn's law). This is attributed to the increasing returns to scale of the manufacturing sector, both static and dynamic. The former refers to output level or sector size, while the latter signifies the effect of learning-by-doing, which is a function of both cumulative past output and/or cumulative production experience over time. Third, the productivity of non-manufacturing is positively correlated with the growth of the manufacturing sector, because of technological spillovers effects from the manufacturing sector to other sectors (Kaldor, 1966).

The superior productivity potential mentioned in Kaldor's second law is an important point (building especially on the work on increasing returns by Young, 1928). Economies of scale are more easily achieved

---

[13]   When neoliberal reforms were imposed in Africa in the 1980s, state support for industrialisation was dismantled and the manufacturing sector went into decline. GDP per capita in Africa also declined, at an annual average rate of 1.6% between 1981 and 1994 (WDI, 2018). Economic growth in Africa has picked up since the mid-1990s, but the growth is highly volatile and tends to swing in tandem with price fluctuations of primary commodities (Pilling, 2016; Taylor, 2015). The share of manufacturing in economic output in Africa is currently the lowest of all regions of developing countries in the world, at around 11% (WDI, 2018).

in the manufacturing sector, as manufacturing activities lend themselves more easily to mechanisation and chemical processing than do other types of economic activities. The ease of spatially concentrating manufacturing production is also an important factor behind the greater productivity potential. Agriculture is more constrained in terms of space, soil and climate. And some services activities are, by their very nature, impervious to productivity increases. Chang (2014, Chapter 7) provides the example of producing music: if a string quartet trots through a 27-minute piece in nine minutes, we will not say that its productivity has trebled.

It is also important to emphasise the third law, as many people tend to forget that productivity growth in other sectors of the economy are often a result of innovations in the manufacturing sector. Think about how the world's most productive agricultural economies are heavy users of chemicals, fertilisers, pesticides and agricultural machinery, and how the world's most productive service economies rely on top-tier computer technology, transport equipment and, in some instances, mechanised warehouses.

These also take form through organisational innovations that originate from the manufacturing sector. For example, many fast food restaurants use assembly techniques in their kitchens, and some even deliver food on a conveyor belt ('YO! Sushi' being the famous example). As another example, large retail chains often apply modern inventory management techniques that were developed in the manufacturing sector (Chang et al., 2013).

The importance of the manufacturing sector for a country's overall innovation infrastructure cannot be highlighted enough. Even in advanced countries, where manufacturing production is supposed to have been on the decline since the early 1990s, the bulk of innovation happens in the manufacturing sector. In the US, firms associated mainly with industrial production still employ 64% of all scientists and engineers, and the manufacturing sector accounts for 70% of industrial R&D (Bonvillan, 2012).

In short, our discussion in this section shows that many services 'import' technology from the manufacturing sector. In the next subsection, we will see not only that many services are productive because of imported technology from the manufacturing sector, but also that their existence is dependent on a manufacturing core.

Counter-Argument 3: The Existence of Services is Largely Dependent on a Manufacturing Core, More Than the Other Way Around

In the previous section, we mentioned how the productivity of manufacturing spills over to services. Additionally, many services are dependent on manufacturing firms as customers, and would not exist without a manufacturing core. Hirschman (1958) made an important contribution to understanding the spillovers from the manufacturing sector to other sectors of the economy. He argued that all sectors are linked to one another through backward and forward linkages, but that the manufacturing sector is characterised by stronger backward and forward linkages than other sectors of the economy, thus acting as the main engine of economic development.

Daniel J. Meckstroth's recent paper, 'The Manufacturing Value Chain is Much Bigger Than You Think!' (Meckstroth, 2017), illustrates Hirschman's point in a useful way. He provides the example of a manufacturing plant, and shows how it stimulates many domestic service activities in the upstream supply chain and the downstream sales chain. The upstream supply chain includes corporate and contract R&D services, outsourced professional services for manufacturers and distributors, transport of inputs used in production, and utilities provision for the manufacturing plant and its distribution facilities (for example, electricity, water and gas). The downstream sales chain includes transport of the manufactured goods to port or market, wholesale and warehousing operations, retail operations, and aftermarket maintenance and repair services of the final product. Based on this framework for understanding how manufacturing stimulates other economic activities, Meckstroth calculates a domestic manufacturing value-added 'multiplier' in the United States of 3.6. This means that for every dollar of domestic manufacturing value-added in the United States destined for manufactured goods for final demand, another $3.60 of value-added is generated elsewhere in the domestic economy.

However, every economic activity stimulates another economic activity. This means that one could also argue that, just as manufacturing stimulates services, services stimulate manufacturing. But evidence shows that manufacturing has a stronger multiplier effect than services. The seminal study on this was conducted by Park and Chan (1989), who found that the manufacturing sector generates two to three times more output in the rest of the economy than the services sector does. More recent studies also confirm this. Pilat and Wolfl (2005) estimate that 29% of the manufacturing workforce in France contribute indirectly to the production of non-manufacturing output, whereas only 13% of the services workforce contribute indirectly to the production of non-services output. Kuan (2017) shows that in Singapore the manufacturing sector has stronger value-added spillovers to the services sector than vice versa: every 100 new manufacturing jobs are associated with 27 new non-manufacturing jobs. By contrast, every 100 new services jobs are associated with only three additional manufacturing jobs.

Not only do many services depended on a manufacturing core, though: some of them are also by their very nature linked to manufacturing. These most importantly include industrial R&D, innovation, product design and other engineering-related services. Such services depend on manufacturing know-how, and one could make a strong case for having such services counted as manufacturing in the national accounts, which is currently not the case.

Berger (2015) shows that, in some industries, the R&D and manufacturing process are close to inseparable. For example, in solar power the most promising R&D and innovation involves cheaper and more efficient ways of manufacturing photovoltaics. The innovation is in the manufacturing. Similarly, Pisano and Shih (2012) argue that it does not make sense to separate manufacturing from many of the services that are embedded in the manufacturing process. They propose that we should think in terms of the 'industrial commons' instead, which they define as: 'The R&D and manufacturing infrastructure, know-how, process-development skills, and engineering capabilities embedded in firms, universities, and other organizations that provide the foundation for growth and innovation in a wide range of industries' (Pisano and Shih, 2012, p. 2). Through various industry case studies, they show how the United States has lost much of its innovation infrastructure to competitor countries in East Asia, because the US initially outsourced manufacturing operations to these countries but failed to realise how closely innovation and design services were linked to the manufacturing process. This has implications for how we understand the smile curve we introduced earlier in the chapter. If we classify industrial R&D and product design as manufacturing activities, this suddenly means that manufacturing value-added increases its share of total value in the value chain.

Counter-Argument 4: The Illusion of De-industrialisation

At the very core of the post-industrial society discourse is the observation that the manufacturing sector is contributing less to total economic output in most of the world's economies. However, a significant part of this decline is an illusion.

First, the declining share of manufacturing in total economic output in many countries is in some part due to reclassification of economic activities rather than an actual change in these countries' productive structures. For example, in the list of economic activities in the Standard Industrial Classification (SIC) codes made by the Office for National Statistics in the UK, companies are classified according to the activity in which their largest number of employees is engaged. This means that a company that both makes and delivers a product will be classified into either manufacturing or services, not both, depending on the number of people working in each category. MMEG (2016) uses the example of ABC Computers Ltd, a company that employs 35 people, 20 of whom are employed to make computers and 15 to deliver computers. This company ends up being classified in the manufacturing category even though it employs almost half of its workforce in a non-manufacturing activity. However, if ABC Computers Ltd outsources the delivery of its products to a delivery company in the same country, there is suddenly an increase in services as share of total output in the economy, without this really being the case.

This outsourcing has actually been happening on a large scale in many countries in the last few years: many services that used to be provided in-house in manufacturing firms (for example, delivery, catering, security guards, design, programming, marketing, analytics, and so on) are now supplied by independent services companies (Chang, 2014, Chapter 7). Additionally, some manufacturing companies that have not started outsourcing their service activities have instead applied to be reclassified as services firms, even though they still conduct some manufacturing. This is mainly because the manufacturing share in their total output is falling. A UK government report estimates that up to 10% of the fall in manufacturing employment between 1998 and 2006 in the UK may be due to this reclassification effect (Chang, 2014, Chapter 7).

Why is the manufacturing share in these companies' total output falling relative to services, though? Looking at countries going through the de-industrialisation process in the 1980s and the 1990s, Rowthorn and Ramaswamy (1999) argue that the main explanation for this trend – and, more generally, the trend of a relative decrease in the size of the manufacturing sector – is that productivity in manufacturing grows faster than in services. A more recent study by Tregenna (2009) similarly shows that the trend of de-industrialisation in some countries is happening because the labour-intensity of manufacturing declines more rapidly over time compared to services; that is, manufacturing has higher productivity.

As a result of this greater productivity potential of manufacturing, prices of manufactured goods have declined relative to that of services, resulting in a falling share of manufacturing in total economic output. This is an important observation: de-industrialisation is not caused by the growing irrelevance of manufacturing, as some proponents of the post-industrial society discourse suggest, but rather because manufacturing is characterised by higher productivity growth potential.

We should also note that the relative price decline of manufactured goods is a result of relative price increases of services as well. Because the services sector has lower potential for productivity growth, income growth in advanced economies, combined with the fact that many services are not tradable, has led to higher wages and prices in the services sector (Baumol, 1967), as well as an increased employment share (Rowthorn and Wells, 1987).

When this relative price effect is taken into account and the shares of different sectors are recalculated in constant prices, as opposed to current prices, the share of manufacturing has in fact not fallen very much in most high-income countries in recent decades. In some of them, such as the US, Switzerland, Finland and Sweden, when calculated in constant prices, it has actually increased (Chang, 2014, Chapter 7).

Counter-Argument 5: Manufactured Goods are Still More Tradable Than Services

In 'Argument 2', we highlighted that services have become more tradable, mainly thanks to advances in ICT. This is great news for developing countries that struggle with developing an internationally competitive manufacturing sector; we cited the examples of India and Rwanda, countries that have found ways to increase their foreign exchange holdings through developing tourism services and information services, respectively.

But while this is good news in part, the bad news for countries that try to specialise only in services is that the increased tradability of some services is little more than a drop in the ocean of international trade. World trade in services as a share of total world trade has more or less remained unchanged since we started counting international trade in services: it increased from 20% in 1980 to 22.5% in in 2016 (WDI, 2018). Yes, this is an increase, but a very small increase for a 36-year time period during which we are supposed to have witnessed the emergence of the post-industrial society. The remainder of international trade is trade in goods.

Trade in goods dominates international trade because, as we have said, most services require the consumer and producer to be in the same location. And even some producer and business services that can in theory be traded will in many instances locate within the national boundaries of the firms that they serve. For example, in the UK and US, software services, information technology services, R&D services and management consultancy services are often developed and specialised to serve a core manufacturing activity in the country (Pisano and Shih, 2012; OLS, 2017).

Countries with very small populations can afford to export only services, such as Lichtenstein, Malta, Monaco and the Seychelles. But once you start moving into the territory of countries with just a few million people, it becomes more difficult. All countries need manufactured goods, and for countries with larger populations it is simply not possible to afford to import all manufactured goods. This is part of the reason why many developing countries have tight capital controls: foreign exchange reserves are smaller because they have to import most manufactured goods (and because what they export is low value).

India, despite experiencing an export boom in services, still has a trade deficit because its trade surplus in services covered only 51% of its trade deficit in goods in 2017. Only a few years earlier, in 2010, its trade surplus in services covered only 31% of its trade deficit in goods (WDI, 2018). A big part of this improvement in the trade balance is that India has started producing more manufactured goods, both for domestic consumption and for export. The UK, which we also highlighted as a service-based success story, has been consistently struggling with a trade deficit since the early 2000s because its trade surplus in services cannot cover its trade deficit in goods, as in India (ONS, 2018).

Countries that want to be successful in international trade and have a healthy trade balance over time have to develop or retain a strong manufacturing base. With the exception of countries with very tiny populations, relying on exports of services is not enough. In the twenty-first century, 'things' are still what mainly cross borders.

Counter-Argument 6: Technological Developments Will Not Steal Manufacturing Jobs

The fear that our jobs will be made redundant by machines is not new. In fact, it has been around since the Luddites protested in England in 1811–16. The Luddites were a group of textile workers who destroyed machinery as a form of protest because they feared that their skills would go to waste as machines gradually replaced their roles in the textile factories.

Two hundred years later, the textile industry is still highly labour-intensive, and so are a range of other manufacturing industries. In fact, the predicted disruption of the so-called fourth industrial revolution on labour markets is mostly hype at this point: for now, 3D printing and robotics are used in relatively few countries. The existence of a certain technology does not translate into an easily applicable technology or a cost-efficient technology. The studies by Manyika et al. (2017) and the World Bank (2016) cited earlier in this chapter, suggesting that more than half of current occupations worldwide stand at risk of automation, have not gone unchallenged. For example, Arnzt et al. (2016) find that the share of current jobs in OECD countries that stand at risk of automation is only 6–12%. In developing countries, the threat to jobs of automation is found to be even lower, at 2–8% of current jobs (Ahmed and Chen, 2017). The reason for this is that the tasks considered most susceptible to automation are those that are done mostly by workers in the middle of the global skills distribution – blue-collar workers in high-income countries – and in countries than can cost-efficiently deploy these new technologies (Acemoglu and Autor, 2011). Hallward-Driemeier and Nayyar (2018) show how the manufacture of electronics, pharmaceuticals, electrical machinery and equipment stand at higher risk of automation than the manufacture of textiles and garments, leather products, wood products and basic metals.

Moreover, the assumption that the adoption of new technologies has a net negative effect on employment is not borne out by evidence. A study by Dutz et al. (2018) on the adoption of new technologies by countries in Latin America actually shows the opposite happening: in Argentina, Chile and Columbia, manufacturing firms that invest in ICT technology have experienced a net increase in employment. Second, even if we assume the 'doomsday' scenario of 3D printers and robots stealing most of our jobs, we do not know whether the manufacturing sector will experience larger job losses than the services sector or the agricultural sector. While, as cited earlier in the chapter, Manyika et al. (2017) show that manufacturing is among the most automatable economic activities, they also show that transportation and warehousing services are at equal risk of automation, and that food services are more susceptible to automation; in fact, sorting of agricultural products is 100% automatable at this point.

In conclusion, we have to be sceptical of the automation hype, especially in the context of developing countries. Most of the studies we have cited on both sides of the debate talk about the risk and possibility of job losses due to automation. They are not based on historical data. The historical data we do have clearly show that in the context of developing countries, the manufacturing sector has been the strongest driver of employment generation (ILO, 2014).

SUMMARY AND CONCLUSION

In the last few decades, both high-income countries and developing countries have seen manufacturing as a share of their economies shrinking: services now dominate most countries' economic structures. This shift has fuelled the discourse of the post-industrial society. This discourse contends that today's economic development strategies need to focus more on developing services, and is rooted in four main arguments: (1) thanks to developments in ICT, services contribute more to productivity growth than they used to, especially digitalised services and services that use digital technology; (2) technological developments and reductions in transport costs have made more services tradable; (3) services account for a higher share of value-added than manufacturing in today's value chains; and (4) automation puts into question the viability of labour-intensive manufacturing strategies.

In this chapter, we have critically evaluated the validity of the post-industrial society discourse, particularly with reference to developing countries. We acknowledge that there are reasons for developing countries to take the post-industrial society discourse seriously. Indeed, some services are characterised by higher tradability and greater productivity growth potential than they were before, and it seems difficult for developing countries to escape the 'middle-income trap' without specialising in at least some high-value services.

However, for many reasons, sustained economic development necessitates the development of an internationally competitive manufacturing sector. First, apart from a few small economies with highly idiosyncratic features, no countries have been able to transform their economies from low- to high-income without industrialisation. This is because, even as services have increased their potential to contribute to economy-wide productivity growth, manufacturing remains the driver of productivity growth and technological development: economies of scale are more easily achieved in the manufacturing sector because manufacturing activities lend themselves more easily to mechanisation and chemical processing. Even for many non-manufacturing activities, manufacturing is the driver of productivity growth: the world's most productive agricultural economies are heavy users of chemicals, fertilisers, pesticides and agricultural machinery, and the world's most productive service economies rely on top-tier computer technology, transport equipment and mechanised warehouses.

Second, the existence of services within an economy is largely dependent on a manufacturing core in that economy, more than the other way around. Studies investigating the multiplier effect of manufacturing and services have made it abundantly clear that manufacturing has a stronger multiplier effect than services. And some services are by definition linked to manufacturing through engineering know-how, such as manufacturing R&D and industrial design. One could question whether these services should be counted as services, instead of manufacturing, in industry classification codes.

Third, the decline of the manufacturing sector across the world – the development that has prompted the post-industrial society discourse – is partly an illusion. Many services that used to be provided in-house in manufacturing firms have been outsourced to independent firms. This has resulted in an increasing share of services in the economy in the industry classifications systems, without this actually being the case. Moreover, part of the manufacturing decline can be explained by the fact that manufacturing has faster productivity growth than services (which has resulted in falling relative prices of manufactured products), not because it is 'less important'.

Fourth, while some services have become more tradable, low tradability still characterises most services because they require consumers and producers to be in the same location. This means that countries that rely on their service sector for economic growth will eventually struggle with trade balance constraints.

Fifth, the prediction that new automation technologies will steal manufacturing jobs is mostly hype without evidence, especially in the context of developing countries. Blue-collar jobs in high-income countries are at higher risk of being made redundant than manufacturing jobs in developing countries. Additionally, evidence does not suggest that the manufacturing sector will suffer larger job losses than the services sector. If jobs are lost to automation, all sectors of the economy will suffer. But this 'if' is a big 'if': as yet, there is no evidence that automation is stealing jobs in developing countries.

In conclusion, we have to take the post-industrial society discourse with a large dose of scepticism. The idea that services is 'knowledge' work and manufacturing is low-value 'grunge' work is simply not correct: most services, in fact, cannot thrive without a vibrant manufacturing sector. Developing countries should not be tricked into thinking that they can skip the industrialisation phase. Factories are what made the modern world, and they will keep remaking it.

REFERENCES

Acemoglu, D. and Autor, D. (2011). 'Skills, Tasks, and Technologies: Implications for Employment and Earnings'. In Card, D. and Orley, A. (eds), *Handbook of Labour Economcis: Volume 4B*. San Diego, CA: North-Holland.

Ahmed, S. and Chen, P. (2017). 'Emerging Technologies, Manufacturing, and Development: Some Perspectives for Looking Forward'. Unpublished manuscript, World Bank, Washington, DC.

Ali-Yrkko, J., Rouvinen, P., Seppala, T. and Yla-Anttila, P. (2011). 'Who Captures Value in Global Supply Chains? Case Nokia N95 Smartphone'. *Journal of Industry, Competition and Trade*, 11(3), pp. 263–278.

Arnzt, M., Gregory, T. and Zierahn, U. (2016). 'The Risk of Automation for Jobs in OECD Countries: A Comparative Analysis'. Social, Employment, and Migration Working Paper No. 189, Organisation for Economic Co-operation and Development (OECD), Paris.

Baer, W. and Samuelson, L. (1981). 'Toward a Service-Oriented Growth Strategy'. *World Development*, 9(6), pp. 499–514.

Bairoch, P. (1982). 'International Industrialization Levels from 1750 to 1980'. *Journal of European Economic History*, 11(2), pp. 269–333.

Baumol, W.J. (1967). 'Macroeconomics of Unbalanced Growth: The Anatomy of Urban Crisis'. *American Economic Review*, 76, pp. 1072–1085.

Bell, D. (1976). *The Coming of Post-Industrial Society*. New York: Basic Books.

Berger, S. (2015). *Making America: From Innovation to Market*. Cambridge, MA: MIT Press.

Bhagwati, J.N. (1984). 'Splintering and Disembodiment of Services and Developing Nations'. *World Economy*, 7(2), pp. 133–144.

Bhagwati, J.N. (2010). 'The Manufacturing Fallacy'. *Project Syndicate*, August 27.

Bonvillan, W.B. (2012). 'Reinventing American Manufacturing: The Role of Innovation'. *Innovation*, 7(3), pp. 97–125.

Bosworth, B. and Collins, S.M. (2008). 'Accounting for Growth – Comparing China and India'. *Journal of Economic Perspectives*, 22(1), pp. 45–66.

Chang, H-J. (2014). *Economics: The User's Guide*. London: Pelican Books.

Chang, H-J., Andreoni, A. and Kuan, M.L. (2013). 'International Industrial Policy Experiences and Lessons for the UK'. London: UK Government Office for Science.

Chang, H-J., Hauge, J. and Irfan, M. (2016). *Transformative Industrial Policy for Africa*. Addis Ababa: UNECA.

Chenery, H. (1960). 'Patterns of Industrial Growth'. *American Economic Review*, 50, pp. 624–654.

Clark, C. (1940). *The Conditions of Economic Progress*. London: Macmillan.

Cruz, M. and Nayyar, G. (2017). 'Manufacturing and Development: What Has Changed?'. Unpublished manuscript, World Bank, Washington, DC.

Davis, G. (2009). *Managed by the Market: How Finance Reshaped America*. New York: Oxford University Press.

Dutz, M.A., Almeida, R.K. and Truman, G.P. (2018). *The Jobs of Tomorrow: Technology, Productivity, and Prosperity in Latin America and the Caribbean*. Washington, DC: World Bank.

Fengler, W. and Rowden, R. (2013). 'How Real is the Rise of Africa'. *The Economist*, 2013 archived debate.

Fisher, A.G.B. (1935). *The Clash of Progress and Security*. London: Macmillan.

Gerschenkron, A. (1962). *Economic Backwardness in Historical Perspective*. Cambridge, MA: Harvard University Press.

Ghani, E. (2010). *The Service Revolution in South Asia*. Oxford: Oxford University Press.

Ghani, E. and Kharas, H. (2010). 'An Overview'. In Ghani, E. (ed.), *The Service Revolution in South Asia*. Oxford: Oxford University Press.

Ghani, E. and O'Connel, S.D. (2014). 'Can Service Be a Growth Escalator in Low Income Countries?'. World Bank Policy Research Working Paper No. 6971, World Bank, Washington, DC.

Hallward-Driemeier, M. and Nayyar, G. (2018). *Trouble in the Making: The Future of Manufacturing-Led Development*. Washington, DC: World Bank.

Haskel, J. and Westlake, S. (2017). *Capitalism Without Capital: The Rise of the Intangible Economy*. Princeton, NJ: Princeton University Press.

Hauge, J. (2018). 'African Industrial Policy in an Era of Expanding Global Value Chains: The Case of Ethiopia's Textile and Leather Industries'. Doctoral thesis. https://doi.org/10.17863/CAM.20781.

Hirschman, A. (1958). *The Strategy of Economic Development*. New Haven, CT: Yale University Press.

ILO (2014). *Global Employment Trends 2014: Risk of a Jobless Recovery?* Geneva: ILO.

IMF (2018). *World Economic Outlook, April 2018: Cyclical Upswing, Structural Change.* Washington, DC: International Monetary Fund.

Kaldor, N. (1966). *Causes of Slow Rate of Growth in the United Kingdom.* Cambridge: Cambridge University Press.

Kaplinsky, R. (2005). *Globalization, Inequality and Poverty: Between a Rock and a Hard Place.* Cambridge: Polity Press.

Kuan, M.L. (2017). 'Manufacturing and Services in Singapore's Economy: Twin Engines of Growth and Their Asymmetric Dependencies'. Ministry of Trade and Industry, Singapore.

Kuznets, S. (1966). *Modern Economic Growth: Rate, Structure and Spread.* New Haven, CT: Yale University Press.

Lewis, W.A. (1954). 'Economic Development with Unlimited Supplies of Labour'. *Manchester School*, 22, pp. 139–191.

Loungani, P., Saurabh, M., Papageorgiou, C. and Wang, K. (2017). 'World Trade in Services: Evidence from A New Dataset'. IMF Working Paper, WP/17/77.

Manyika, J., Chui, M., Miremadi, M., Bughin, J., George, K., Willmott, P. and Dewhurst, M. (2017). *A Future that Works: Automation, Employment and Productivity.* San Francisco, CA: McKinsey Global Institute.

McCormack, R. (2006). 'Council on Competitiveness Says US has Little to Fear but Fear Itself; by Most Measures, US is Way Ahead of Global Competitors'. *Manufacturing and Technology News*, November 30.

McMillan, M. and Rodrik, D. (2011). 'Globalization, Structural Change and Productivity Growth'. In Bacchetta, M. and Jansen, M. (eds), *Making Globalization Socially Sustainable.* Geneva: WTO and ILO.

McMillan, M., Rodrik, D. and Sepulveda, C. (2017). 'Structural Change, Fundamentals, and Growth: A Framework and Country Studies'. Policy Research Working Paper 8041, World Bank, Washington, DC.

Meckstroth, D.J. (2017). 'The Manufacturing Value Chain is Much Bigger than You Think!'. MAPI Foundation, Arlington, VA.

Milberg, W. and Winkler, D. (2013). *Outsourcing Economics: Global Value Chains in Capitalist Development.* Cambridge: Cambridge University Press.

MMEG (2016). 'Manufacturing Metrics Review Report'. Report prepared by the Manufacturing Metrics Experts Group for the UK Department for Business, Innovation and Skills.

Myrdal, G. (1957). *Economic Theory and Underdeveloped Regions.* London: Duckworth.

Nayyar, D. (2013). *Catch Up: Developing Countries in the World Economy.* Oxford: Oxford University Press.

Nurkse, R. (1961). *Problems of Capital Formation in Underdeveloped Countries.* New York: Oxford University Press.

Ocampo, J., Rada, C. and Taylor, L. (2009). *Growth and Policy in Developing Countries: A Structuralist Approach.* New York: Columbia University Press.

OLS (2017). *Strength and Opportunity 2017: The Landscape of the Medical and Biopharmaceutical Sectors in the UK.* London: Office for Life Sciences.

ONS (2018). *Statistical Bulletin: UK Trade: April 2018.* UK Office for National Statistics. Newport: Office for National Statistics.

Palma, J.G. (2005). 'Four Sources of De-industrialisation and a New Concept of the Dutch Disease'. In Ocampo, J.A. (ed.), *Beyond Reforms: Structural Dynamic and Macroeconomic Vulnerability*. Palo Alto, CA: Stanford University Press; Washington, DC: World Bank.

Palma, J.G. (2014). 'De-industrialisation, Premature De-industrialisation and the Dutch Disease'. *Revista NECAT*, 3(5). http://stat.ijie.incubadora.ufsc.br/index. php/necat/article/view/3118/4060.

Park, S-H. and Chan, K. (1989). 'A Cross-Country Input–Output Analysis of Intersectoral Relationships between Manufacturing and Services and their Employment Implications'. *World Development*, 17(2), pp.199–212.

Pilat, D. and Wolfl, A. (2005). 'Measuring the Interaction Between Manufacturing and Services'. OECD Science, Technology and Industry Working Papers 2005/05, OECD, Paris.

Pilling, D. (2016). 'Africa: Between Hope and Despair'. *Financial Times*, April 24.

Pisano, G. and Shih, W. (2012). *Producing Prosperity: Why America Needs a Manufacturing Renaissance*. Cambridge, MA: Harvard Business Review Press.

Prebisch, R. (1950). *The Economic Development of Latin America and its Principal Problems*. New York: United Nations.

Rodrik, D. (2007). 'Industrial Development: Some Stylized Facts and Policies'. In United Nations (ed.), *Industrial Development for the 21st Century*. New York: United Nations.

Romer, C.D. (2012). 'Do Manufacturers Need Special Treatment?'. *New York Times*, February 4.

Rowthorn, R. and Ramaswamy, R. (1999). 'Growth, Trade and Deindustrialization'. *IMF Staff Papers*, 46(1), pp.18–41.

Rowthorn, R. and Wells, J.R. (1987). *De-Industrialization and Foreign Trade*. Cambridge: Cambridge University Press.

Statista (2018). Online statistics portal, https://www.statista.com/. Accessed April 2017.

Szirmai, A. (2009). 'Industrialization as an Engine of Growth in Developing Countries'. UNU-MERIT Working Paper Series 2009-010.

Szirmai, A. and Verspagen, B. (2011). 'Manufacturing and Economic Growth in Developing Countries, 1950–2005'. UNU-MERIT Working Paper Series 2011-069.

Taylor, I. (2015). 'Dependency Redux: Why Africa is Not Rising'. *Review of African Political Economy*, 43(147), pp.8–25.

Tregenna, F. (2009). 'Characterising Deindustrialisation: An Analysis of Changes in Manufacturing Employment and GDP Internationally'. *Cambridge Journal of Economics*, 33(3), pp.433–466.

UNCTAD (2016a). *Trade and Development Report, 2016: Structural Transformation for Inclusive and Sustained Growth*. Geneva: United Nations Conference on Trade and Development.

UNCTAD (2016b). 'Robots and Industrialization in Developing Countries'. Policy Brief No. 50, United Nations Conference on Trade and Development, Geneva.

UNECA (2015). *Economic Report on Africa 2015: Industrializing through Trade*. Addis Ababa: United Nations Economic Commission for Africa.

WDI (2018). World Development Indicators online database. https://databank.world bank.org/data/reports.aspx?source=world-development-indicators (accessed March 2018).

WIPO (2017). *World Intellectual Property Report 2017: Intangible Capital in Global Value Chains*. Geneva: World Intellectual Property Organization.

World Bank (2008). *The Growth Report: Strategies for Sustained Growth and*

Inclusive Development. Washington, DC: Commission for Growth and Development.

World Bank (2016). *World Development Report 2016: Digital Dividends*. Washington, DC: World Bank.

WTO (2013). *World Trade Report 2013: Factors Shaping the Future of World Trade*. Geneva: World Trade Organization.

Young, A.A. (1928). 'Increasing Returns and Economic Progress'. *Economic Journal*, 38(12), pp. 527–542.

2. The "lightness" of Industry 4.0 lead firms: implications for global value chains

Lukas Brun, Gary Gereffi and James Zhan

INTRODUCTION

Global value chains (GVCs) have become a dominant feature of the post-Cold War industrial production and trading system. Value chains, organized by global manufacturers and brands, have increasingly divided component production and final assembly into separate, geographically dispersed production locations to take advantage of the comparative and competitive advantages of regions, accelerating a trend of offshored and outsourced production in the 1990s that began in the 1970s. Global value chains have undergone several changes in the post-Cold War period, including efforts to rationalize the number of suppliers, regionalize production, enhance resiliency, improve environmental sustainability and, most recently, digitization. Digitization, due in large part to the suite of technologies commonly referred to as Industry 4.0 or the Fourth Industrial Revolution, is changing the frontier of what tasks can be performed by machines and what must be completed by humans, challenging the extensiveness of production in geographic space and the density of interactions among buyers and suppliers. In this chapter, we argue that technological change is introducing new, highly capable digital technology multinational enterprises ("digital economy MNEs") into the manufacturing and service sectors. These firms are unique in that they value non-physical assets higher than physical assets, indicative of a competitive strategy valuing more asset-light forms of international production. "Lightness" among these firms has development implications for regions, especially if lightness among digital economy MNEs is a harbinger of increased lightness among all industries.

To develop this argument, we organize our discussion into four sections. The first reviews the rise of and recent dynamics in GVCs. The second section defines the suite of technologies making up Industry 4.0 and allied concepts. This section also discusses the characteristics of digital economy MNEs, the lead firms in the digital economy, focusing on "lightness" as a unique characteristic of these firms that is enabled by Industry 4.0 technological change. The third section explores the implications of light lead firms on GVCs, exploring three scenarios about the impact of more asset-light forms of international production and alternative modes of governance. The final section concludes with a summary of points made in the chapter and areas for future research.

THE RISE AND RECENT DEVELOPMENTS IN GVCs

Multinational corporations in the West began extending their supply chains overseas in the 1970s and 1980s, following the earlier trend of multinationals in extractive industries, as differences in factors of production made developing countries attractive locations for the production of some industrial goods, notably aircraft and automobiles (Gereffi, 2014). Although international trade of raw materials and finished goods has occurred since ancient times, the division of component production and final assembly into separate, geographically dispersed production locations removed from the site of final consumption is a feature unique to the global economy accelerating since the 1990s. Global value chains, defined as the full range of activities that firms and workers carry out to bring a product from conception to its end use and beyond, today make up 80% of global trade (UNCTAD, 2013). Global value chains extend production both in terms of geographic space and in terms of the density of interactions among buyers and suppliers required for designing, producing and delivering products to the final customer.

   In addition to the expansion of supply chains abroad by multinational producers, large United States (US) retailers began contracting with manufacturers abroad to supply the products sold in their stores (Gereffi, 1994). JC Penney and Sears, for example, contracted with Samsung to produce microwaves and refrigerators for the US market in the 1970s (Magaziner and Patinkin, 1989). Walmart, despite a "Buy American" commitment in the mid-1980s (Hayes, 1992), began sourcing many of its products abroad, notably from China, especially after its accession to the World Trade Organization (WTO) in 2001. Global brands, especially in the apparel and consumer products segments, during the 1990s began using contract manufacturers to produce many of their products abroad, and importing them to major consumer markets in the US and Europe. As a result of these changes, new global trade and investment patterns emerged in which large retailers and global brands sourced goods from overseas factories, specifying the production, price and quality standards for the goods, and then import products for sale in major end markets located in advanced industrial countries. The expansion of value chains globally meant that trade in intermediate goods increased as imports became necessary for exporting. Intermediate goods trade increased with the development of outsourced and offshored production systems of global buyers and brands. The import content of exports rose from 20% in 1990, to 40% in 2010, and has remained around 30% in the most recent period (UNCTAD, 2018).

The global commodity chain (GCC) and global value chain (GVC) literatures within economic sociology highlighted that industries were increasingly characterized by the "unparalleled fragmentation and reintegration of global production and trade patterns since the 1970s" (Gereffi, 2005, p. 167). These changes were caused by the rise of global buyers, that is, large retailers and other branded firms that did not own manufacturing capabilities of their own. The GCC literature contrasted buyer-driven and producer-driven chains as having different production methods and, consequentially, power structures (Gereffi, 1994, 1999). Producer-driven chains were characterized by large, vertically integrated global manufacturing companies producing technology and capital-intensive items, while buyer-driven chains were characterized by global networks of formally independent companies producing less technology- and capital-intensive items. In buyer-driven chains, design and marketing were the key features of value-adding activities, in contrast to the technology and production expertise of producer-driven value chains. Thus, the GCC framework drew attention to the power dynamics within global production networks as chiefly residing in either the large producers or the larger purchasers of goods and services (Gereffi, 2005). Global commodity chains also provided an explanation for the observed increase in trade of components and other intermediate goods, and pointed to the role of interfirm and intrafirm trade caused by global outsourcing, which trade theory was just beginning to understand but trade statistics were unable to differentiate (Gereffi, 2014) until the development of trade in value-added statistics by the Organisation for Economic Co-operation and Development (OECD), WTO (OECD, 2015) and the United Nations Conference on Trade and Development (UNCTAD, 2013).

Complimentary innovations such as containerized cargo shipment and information and communication technology (ICT) made international transportation and communication faster and less expensive, extending further the reach of global producers and retailers vying for improved products that were faster and cheaper to produce than before. As the end of the Cold War opened new countries to Western firms, an increasing number of countries became potential production and sales sites for Western firms and brands. The relative costs of transportation and labor as a share of product price became a key determinant across industries for the decision on whether to offshore production (Sirkin et al., 2012).

Recent Dynamics in GVCs

In the aftermath of the 2008–2009 Global Financial Crisis, four broad global value chain dynamics are occurring: rationalization, regionalization, resiliency and digitization.[1] We briefly touch on each of these trends, before focusing our discussion on how digitization, or Industry 4.0, is affecting both suppliers and lead firms in global value chains.

In the first trend, rationalization, global lead firms, whether in producer- or buyer-driven chains, are consolidating their supply chains to include fewer, but more capable, suppliers (Gereffi and Lee, 2012). Lead firms have reduced the number of suppliers due to the realization that, firstly, only a few suppliers were providing the majority of valuable components; and secondly, that auditing requirements could be done more efficiently and frequently if a smaller number of highly capable suppliers existed. Auditing is important to firms as a means to certify that products meet technical specifications, but also as a compliance mechanism to ensure that products are meeting social and environmental responsibility requirements.

A second trend in global value chains is regionalization (Gereffi, 2014). Rather than extending supply chains globally, the trend has been for firms in North America, Europe and Asia to find low-cost areas of production in their region. In North America, supply chains are extending to Mexico; in Europe, supply chains are extending to Eastern European countries; and in Asia, supply chains are moving to countries outside of China, including Vietnam, Indonesia and Myanmar (Burma). The second aspect of supply chain regionalization is the growth of South–South trade. The general pattern of trade throughout the twentieth and twenty-first centuries has been between countries in the northern hemisphere, and between countries in the northern and southern hemispheres. However, the fastest-growing corridors of trade are all among regions in the southern hemisphere, notably between Asia and the Middle East and North Africa, Asia and sub-Saharan Africa, and Asia and Latin America (Jha et al., 2014). The WTO expects that South–South trade could make up around 43% of global trade, double its current percentage (WTO, 2013). The Asian

---

[1] Improved environmental sustainability is arguably another important trend in global value chains in the post-2008 crisis period. See De Marchi et al. (2013) and Seuring and Müller (2008) for additional discussions.

Development Bank projects that South–South trade could increase from 33% in 2004 to 55% in 2030, and that the South's share of global trade could overtake North–North trade by 2030 (Anderson and Strutt, 2011).[2]

A third dynamic in global value chains has been a focus on resiliency. Supply chain resiliency is important due to the potential of disruptive events hampering the ability of companies to produce goods and provide services (Lynn, 2005). Supply chain resiliency can be developed by increasing the number of production sites of key suppliers and increasing inventory to reduce the risk of disruption. For example, Apple's key supplier, Foxconn, has increased its locations due not only to a desire to produce outside of China, but also to serve local demand in South America. The previous two supply chain dynamics discussed, rationalization and regionalization, may also contribute to supply chain resiliency.

The focus of this chapter is on an important fourth trend in global value chains: digitization. Supply chain digitization is defined as the use of advanced data analytical tools and physical technologies to improve the digital connectivity and technological capabilities of supply chains (Mussomeli et al., 2016). Advanced data analytical tools include visualization, scenario analysis and predictive learning algorithms, which are typically called information technology (IT). Advanced physical technologies include robotics, drones, additive manufacturing (three-dimensional – 3D – printing) and autonomous vehicles, typically called operations technology (OT). The combination of IT and OT, made possible by improved processing capabilities, increased computing power, and reduced costs of computing, storage and bandwidth since 2001, has allowed for real-time access to data, analysis, and optimization in the production system (Figure 2.1).

INDUSTRY 4.0 AND GLOBAL VALUE CHAINS

Industry 4.0 and Allied Terms

Industry 4.0 is a collection of technologies and enhanced capabilities that, when combined, are expected to change the way products and services are created, produced and delivered. Industry 4.0 has multiple allied concepts, including the "fourth industrial revolution" and Industrie 4.0. A summary

---

[2] Delving into what lies behind some of these figures, first, South–South exports grew at an annual average rate of 13% between 1995 and 2016, far outpacing total world exports, at 8%. The value of South–South trade increased almost seven-fold, from just $0.6 trillion in 1995 to $4 trillion in 2016. The share of South–South trade in developing countries' total exports rose from 42% to 57%. In 2016, one quarter – 25% – of world total trade took place among developing countries. (See UNCTAD, 2018, Global South, 1.1.)

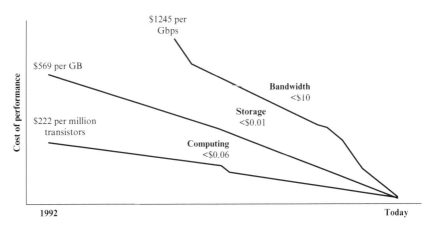

Source: Mussomeli et al. (2016).

Figure 2.1   *Declining costs in bandwidth, storage, and computing led to Industry 4.0*

of the terms used to describe the increased availability, collection and analysis of data for goods and service producing systems is provided in Table 2.1.

The key parameters of Industry 4.0 are big data, advanced analytics, human–machine interface, and digital-to-physical transfer (Baur and Wee, 2015). Big data is "the astonishing rise in data volumes, computational power, and connectivity, especially new low-power wide-area networks"; advanced analytics refers to "the emergence of analytics and business-intelligence capabilities"; human–machine interface refers to "new forms of human–machine interaction such as touch interfaces and augmented-reality systems"; and digital-to-physical transfer refers to "improvements in transferring digital instructions to the physical world, such as advanced robotics and 3-D printing" (Baur and Wee, 2015).

Boston Consulting identifies nine technologies that comprise Industry 4.0: big data and analytics, autonomous robots, simulation, horizontal and vertical system integration, the industrial Internet of Things, cybersecurity, the Cloud, additive manufacturing and augmented reality (Figure 2.2):

- Big data and analytics are used to collect and evaluate data from production equipment and systems, enterprise and customer management systems to support decision-making.
- Autonomous robots are developing to become flexible and cooperative with one another, and able to learn and work with humans;

Table 2.1   Industry 4.0 and allied terms

Term	Definition	Key parameters
Industry 4.0	A term extensively used by McKinsey & Company to describe: "The next phase in the digitization of the manufacturing sector, driven by four disruptions: the astonishing rise in data volumes, computational power, and connectivity, especially new low-power wide-area networks; the emergence of analytics and business-intelligence capabilities; new forms of human–machine interaction such as touch interfaces and augmented-reality systems; and improvements in transferring digital instructions to the physical world, such as advanced robotics and 3-D printing" (Baur and Wee, 2015).	Big data Advanced analytics Human-machine interfaces Digital-to-physical transfer
Industrie 4.0	A German strategic initiative, described in the German Trade and Investment Ministry's 2010 "High-Tech Strategy 2020" plan, seeking a "fusion of the online world and the world of industrial production" (Merckel, 2015) as a "means to establish Germany as a lead market and provider of advanced manufacturing solutions . . . Cyber-physical production systems (CPPS) made up of smart machines, logistics systems and production facilities allow peerless ICT-based integration for vertically integrated and networked manufacturing" (GTAI, 2017).	Smart industry Smart factory
Fourth industrial revolution (4IR)	Championed by the World Economic Forum and its founder Klaus Schwab, the term "Fourth Industrial Revolution" (4IR) describes the range of new technologies fusing the physical, digital and biological worlds into "cyber-physical systems." The emerging technology breakthroughs in artificial intelligence, robotics, the Internet of Things, autonomous vehicles, 3D printing and nanotechnology are a part of the 4IR. The 4IR is distinguished from the first, second, and third industrial revolutions in which mechanization, electricity and information technology, respectively, powered industrial change (Davis, 2016; Schwab, 2017).	Cyber-physical systems

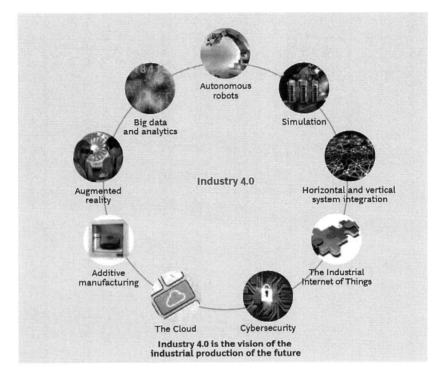

Source: Rüßmann et al. (2015).

Figure 2.2   Nine technologies in Industry 4.0

robots will cost less and have a greater range of capabilities than
those that currently exist in manufacturing sites.

- Simulations, although already used extensively in the engineering
  phase, are expected to create a real-time virtual model of machines,
  products and humans mirroring the physical world. These virtual
  models allow operators to test and optimize machine settings for the
  next product in line before a physical changeover, reducing machine
  set-up times and improving quality.
- Horizontal and vertical systems integration will combine companies, suppliers and customers; and within companies, departments,
  functions and capabilities.
- The industrial Internet of Things (IoT) embeds objects with technology that can communicate with IT systems and be detected by sensors. The IoT will increase the connectivity of machines and
  products through distributed systems, allowing real-time response.

- Cybersecurity will become more important as increased connectivity and use of standard communications protocols by industrial and manufacturing systems will require secure, reliable communications, identity and access management systems.
- The Cloud will become a key feature of increasing the connectivity and data access sharing across sites and company boundaries as part of the Internet of Things. The Cloud will improve to be capable of faster reaction times and may also hold monitoring and control processes.
- Additive manufacturing is currently used to create prototypes and individual components. As the Internet of Things becomes more pervasive, it can be used to create small batches of customized products that can be produced on site and reduce transportation distances and inventory.
- Augmented reality supports parts selection in warehouses and sending repair instructions. Although currently in its infancy, augmented reality may allow workers to receive repair instructions in real time while looking at the system needing repair. Virtual training through augmented reality may also be used increasingly.

The overall vision of Industry 4.0 systems is to automate and integrate production lines, and to design and produce collaboratively and virtually. As a result of Industry 4.0 technologies, manufacturing processes will become more automated and flexible to allow for smaller lot sizes and to allow for learning, self-optimization, and adjustment; automated logistics will use autonomous vehicles and robots to adjust automatically to production needs (Rüßmann et al., 2015).[3]

The Effects of Digitization on Global Supply Chains

Digitization is leading to three broad trends in value chains: extended dis-intermediation, servicification, and distributed and flexible production.[4] Together, these three trends are reshaping the supply chains and affecting the role of suppliers in GVCs (Table 2.2). We discuss each trend below.

Digitization is permitting extended disintermediation of supply chains, that is, allowing goods and service producers to produce and deliver

---

[3] Manyika et al. (2013) identify 12 technologies that are part of Industry 4.0. In general, they overlap later efforts at defining Industry 4.0, such as those by Rüßmann et al. (2015) and Baur and Wee (2015), although they also include genomics and energy-related technologies (storage, enhanced oil and gas exploration and recovery, and renewable technologies), which are now not considered as part of Industry 4.0 technologies.

[4] On distributed manufacturing, see Srai et al. (2016a) and Srai et al. (2016b).

Table 2.2   Digital transformation and implications for value chains

Value chain stage	Description	Industries	Potential GVC implications
Upstream/ supplier relations	E-auctions, with open or closed systems Supplier or vendor managed inventory Collaborative product or production process design	Automotive, aerospace, maritime, consumer electronics (discrete assembly industries)	New entry modes into GVCs by suppliers due to distributed production (more, smaller production locations) Increased supplier proximity to clients Increased coordination and information exchange by lead firms (more sophisticated centralized coordination and quality control)
Internal production processes	Digitally enabled automation of factory operations that allow customization and production to order (volume flexibility) Digital replication, with production closer to consumption Advanced digitally enabled manufacturing technologies (3D printing, continuous processing)	Oil, mining, shipbuilding, steel, chemicals, machinery manufacturing, automotive, aerospace (production-asset intense industries; inventory-heavy industries) Food and beverage, chemical, nutraceutical (batch process industries that benefit from volume flexibility)	Shift to capital-intensive production due to automation, net job loss, improved job quality Servicification of production, production assets, and product Flexible production: increased use of contract manufacturing and outsourcing of ancillary operations
Downstream/ customer relationships	Disintermediation in product delivery and distribution models;	Media, financial services Sharing economy E-commerce business-to-consumer (B2C)	Disintermediation: Increased value capture by MNEs in downstream segments

Table 2.2   (continued)

Value chain stage	Description	Industries	Potential GVC implications
	monitoring of product use by the end-user Digitally enabled product customization Mass connectivity between customers and suppliers	firms, retailers, fast-moving consumer goods with last-mile distribution, health care solutions	Fewer local distribution partnerships, new service partnership opportunities Increased competition as downstream firms challenge established players
End-to-end processes	Transparency and traceability; digital quality and compliance systems Big-data predictive supply chains Use of new data management providers and system integrators	Pharmaceuticals, food (regulated industries requiring conformance) Aerospace and white goods (through-life servicing)	Footloose production due to frequent reconfiguring of production locations Increased compliance requirements for suppliers and users Enterprise data system providers increasingly important to drive predictive supply chains, through-life product servicing, and integrating systems

Source: Adapted from UNCTAD (2017c, pp. 180–181).

their products directly to end-users, bypassing supply, distribution and sales networks. For example in business-to-business (B2B) transactions, downstream disintermediation is exemplified by a firm's ability to bypass wholesale and distribution functions performed by external service providers and conducting the functions themselves. Digitization can change the firm's decision from "buy" to "make," resulting in shorter supply chains. For business-to-consumer (B2C) interactions, disintermediation due to supply chain digitization is exemplified by direct service provision. For example, as media companies became digital media firms with data streaming services, traditional distribution channels were bypassed altogether, allowing consumers to access digital content directly. Similarly, firms leading in the "sharing economy," companies such as Uber and Airbnb, place pressure on traditional taxi service, hotel and short-term real-estate leasing companies by connecting asset owners directly with those who need services in the short term. These companies also have a remarkable potential to create network effects that bring very small enterprises into value chains. Furthermore, digitization is also affecting disintermediation in supporting industries, notably financial services and other "trusted third party" data and verification service providers, as technology allows parties to instantly verify transactions. As transactions between businesses move from third-party verification to direct, instant digital transactions (that is, blockchain technology), the role of financial intermediaries and other trusted third-party actors changes.

Second, digitization is increasing the role of services as a business model for both manufacturing and service sector GVCs, a trend somewhat awkwardly termed "servicification." Servicification comes in three forms: unbundling capital equipment into a service provided by external providers, unbundling manufacturing-related activities into services provided by external providers, and the capture of production and use data into a value-added service. Unbundling capital equipment into a service provided by external providers is becoming increasingly common. Both pay-by-use ("power-by-the-hour") and subscription services have become more common due to the rapidly changing technology and service requirements of Industry 4.0 capital equipment, turning capital expenditures into operational expenditures (Baur and Wee, 2015; Mussomeli et al., 2016; Porter and Heppelmann, 2014). The model means that some manufacturers no longer own their production equipment, but pay either a fixed subscription cost or variable "per-use" fee to equipment manufacturers to use and maintain the equipment. For example, Chesbrough (2012) writes of the "long tail" in aircraft engines in which the majority of the profits derived from GE are in the maintenance and service of its engines, rather than their outright sale. After realizing that engines were only a means to getting the more valuable service income stream, GE changed its business model from being a product and component supplier to being a power and propulsion provider, in which it leased equipment on a "power by the hour" basis. The shift from thinking of equipment as a capital cost to an operations cost is a major change in the way capital equipment producers and buyers in a number of industries relate to one another. It can also align the incentives of buyers and producers to make products more reliable, durable and simple to fix (Porter and Heppelmann, 2014).[5]

---

[5]   Porter and Heppelmann (2014, p. 84) note that hybrid business models exist between the extremes of traditional product sales and the product-as-service or product-sharing

Unbundling manufacturing-related activities into services is due to the fragmentation of value chains into separate tasks, which revealed that manufacturing value chain activities, including manufacturing, are actually service activities ("manufacturing as service"). Digitization allows these services to be unbundled either as separate business entities or outsourced to contact manufacturers (UNCTAD, 2017c). For example, technical support services, including production machine maintenance and service, specialist diagnostics and quality testing are increasingly outsourced to specialized service firms in manufacturing value chains.

The capture of production and product-use data into a value-added service is also an increasingly common form of servicification. Licensing intellectual property may become a more important revenue stream for many companies as they monetize data related to the production and use of their products. As sensors and communication capabilities are embedded in products, they can be used to create system platforms of similar products, optimize their individual or combined use, or be sold to develop new information products to new customers (Porter and Heppelmann, 2014). For example, data about the fuel efficiency of a vehicle under different operating conditions and the current driving conditions on roads could be valuable to a number of potential customers, including other drivers, transportation and logistics companies, and insurance companies. Data about how, when and where the product is used could be valuable to product manufacturers to segment customers, customize features and provide specialized service plans or discounts for additional products to highly specific niche customers (Porter and Heppelmann, 2015).

The third effect of digitization on supply chains is the capital substitution of labor due to automation. Expected productivity gains incentivize the automation of production. As investment in automation and robotics increases, the capital intensity of production rises, changing the type and amount of activities performed by human labor. In general, overall productivity is expected to increase between 5% and 8% due to the adoption of Industry 4.0 innovations, although this will vary by industry (Rüßmann et al., 2015). Based on the experience in Germany, Rüßmann et al. (2015) expect that the automotive industry will achieve 6–9% productivity gains, machinery industry will achieve 10–15% productivity increases, food and beverage 5–10%, and mechanical component suppliers 4–7%. Adopting productivity-enhancing technologies will require a 35% capital investment increase over the next five to ten years, but is expected to yield 30%

---

model. Product sales can be bundled with warranties, service contracts or performance-based contracts in which the manufacturer maintains the responsibility and risk for product performance.

reductions in labor, operating and overhead costs, and 50% reductions in logistics costs. Revenue growth due to the adoption of Industry 4.0 innovations is expected to contribute 1% to Germany's gross domestic product (GDP), as manufacturers increase their investment into enhanced equipment and new data applications.

As adoption of Industry 4.0 technologies increases, some tasks routinely performed in current occupations and industries will be replaced by technology, affecting the nature of work. Industrial robots are expected to affect 36–60 million full-time equivalents (FTEs) by 2025 of the 355 million applicable industrial workers and increase productivity 75% for each FTE (Manyika et al., 2013). The change in the nature of work due to the introduction of robots has already been dramatic, as have common business functions such as clerical and bookkeeping positions across industries (Autor et al., 2003; Manyika et al., 2013). The likelihood that this trend will continue is high, resulting in workers and automated systems working together hand in hand, at times quite literally. As automation capabilities increase, the skills required by workers and professionals across most sectors of the economy will shift to performing non-routine physical activities and operating machinery in unpredictable environments, interfacing with stakeholders, managing and developing people, and applying expertise to decision-making, planning and creative tasks (Bughin et al., 2017a; Chui et al., 2015). The question currently unanswered is the degree to which the adoption of Industry 4.0 technologies will complement rather than substitute labor. Both are likely to occur simultaneously. Although much of the focus of the early work on Industry 4.0 (Frey and Osborne, 2013) has been on the substitution effect of labor by technology, less focus has been given to the complementary effects of technology on labor and the new occupations and skills needed, notably maintenance of autonomous systems, as industries across the world adopt Industry 4.0 technologies.[6]

Supply chain digitization affects all stages of the value chain because it reduces transaction costs for both internal and external business operations. Supplier, or upstream, relationships are affected by e-auctions, vendor managed inventory, and collaborative product or production

---

[6]   Autor et al. (2003) argue that the "middle-skills" segment of the workforce has already experienced increasing job displacement over the past two decades. Since 2000, the United States has created 8 million net new full-time equivalent positions; two-thirds of those have been in low-skill interactive work and the remaining one-third in high-skill interactive work. About 2.5 million net production and transaction positions were lost since 2000. Robots have replaced assembly line workers, and software performs many of the tasks once completed by bookkeepers, secretaries, and file clerks. Thus, increased job displacement in recent decades was primarily due to improvements in information technology and the decreasing price of computer processing devices. See also Manyika et al. (2015, p. 57).

process design (UNCTAD, 2017c). B2B digital services affecting upstream relationships include digitally enabled markets connecting buyers with suppliers, such as digital bid-ask or auction markets, digital payments and digitized enterprise resource planning software. E-auctions reduce trans-action costs from external business operations because of "on-demand" supply chain partner models, resulting in scattered and on-demand supply. However, the impact of e-auctions on vendors needs additional study. On one hand, they may permit new entrants and smaller firms to compete on a more equal footing with larger firms (Mussomeli et al., 2016). On the other hand, if the vendor platforms are complex, require qualifying capabilities or certifications, or are closed by design, then they can reduce the opportunities for new entrants in favor of established suppliers (UNCTAD, 2017c). Vendor managed inventory and collabora-tive product and process design also increase the efficiency of the firm's supply chain due to digitization. Internal production processes are made more efficient by digitally enabled automation of factory operations (that is, continuous processing) and manufacturing technologies that permit production closer to consumption (that is, 3D printing).

Customer, or downstream, relationships are affected by mass connectiv-ity between manufacturers and customers, allowing direct sales and mass customization. Additional downstream relationships affected by digitizing the supply chain are B2C digital services including advertising, sales, payment and customer service delivered through social media or other electronic means (Manyika et al., 2015). As electronic means provide a direct connection to customers, the distribution function can be provided by the manufacturer or outsourced to specialized new firms providing digitized distribution services.

Digital Economy Lead Firms

New firms are leading the change in the digital economy. These new actors are leading the twin forces of disruption and disintermediation characterizing the change in global manufacturing and service GVCs due to the adoption of Industry 4.0 technologies. The purpose of this section is to better understand these new firms, which we call the "digital economy MNEs."

The architecture of the digital economy can be divided into two major categories: digital and ICT MNEs (see Figure 2.3 and Table 2.3). Digital MNEs are characterized by the use of the Internet as their central operating and service delivery model. Digital MNEs include pure digital companies, such as Internet platform companies and digital solutions firms (for example, electronic payment companies), that rely entirely on

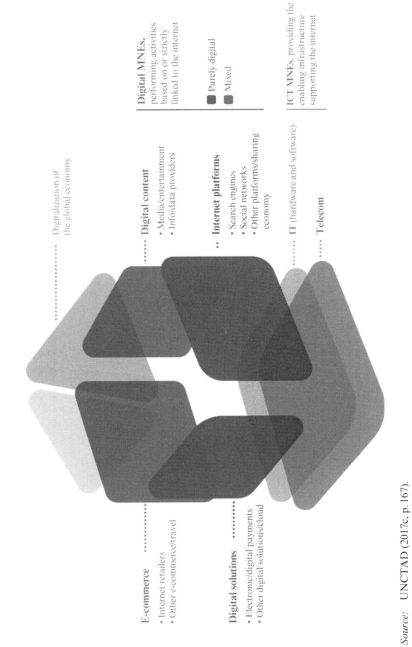

Digital MNEs, performing activities based on or strictly linked to the internet

■ Purely digital
■ Mixed

ICT MNEs, providing the enabling infrastructure supporting the internet

Digitalization of the global economy

Digital content
• Media/entertainment
• Info/data providers

Internet platforms
• Search engines
• Social networks
• Other platforms/sharing economy

IT (hardware and software)

Telecom

E-commerce
• Internet retailers
• Other e-commerce/travel

Digital solutions
• Electronic/digital payments
• Other digital solutions/cloud

Source: UNCTAD (2017c, p.167).

Figure 2.3   The architecture of the digital economy

Table 2.3 The digital economy: digital and ICT MNEs

Category	Subcategory	Description	Examples
Digital MNEs	Internet platforms	Companies providing digital services through Internet and Cloud-based platforms, search engines and social networks	Alphabet/Google, Facebook, eBay
	Search engines	Includes sharing economy platforms (e.g., transaction platforms – eBay; and open-source platforms – Red Hat)	
	Social networks		
	Other platforms		
	Digital solutions	Includes a variety of players with core activities based on or strictly linked to Internet technologies	Automatic Data Processing, Paypal, Akamai
	Electronic payments	Providers of electronic and digital payments, Cloud hosting and computing, web hosting and e-mail services, digital solutions for business management and for financial applications (fintech)	
	Other digital solutions		
E-commerce	Internet retailers	Specialized and non-specialized online stores and online travel and booking agencies	Amazon, Alibaba, Priceline
	Other e-commerce	Includes agencies specialized in online marketing and advertising	
Digital content	Digital media	Producers and providers of digital content: media (e.g., music, video, e-books, online magazines) and gaming (e.g., "classic" video games, online games, mobile games, multiplayer interactive games)	Netflix, Activision, Thomson-Reuters
	Games	Production relying on digital formats or files; delivery through both traditional channels (e.g., cable TV for digital media) and online channels (e.g., Internet TV and "over-the-top" – OTT)	
	Information and data	Database-related products and services: big data providers, marketing and customer intelligence, and providers of economic, business and credit information	

Table 2.3 (continued)

Category	Subcategory	Description	Examples
ICT MNEs	IT Devices and component	Manufacturers of ICT hardware (computer brands) but also components (e.g., semiconductor industry)	Apple, Samsung, Sony, Microsoft, Accenture, SAP
	Software and services	Developers of software; providers of assistance and IT consultancy	
		Major software houses, turning from a physical delivery model (with physically installed applications) to remote service applications delivered on demand	
		Category bordering "digital solutions"	
	Telecom	Owners of the telecommunication infrastructure on which Internet data is carried	AT&T, Deutsche Telekom, Vodafone
		Increasingly active also as providers of Internet services and direct OTT content	

Source: UNCTAD (2017a, p. 3).

the Internet for conducting business. Digital MNEs also include mixed players, such as e-commerce and digital content firms (for example, digital media and games), that have a prominent presence online but retain some portion of their business in non-digital forms. For example, digital media and e-commerce firms can deliver their content or fulfill orders entirely through the Internet, but can also deliver it to customers through more traditional, non-digital channels if the content or product is tangible.

ICT MNEs include legacy telecom providers, device and component manufacturers, and software development firms. This group of firms creates the infrastructure enabling access to the Internet by companies and people. Telecom firms own the telecommunication infrastructure through which Internet data are carried. Device and component manufacturers produce ICT hardware and the components necessary to run them. Software firms develop the programming code and deliver the software to customers, increasingly through digital means. Software services firms offer assistance and consultation on technical and digital market topics.

An important characteristic of the new digital economy MNEs is a preference for being foreign-asset-light (see Table 2.4).[7] Companies may derive foreign sales as a result of having a significant portion of their productive assets abroad ("asset heavy") to reach foreign customers, or they may achieve the same level of foreign sales with few foreign assets abroad ("asset light"). Table 2.4 demonstrates that in comparison to non-digital MNEs, digital economy MNEs possess fewer foreign assets, indicating a reduced international physical footprint even though they derive a significant portion of their sales abroad. The implication of fewer foreign assets is a reduced need for digital economy MNEs to conduct manufacturing and service activities outside the home country to achieve foreign sales. Instead, they can be performed by the firm itself (insourcing) in the home country (reshoring), reversing value chain trends occurring since the 1970s.

Lightness also varies significantly within digital economy MNEs (Table 2.5). For example, although Internet platforms are the "lightest" category of firms, eBay has an 8.87 ratio of foreign sales to assets (very light), while Alphabet and Facebook have lightness ratios around 2 (2.25 and 2.51, respectively), which are close to the average levels of lightness for the Internet platform category.

These vastly different lightness ratios indicate firm-level differences in

---

7   Digital economy MNEs are also fast growing, keep cash reserves overseas, and concentrate investments in few countries, especially in the US. For a discussion of these other characteristics, see UNCTAD (2017b, pp. 156–175).

Table 2.4   Lightness ratio of sectors in the digital and non-digital economy

	Industry	Share of foreign sales (A)	Share of foreign assets (B)	Lightness ratio (A/B)
High digital impact	**Internet platforms**	**0.50**	**0.19**	**2.63**
	IT devices & components	**0.75**	**0.39**	**1.91**
	Digital solutions	**0.32**	**0.17**	**1.90**
	Total digital	**0.40**	**0.27**	**1.49**
	Total ICT	**0.63**	**0.43**	**1.48**
	IT software & services	**0.63**	**0.46**	**1.38**
	Automotive and aircraft	0.53	0.71	1.30
	Digital content	**0.36**	**0.32**	**1.14**
	E-commerce	**0.42**	**0.38**	**1.11**
Low digital impact	Other manufacturing*	0.62	0.71	1.10
	Chemicals and pharma	0.64	0.68	1.10
	Food, beverages, tobacco	0.90	0.87	1.00
	Telecom	**0.42**	**0.46**	**0.92**
	Primary sector	0.76	0.68	0.90
	Utilities	0.55	0.47	0.90
	Petroleum and refining	0.73	0.60	0.80
	Others	0.67	0.38	0.60

Notes: Bolded sectors are digital economy sectors. See UNCTAD (2017a) for discussion on data, methods, and procedures in deriving lightness ratio.
* "Other manufacturing" includes machinery and electric equipment

Source: UNCTAD (2017a, pp. 8–11), UNCTAD (2017b, p. 172).

the importance of foreign assets used to achieve foreign sales. Although eBay is able to achieve a share of foreign sales similar to those of Facebook and Alphabet (58% versus 53–54%), it has less than a third of their share in foreign assets. Differences in where data centers (server farms), foreign operations, research and development, and customer service centers are located help to explain the reasons for the variation among these firms. For example, Alphabet maintains data centers in the US, Europe and

Table 2.5   Lightness ratio of selected top 20 digital economy MNEs

Category	Company name	Total sales (billion USD)	Total assets (billion USD)	Share of foreign sales (2015)	Share of foreign asset (2015)	Lightness ratio
Internet platforms	Alphabet	75.0	147.5	0.54	0.24	2.25
	Facebook	17.9	49.4	0.53	0.21	2.51
	eBay	8.6	17.8	0.58	0.07	8.89
	Average	*11.3*	*26.4*	*0.50*	*0.19*	*2.63*
Digital solutions	Automatic Data Processing	11.7	43.7	0.15	0.10	1.50
	First Data Corporation	11.5	34.4	0.14	0.11	1.36
	PayPal	9.2	28.9	0.50	0.07	7.61
	Average	*4.2*	*9.7*	*0.32*	*0.17*	*1.90*
E-commerce	Amazon.com	107.0	65.4	0.36	0.32	1.13
	Priceline Group	9.2	17.4	0.80	0.17	4.77
	Expedia	6.7	15.5	0.44	0.11	3.95
	Average	*9.9*	*13.5*	*0.42*	*0.38*	*1.11*
Digital content	21st Century Fox	27.3	48.2	0.29	0.10	2.98
	Liberty Global	18.3	67.9	0.61	0.65	0.97
	Sky	16.1	23.5	0.30	0.07	4.55
	Average	*11.1*	*19.3*	*0.36*	*0.32*	*1.14*
IT devices and components	Apple	215.6	321.7	0.65	0.39	1.65
	Sony	72.0	148.0	0.71	0.24	3.00
	Taiwan Semiconductor	25.6	50.3	0.89	0.03	31.30
	Flextronics	24.4	12.4	0.70	0.20	3.43
	Average	*31.5*	*36.3*	*0.75*	*0.39*	*1.91*
IT software and services	Microsoft	85.3	193.7	0.52	0.43	1.22
	Qualcomm	23.6	52.4	0.98	0.18	5.61
	Adobe Systems	5.9	12.7	0.47	0.21	2.23
	Average	*19.5*	*32.2*	*0.63*	*0.46*	*1.38*
Telecom	AT&T	146.8	402.7	0.04	0.05	0.94
	Vodaphone	59.0	192.6	0.85	0.90	0.94
	Telecom Italia	21.5	77.6	0.25	0.12	2.08
	Average	*31.3*	*74.8*	*0.42*	*0.46*	*0.92*

Source: UNCTAD (2017a, pp. 8–11).

Asia, and has major foreign office locations in Ireland and Switzerland.[8] Facebook similarly has significant operations and office locations abroad, while eBay's foreign presence is largely limited to government relations staff. Presumably, companies with a "heavier" presence abroad provide in the aggregate greater macroeconomic benefits for host countries than companies with "lighter" business models. We discuss the implications of light lead firms on the development prospects of regions in the next section.

THE IMPLICATIONS OF LIGHT LEAD FIRMS ON GVCs: THREE SCENARIOS

Since their origin, the GCC and GVC literatures have been concerned not only with accurately describing varieties of firm governance and the factors of change, but also to understand their implications for improving the economic, social and environmental prospects of regions. While the development implications of expansion abroad by global producers corresponded with foreign direct investment and factory ownership, the rise of global buyers led to the separation of manufacturing and production facility ownership. Buyer-driven value chains and the mode of production they engendered led to indigenous component and final goods production capacity development, which was facilitated by global lead firms. The development prospects of countries in a buyer-driven world increased, as there was hope that production or service niches existed in the production chain for actors with a range of capabilities.

Development within the context of value chains meant finding a domestic toehold in a global value chain, which could then be used to capture more of the value-added in a product or service through various ways of "upgrading."[9] Capturing economic value is a dynamic process which ultimately is subject to the profitability of the bundle of activities performed by the companies in a region, relative to other regions. When value chain

---

8 See https://www.google.com/intl/en/about/locations/ for a list of global locations for Google/Alphabet. Facebook's international presence can be found here: https://newsroom. fb.com/company-info/. The international locations for eBay are given at https://www.ebay mainstreet.com/offices.

9 "Upgrading" can mean increasing the unit price of goods sold ("product upgrading"), improving productivity ("process upgrading"), increasing the number of activities in a value chain conducted by a firm or firms in a geographic region ("functional upgrading"), or economic diversification into new or related industries ("chain upgrading") (Humphrey and Schmitz, 2002). Non-economic forms of upgrading include "social" upgrading, defined as the improvement of working conditions, wage rates and greater participation by gender, race or age groups; and "environmental" upgrading, defined as reducing the environmental footprint of production, including the carbon footprint.

activities are no longer profitable, or less profitable than in other regions, they either shift to other regions or are shed entirely from the value chain. The implication of this global dynamic is that it was increasingly unlikely that all value-adding activities could be conducted by any single company or region, but this would depend on relative input and logistics costs among regions (Sirkin et al., 2012).[10]

For developing regions of the world, the consequence of this global dynamic was the development and growth of economies, as segments previously conducted in higher-cost areas moved to areas with lower relative costs. For developed regions, lower-value-adding areas of the value chain, notably manufacturing in mature industries and routinized codifiable service tasks, were increasingly performed offshore. Combined, globalization and the logic of value-added production meant that industries were "hollowed out" (Goos and Manning, 2007; Goos et al., 2009, 2014) from the perspective of the developed world, with the advanced industrialized world capturing more value but fewer jobs in an industry; while nations in the developing world competed on low relative costs and attracting segments of the value chain that were previously conducted elsewhere.[11] Ongoing debates exist about the benefits of the global production system, particularly on how those benefits are distributed, and the implications for the middle class in both the developed and developing worlds (Milanovic, 2016a, 2016b).

The increasing digitization of supply chains and the emergence of new lead firms at the forefront of the change in the digital economy could signal a new era in the global economy. To the extent that digitization increases the "lightness" of other industries, the impact upon workers, regions and governments could be significant, even disruptive.[12]

---

[10]   Exceptions from this general statement may include very new products or industries, which may be dominated by a single firm with a vertically integrated production system. Public policy interventions, notably "supply chain cities" created in China, may also be an exception. Industry 4.0 technologies may change the "make or buy" calculus due to the disruptive nature of technological change, especially in regard to disintermediation.

[11]   See Hallward-Driemeier and Nayyar (2017) for a more detailed discussion regarding the history of manufacturing-led development.

[12]   Estimates of the automation potential of industries are available from multiple sources, especially Bughin et al. (2017a, 2017b). Complementary analysis in Manyika et al. (2013) estimates the employment effects of three Industry 4.0 technologies (advanced robotics, autonomous vehicles and 3D printing) particularly relevant to the manufacturing sector. See also Arntz et al. (2016), Davis (2016), Frey and Osborne (2013, 2017) and WEF (2016) for contrasting employment methodologies and impacts. Regional impacts of automation and technology adoption scenarios are provided by Bughin et al. (2017a). UNCTAD (2017b, p. 176) finds that "to date, the adoption of digital technologies in non-ICT MNEs is not yet visible in international production patterns in the way it is for ICT and digital MNEs . . . the relative contributions of foreign sales and assets have not substantially changed over the past 10 years."

The ability of digital economy MNEs to penetrate other product and service sectors is likely to be a function of the automation potential of industries. The estimated employment effects of automation are staggering. Early work by Frey and Osborne (2013) estimated that between 47% and 57% of occupations are susceptible to automation, and that 47% of US occupations were at high risk of automation in the next 10–20 years. A follow-up study by Frey and Osborne sponsored by Citibank (Citi, 2016) estimated that 57% of jobs in OECD countries, 69% of jobs in India, and 77% of jobs in China could be automated. In contrast, a study by the OECD (Arntz et al., 2016) found that only 9% of jobs across 21 OECD countries are automatable, with notable differences between countries. Caution regarding the impact of automation on employment is warranted, as what is technically feasible is not always also economically profitable (UNCTAD, 2017b).

Estimates continue to vary in the two most recent analyses by the World Economic Forum's "Future of Jobs" report (WEF, 2016) and McKinsey's "A Future that Works" report. The World Economic Form's report (WEF, 2016), based on a survey of major global employers, concludes that 7.1 million jobs will be lost globally between 2015 and 2020 due to technological changes, while 2 million jobs will be gained. In contrast, McKinsey's report (Bughin et al., 2017a) concludes that almost 50% of work activities can be automated, given existing technology; that 60% of occupations have at least 30% of automatable activities; and that about 5% of occupations can be automated entirely. McKinsey uses US Department of Labor O*NET task-level data to determine what tasks within sectors can be automated, given the current level of technology, and uses this baseline to estimate global impacts (Bughin et al., 2017a).[13] The authors find that technically automatable activities affect 1.2 billion workers worldwide and US$14.6 trillion in wages, with China, India, Japan and the US contributing to more than half of these figures. Within the manufacturing sector, employment in low-skill labor-intensive tradable industries, such as textiles, apparel and furniture manufacturing (Hallward-Driemeier and Nayyar, 2017), may be at a higher risk for automation due to the automation potential of low-skill tasks.

The impact of digitization on GVCs could also result from changes in foreign investment behavior by MNEs, especially if foreign-asset-light business models become more prevalent for both digital and non-digital economy MNES. The incentives to invest in production-related assets abroad decrease as firms are able to competitively produce closer to final demand markets, which still largely reside in the developed world. In the

---

[13]   The methodology used to determine the automation potential of job groups is provided in Bughin et al. (2017a, pp. 4, 119–131).

place of production-related investments by MNEs or their suppliers, other forms of investment may become more important for businesses with foreign-asset-light business models, including knowledge-seeking foreign investments and financial- or tax-driven foreign investments (UNCTAD, 2017c). These forms of foreign investment have fewer beneficial macroeconomic impacts for the recipient country than investments by lead firms or their suppliers in production-related assets.

The question from a value chain firm governance standpoint is whether digital economy MNEs will complement, displace or lead to the adaptation of existing lead firms (Gereffi, 2001; Rehnberg and Ponte, 2017). Three scenarios are possible: complementary, displacement and adaptation (Table 2.6).

The first is a complementary scenario in which digital economy MNEs create dramatic new additional value in the global economy, enhancing existing levels of employment and investment across industries, but do not replace existing lead firms. In this scenario, the new digital economy firms create new products, new employment and new investment that augment the existing structure of trade, investment and development occurring since the 1970s.

Table 2.6   Three scenarios for digital economy MNEs and lead firm governance

Scenario	Description	Example
Complementary	Digital economy MNEs create dramatic new value in the global economy, increasing levels of employment and investment across industries; digital economy MNEs compete alongside but do not replace existing lead firms	"Bricks and mortar" and e-commerce business models (Walmart and Amazon; Rooms to Go and Conn's)
Displacement	Digital economy MNEs disrupt existing industries, challenging existing lead firms' business models; displacement could be rapid or gradual	Rapid: Kodak, Blockbuster. Gradual: Apple, Alphabet, Amazon, Uber in separate product markets
Adaptation	Traditional buyer and producer lead firms successfully adopt Industry 4.0 technologies to maintain competitiveness	Automotive: Ford and Google. Heavy industry: GE

A second, displacement, scenario could occur, in which digital economy MNEs disrupt existing industries, challenging existing lead firms' business models. Displacement could be rapid or gradual. In the rapid displacement version, technology change challenges the firm's business model to such an extent that it does not have time to undergo the organizational changes needed to adapt. In the gradual displacement version, digital economy MNEs become the increasingly powerful interconnection point, or "digital hub," between the customer, manufacturer and supplier due to their ability to use Industry 4.0 technologies to synchronize purchasing, manufacturing and delivery. Due to their ability to achieve foreign sales with reduced foreign assets, digital economy MNEs in this scenario eventually displace the "heavier" existing lead firms.

A third, adaptation, scenario could occur in which Industry 4.0 technologies are successfully adopted by the existing lead firms to improve the efficiency of production. In this scenario, efficiency gains due to Industry 4.0 technologies are adopted by existing firms to achieve new levels of efficiency and competitiveness.

Which scenario will emerge as dominant is currently uncertain, largely because evidence exists to support all three. For example, with regard to the complementary scenario, the current state of retail in the US supports both "bricks and mortar" and e-commerce business models. Traditional retailers, such as Sears, JC Penney, and discount retailers such as Walmart, co-exist with e-commerce sites such as Amazon, although questions admittedly exist about their ability to maintain their market share and profits in light of e-commerce challenges over the long run. An additional example of the complementary scenario is in the furniture industry, whereby the majority of furniture is sold by bricks and mortar retailers meeting the consumer's desire to touch, feel and customize the product prior to purchase. However, online discount retailers, including Rooms to Go and Ashley Furniture, provide online portals to allow direct-to-the-consumer purchases of furniture, rapid delivery and easy returns (Brun et al., 2013).

Evidence for the displacement scenario also exists. Rapid disruption of existing firms due to digitization has occurred in a number of industries, as exemplified by Kodak, Polaroid and Blockbuster. In these cases, technology change undercut the business models of these firms, leaving the organizations with insufficient time to adapt. The key challenge for legacy lead firms is to ensure that they are at the forefront of anticipating disruptive technology and business model changes, while maintaining leadership in more incremental change technologies that are likely to attract more immediate product and service demand from customers. The balance can be difficult, as illustrated by these former lead firms who were "disrupted" out of business.

Evidence for gradual displacement of existing lead firms by digital economy firms also exists. Some very large digital economy firms are aggressively expanding through acquisitions and product development to become important actors in other areas of the economy, blurring traditional industry boundaries. For example, Apple is expanding from its core expertise in designing, marketing and selling consumer electronic devices to becoming a digital media firm through its iTunes platform.[14] Alphabet, Google's parent company, has divisions in biotechnology (Verily), artificial intelligence research (Deepmind) and self-driving cars (Waymo). Amazon's founder, Jeff Bezos, not only holds the large e-commerce site, but also holds asset-heavy firms such as Whole Foods and the *Washington Post*.

An interesting dynamic from a value chain standpoint is that these companies are both powerful new suppliers in traditional industries and lead firms in their own core markets. Take the example of the automotive industry. Google is entering the car industry with its Android operating system adopted by GM, Hyundai, Honda and Audi as part of the Open Automotive Alliance (Porter and Heppelmann, 2014) and driverless car technology, due to its ability to integrate sensors, software and data with the physical testing and development of products. Similarly, Uber is moving from an on-demand transportation company to a food delivery company, while also developing its own driverless car technology (Manyika et al., 2015).

At the same time, traditional car manufacturers are investing more heavily into the new technologies affecting the production and use of their products (the adaptation scenario). Traditional car manufacturers such as GM also are entering new consumer-facing markets as they see the oncoming shift in driverless vehicles and competition from shared-use companies such as ZipCar as an opportunity to change from a product supplier to a capability provider (Gauger et al., 2017; Porter and Heppelmann, 2014).[15] What remains uncertain is whether the car manufacturer (such as GM or Ford) or the digital economy MNE company (such as Uber, Lyft, ZipCar or Google) will be the lead consumer-facing company.[16] General Electric, the grandfather of heavy industry, is also rapidly adopting new Industry 4.0 production and service technologies to maintain its competitiveness.

---

[14] Sales of Apple's digital content services grew 35% from 2014 to 2016, in contrast to 11% of total sales (2016 Apple 10-k, https://www.sec.gov/Archives/edgar/data/320193/000162828016 020309/a201610-k9242016.htm).

[15] The on-demand use programs by auto manufacturers are RelayRides (GM), DriveNow (BMW) and Dash (Toyota).

[16] See, for example, https://www.wsj.com/articles/google-takes-on-uber-with-new-ride-share-service-1472584235 and https://techcrunch.com/2016/11/01/uber-and-gm-partner-to-off er-drivers-car-sharing-through-maven/.

CONCLUSION

The purpose of this chapter was to review the dynamics global value chains have undergone over the past several decades, focusing on the changes that digitization continues to introduce to where and how goods and services are produced in the global economy. Digitization, due in large part to the suite of technologies commonly referred to as "Industry 4.0," is changing the frontier of what tasks can be performed by machines and what must be completed by humans, changing how value chains function, and challenging the extensiveness of production in geographic space, and the density of interactions among buyers and suppliers.

In this chapter, we have argued that technological change is introducing new, highly capable digital technology multinational corporations (digital economy MNEs) into the manufacturing and service sector. These firms are unique in that they can achieve foreign market sales with fewer assets and employees overseas, indicative of a competitive strategy valuing more asset-light forms of international production. We explored how "lightness" among these firms has development implications for regions, especially if lightness among digital economy MNEs is a harbinger of increased lightness among all industries. We also pointed out that despite predictions and scenarios about the effects of digitization on employment, trade and investment, little effort has been exerted to understand the conditions under which digital economy MNEs will supplant, support or be replaced by existing lead firms, and how the dynamics will differ between producer-driven and buyer-driven value chains. We explored three scenarios of how lead firm governance could change as a result of digital economy MNEs. Although we have begun the exploration of the role of light lead firms in transforming the global economy, additional work is needed. In particular, we pointed out that more research is required to better understand why firms have different levels of lightness, even within the same category or subcategory; the firm-specific implications for trade, investment and regional development; and the conditions under which existing lead firms will complement, adapt, or be displaced by digital economy MNEs.

REFERENCES

Anderson, K., and Strutt, A. (2011). Asia's changing role in world trade: prospects for South–South trade growth to 2030. Background Paper for Asian Development Bank's *Asian Development Outlook*.

Arntz, M., Gregory, T., and Zierahn, U. (2016). The risk of automation for jobs in OECD countries: A comparative analysis. OECD Social, Employment, and Migration Working Papers (189), 0-1.

Autor, D.H., Levy, F., and Murnane, R.J. (2003). The skill content of recent technological change: An empirical exploration. *Quarterly Journal of Economics*, 118(4), 1279–1333.

Baur, C., and Wee, D. (2015). Manufacturing's next act. *McKinsey Quarterly*, Jun.

Brun, L., Buciuni, G., Frederick, S., and Gereffi, G. (2013). *The Furniture Value Chain in North Carolina*. Durham, NC: Duke GVC Center. Retrieved from https://gvcc.duke.edu/wp-content/uploads/2013-09-30-The-Furniture-Value-Chain-in-North-Carolina.pdf.

Bughin, J., Manyika, J., and Woetzel, J. (2017a). *A Future That Works: Automation, Employment, and Productivity*. San Francisco, CA: McKinsey Global Institute. Retrieved from http://www.mckinsey.com/global-themes/digital-disruption/harnessing-automation-for-a-future-that-works.

Bughin, J., Manyika, J., and Woetzel, J. (2017b). Where machines could replace humans – and where they can't (yet). *Tableau*. Retrieved from https://public.tableau.com/profile/mckinsey.analytics#!/vizhome/InternationalAutomation/WhereMachinesCanReplaceHumans.

Chesbrough, H. (2012). Open services innovation. Retrieved May 26, 2017, from http://innovationexcellence.com/blog/2012/11/04/open-services-innovation/.

Chui, M., Manyika, J., and Miremadi, M. (2015). Four fundamentals of workplace automation. *McKinsey Quarterly*, 29(3), 1–9.

Citi, G. (2016). Technology at work V 2.0: The future is not what it used to be. *Citi GPS: Global Perspectives and Solutions* (January). https://www.oxfordmartin.ox.ac.uk/publications/view/2092.

Davis, N. (2016). What is the fourth industrial revolution? *World Economic Forum*. Retrieved from https://www.weforum.org/agenda/2016/01/what-is-the-fourth-industrial-revolution/.

De Marchi, V., Di Maria, E., and Micelli, S. (2013). Environmental strategies, upgrading and competitive advantage in global value chains. *Business Strategy and the Environment*, 22(1), 62–72.

Frey, C.B., and Osborne, M.A. (2013). The future of employment. How susceptible are jobs to computerisation. Retrieved from https://www.oxfordmartin.ox.ac.uk/downloads/academic/The_Future_of_Employment.pdf.

Frey, C.B., and Osborne, M.A. (2017). The future of employment: How susceptible are jobs to computerisation? *Technological Forecasting and Social Change*, 114, 254–280.

Gauger, C., Gehres, B., Quinn, M., Schmieg, F., and Xu, G. (2017). Building the digital car company of the future. Boston Consulting Group Publications. www.bcg.com/publications/2017/automotive-digital-transformation-building-digital-car-company-future.aspx.

Gereffi, G. (1994). The organization of buyer-driven global commodity chains: How US retailers shape overseas production networks. In G. Gereffi and M. Korzeniewicz (eds), *Commodity Chains and Global Capitalism* (pp. 95–122). Westport, CT: Greenwood Press.

Gereffi, G. (1999). International trade and industrial upgrading in the apparel commodity chain. *Journal of International Economics*, 48(1), 37–70.

Gereffi, G. (2001). Beyond the producer-driven/buyer-driven dichotomy: The evolution of global value chains in the internet era. *IDS Bulletin*, 32(3), 30–40.

Gereffi, G. (2005). The global economy: Organization, governance, and development. In N.J. Smelser and R. Swedberg (eds), *The Handbook of Economic Sociology* (2nd edition, pp. 160–182). Princeton, NJ: Princeton University Press.

Gereffi, G. (2014). Global value chains in a post-Washington Consensus world. *Review of International Political Economy*, 21(1), 9–37.

Gereffi, G., and Lee, J. (2012). Why the world suddenly cares about global supply chains. *Journal of Supply Chain Management*, 48(3), 24–32. doi: 10.1111/j.1745-493X.2012.03271.x.

Goos, M., and Manning, A. (2007). Lousy and lovely jobs: The rising polarization of work in Britain. *Review of Economics and Statistics*, 89(1), 118–133.

Goos, M., Manning, A., and Salomons, A. (2009). Job polarization in Europe. *American Economic Review*, 99(2), 58–63.

Goos, M., Manning, A., and Salomons, A. (2014). Explaining job polarization: Routine-biased technological change and offshoring. *American Economic Review*, 104(8), 2509–2526.

GTAI (2017). Industrie 4.0 what is it? Retrieved May 25, 2017, from https://industrie4.0.gtai.de/INDUSTRIE40/Navigation/EN/Topics/Industrie-40/what-is-it.html.

Hallward-Driemeier, M., and Nayyar, G. (2017). *Trouble in the Making? The Future of Manufacturing-Led Development*. Washington, DC: World Bank. Retrieved from https://openknowledge.worldbank.org/handle/10986/27946.

Hayes, T.C. (1992). Wal-Mart disputes report on labor. *New York Times*, December 24.

Humphrey, J., and Schmitz, H. (2002). How does insertion in global value chains affect upgrading in industrial clusters? *Regional Studies*, 36(9), 1017–1027.

Jha, M., Amerasinghe, S., Narayanan, C., Calverley, J., and Chrysostomou, A. (2014). *Global Trade Unbundled*. [Special report], April 9. https://www.sc.com/en/resources/global-en/pdf/Research/2014/Global_trade_unbundled_10_04_14.pdf.

Lynn, B.C. (2005). *End of the Line: The Rise and Coming Fall of the Global Corporation*. New York: Doubleday.

Magaziner, I.C., and Patinkin, M. (1989). *Silent War*. New York: Random House.

Manyika, J., Chui, M., Bughin, J., Dobbs, R., Bisson, P., and Marrs, A. (2013). *Disruptive Technologies: Advances that will Transform Life, Business, and the Global Economy* (Vol. 180). San Francisco, CA: McKinsey Global Institute.

Manyika, J., Ramaswamy, S., Khanna, S., Sarrazin, H., Pinkus, G., et al. (2015). *Digital America: A Tale of the Haves and Have-mores*. San Francisco, CA: McKinsey Global Institute.

Merckel, A. (2015). Speech given by German Chancellor Angela Merkel to the 2015 World Economic Forum, Davos. https://www.link-labs.com/blog/iot-vs-industry-4.0.

Milanovic, B. (2016a). *Global Inequality*. Cambridge, MA: Harvard University Press.

Milanovic, B. (2016b). Global inequality: A new approach for the age of globalization. *Panoeconomicus*, 63(4), 493–501.

Mussomeli, A., Gish, D., and Laaper, S. (2016). The rise of the digital supply network: Industry 4.0 enables the digital transformation of supply chains. *Deloitte Insights*, December, 1.

OECD (2015). Trade in value added. Retrieved May 18, 2017, from http://www.oecd.org/industry/ind/measuringtradeinvalue-addedanoecd-wtojointinitiative.htm.

Porter, M.E., and Heppelmann, J.E. (2014). How smart, connected products are transforming competition. *Harvard Business Review*, 92(11), 64–88.

Porter, M.E., and Heppelmann, J.E. (2015). How smart, connected products are transforming companies. *Harvard Business Review*, 93(10), 96–114.

Rehnberg, M., and Ponte, S. (2017). From smiling to smirking? 3D printing, upgrading and the restructuring of global value chains. *Global Networks*, 18(1), 57–80.

Rüßmann, M., Lorenz, M., Gerbert, P., Waldner, M., Justus, J., et al. (2015). Industry 4.0: The future of productivity and growth in manufacturing industries. *Boston Consulting Group*, 9(1), 54–89.

Schwab, K. (2017). *The Fourth Industrial Revolution*. New York: Crown Business.

Seuring, S., and Müller, M. (2008). From a literature review to a conceptual framework for sustainable supply chain management. *Journal of Cleaner Production*, 16(15), 1699–1710.

Sirkin, H.L., Zinser, M., Hohner, D., and Rose, J. (2012). US manufacturing nears the tipping point. Which Industries, why and how much? BCG Perspectives, March. http://image-src.bcg.com/Images/BCG_US_Manufacturing_Nears_the_Tipping_Point_Mar_2012_tcm9-106751.pdf.

Srai, J.S., Harrington, T.S., and Tiwari, M.K. (2016a). Characteristics of redistributed manufacturing systems: A comparative study of emerging industry supply networks. *International Journal of Production Research*, 54(23), 6936–6955.

Srai, J.S., Kumar, M., Graham, G., Phillips, W., Tooze, J., et al. (2016b). Distributed manufacturing: scope, challenges and opportunities. *International Journal of Production Research*, 54(23), 6917–6935.

UNCTAD (2013). *World Investment Report 2013: Global Value Chains: Investment and Trade for Development*. New York: United Nations.

UNCTAD (2017a). Chapter IV Technical Annex: The Top 100 Digital MNEs: United Nations Committee on Trade and Investment. Retrieved from http://unctad.org/en/PublicationChapters/wir2017ch4_Annex_en.pdf.

UNCTAD (2017b). *Trade and Development Report*. Retrieved from https://unctad.org/en/PublicationsLibrary/tdr2017_en.pdf.

UNCTAD (2017c). *World Investment Report*. Geneva: United Nations Committee on Trade and Development (UNCTAD).

UNCTAD (2018). *World Investment Report*. Retrieved from https://unctad.org/en/PublicationsLibrary/wir2018_en.pdf.

WEF (2016). The future of jobs: employment, skills and workforce strategy for the fourth industrial revolution. In *Global Challenge Insight Report*, Geneva: World Economic Forum.

WTO (2013). *World Trade Report: Factors Shaping the Future of World Trade*. Geneva: World Trade Organization.

3. The National Innovation System (NIS) and readiness for the fourth industrial revolution: South Korea compared with four European countries

Keun Lee and Jongho Lee

INTRODUCTION

Lundvall (1992) defines the National Innovation System (NIS) as "elements and relationships which interact in the production, diffusion and use of new, and economically useful, knowledge." Specifically, the NIS is a concept related to the efficiency of production, diffusion and use of knowledge. Scholars from the Schumpeterian school, such as Lundvall and Nelson, have advocated the NIS concept. They argued that the differences in NIS among countries have given birth to the differences in innovation performance, and thus in the countries' economic performance. In this sense, Schumpeterian economics differs from the emphasis on the political institution, as in Acemoglu and Robinson (2012), who suggested that political institutions determine the growth rate of countries, in particular inclusive rather than extractive institutions. In general, political institutions are more binding critically in pre-modern societies or low-income countries than in upper-middle- or high-income societies. Using the number of granted United States (US) patents and research and development (R&D) expenditure as a proxy for innovation, Lee and Kim (2009) find that innovation capability is important for economic growth in countries beyond the middle-income stage, whereas political institutions are binding for economic growth in lower-middle- or low-income countries.

This chapter analyzes and compares the National Innovation System of Korea against the four European economies of Italy, the United Kingdom (UK), France and Germany. One focus of the comparative analysis is to determine the extent to which each country is better prepared for the fourth industrial revolution (4IR). As popularized by Schwab (2016) at the 2016 World Economic Forum, the 4IR refers to the new waves of innovation consisting of several technologies comprising three-dimensional (3D) printing, the Internet of Things (IoT), artificial intelligence (AI), smart cars, big data and on-demand economy (sharing economy). In general, the 4IR is regarded as making innovation based on a broad spectrum of technologies from diverse fields and is thus becoming more convergent. The chapter attempts to address which aspect of the NIS is friendlier to the 4IR, and which countries have a more adequately prepared NIS for the coming 4IR. The next section briefly describes the methodology for analyzing NISs, because we need to study the variables that can reveal various aspects of NISs. The chapter then compares the NISs of Korea and four European countries. A final section concludes.

FIVE ASPECTS OF THE NIS AND READINESS FOR THE 4IR

Empirical analysis of innovation and knowledge is challenging because of the difficulty in measuring innovation and knowledge and the lack of data. However, patent data have increasingly become available and used for this purpose because they (especially patent citation data) can be considered as a proxy for the paper trail of knowledge flows. Like academic articles citing each other, patent citations are about which patents cite which other patents, and are presumed to be informative links between patented inventions. In other words, knowledge flows among inventors leaving a paper trail in the form of citations in patents (Jaffe et al., 1993). By conducting a survey of inventors, Jaffe et al. (2000) investigate the extent to which citations actually reflect knowledge flows, and find that a significant proportion do so. This condition makes it possible to use the probability of citation as a proxy for the probability of a useful knowledge flow.

A methodology has been developed for quantifying NISs by using patent citation data extracted from the USPTO (US patents and trademark office) site, and here we will briefly introduce it and explain the usage.[1] In the Korean patent system, only recently has the database included information regarding which patents cited which other patents, but the United States Patent and Trademark Office has been collecting citation data for a long time. Citation data of patents represent how existing knowledge is used for subsequent inventions, and thus contain valuable information

---

[1] For further details on the methodology, please refer to Lee (2013) and Lee et al. (2017).

for the flow of knowledge (acquisition and usage). For this reason, patent citation data are useful for innovation system studies trying to capture efficiency in the creation and usage of knowledge.

Jaffe and Trajtenberg (2002) provide extensive US patent data for researchers, conveniently in the form of a CD. Their book also contains a description of the data and methodologies for econometric analysis using patent data, over the period 1999 to 2006. In this chapter we use more updated data, up to mid-2010 or 2015, so that the more recent evolution of the NIS is highlighted. The methodology for building the database of up-to-date patents and their citations is explained in the Appendix.

In comparing the NIS of countries, it would be problematic to use patent data from different patent offices because they use different standards. It is therefore important to use patent data collected by a particular country to which the largest number of other countries apply for patents. US patents data are a perfect example of such a case, and thus we use patents filed in the US by countries for international comparison. Now let us introduce the main variables describing the NIS, which were also used in Lee (2013) and Lee et al. (2017), while the detailed technical definitions of these variables are presented in the Appendix.

The first NIS variable is related to the source in the acquisition of knowledge and the degree of localization in the production of knowledge. That is, it regards how much knowledge being created relies on foreign or domestic knowledge bases. In other words, it measures how much knowledge is created domestically by citing the patents owned by inventors of the same nationality. It can be referred to as a measure of the localization of knowledge creation, and is a proxy for how often a patent filed by a country cites other patents filed by its citizens. At the firm level, it can be self-citation of patents belonging to a firm, and is a variable that represents how independently firms produce knowledge. According to Lee (2013), Korea and Taiwan showed a low degree of localization in knowledge creation in the early 1980s, which was similar to that of other middle-income countries but much lower than that of advanced countries. However, the degree of localization increased rapidly after the mid-1980s and reached the average level of advanced countries by the late 1990s, indicating a significant catch-up in this regard.

The second NIS variable regards the concentration of actors or patent holders in knowledge creation. It indicates whether the producers of knowledge are led by a few big businesses or evenly distributed among a variety of inventors. Clearly, this variable shows a quite even distribution of knowledge producers for advanced countries, while knowledge creation is concentrated among a few inventors in the case of typical developing countries.

The third NIS variable is originality. Existing literature describes it as how wide the range of the source of knowledge is when a patent cites preceding patents. That is, we say that knowledge has a high degree of originality if it relies on knowledge from a variety of fields. We may reason that the NIS featuring a higher degree of originality can be considered better or more prepared for the 4IR, to the extent that the 4IR requires more convergence technologies which are more broadly based and tend to be fusion technologies. Similar to the concentration variable, advanced countries show a relatively higher degree of originality than developing countries. Interestingly, countries from Latin America show higher degrees of originality compared to South Korea and Taiwan (Lee, 2013).

The fourth NIS variable is technological diversification. This measure is about whether countries or firms produce patents in a wide variety of fields or in a few limited areas. A country with a more diversified NIS can be regarded as better prepared for the 4IR, because a broad portfolio in its technological resources may mean a higher possibility of innovation in the era of the 4IR, which also means broadening of the scope of innovation activities. Lee (2013) shows that advanced countries have a higher degree of technological diversification than developing countries. In the case of South Korea and Taiwan, the degree of technological diversification has increased since the mid-1980s. Although still lower than that of Germany or Japan, the degree of technological diversification for South Korea and Taiwan has reached the average of high-income countries.

The fifth NIS variable is related to whether or not countries specialize in sectors with fast obsolescence of knowledge or slow obsolescence of knowledge. This notion is expressed as the cycle time of technologies. It represents the length of the life expectancy of the particular knowledge being used. A short cycle time of technology means that the life span of the knowledge lasts only a few years, and after that the usage declines dramatically as it soon becomes outdated or less used. The cycle time of technology is calculated by measuring average time lags between the application (grant) years of the citing and cited patents. That is, it shows how much on average a patent relies on old technologies for invention of new knowledge. Lee (2013) shows that major advanced countries are specialized in sectors with relatively longer cycle times of technology, while since the mid-1980s South Korea and Taiwan have shown a tendency to focus on sectors with relatively shorter cycle times of technology, as their patents tend to cite other relatively recent patents.

THE NIS DURING THE CATCH-UP STAGES IN KOREA

Lee (2013) investigated the major characteristics of the NIS catch-up stage by comparing the NISs of South Korea and Taiwan with the NISs of both other developing and developed countries. He uses the above five variables to empirically test the determinants of per capita gross domestic product (GDP) growth. One of the most important findings of Lee (2013) is that successful catching-up countries and firms have specialized in sectors with short cycle times of technology.

The reasons that specializing in sectors with short cycle times is more advantageous for catching-up growth are explained as follows. First, specializing in fields with short cycle times of technology means that existing knowledge becomes obsolete fast. This would mean lower entry barriers for latecomers because they can afford to rely less on the existing knowledge dominated by advanced countries. Second, having short cycle times of technology, as in information technologies, means that new technology arrives more frequently, resulting in high growth potential. Additionally, specializing in sectors with short cycle times of technology would facilitate quickly raising the degree of knowledge localization (measured by self-citation at the country level). That is, it would be advantageous in achieving fast and successful localization of knowledge creation, because reliance on old or existing knowledge controlled by advanced countries would be relatively low.

In country-level empirical studies, Lee (2013, Chapter 3) demonstrates that there is a significant correlation between having more patent applications in fields related to shorter cycle times of technology and a higher per capita GDP growth rate, such as in East Asian countries including South Korea and Taiwan. In contrast, economic growth in high-income countries as well as in other middle-income countries is positively related to specialization in technologies with long cycle times, although they differ in that advanced economies specialize in high value-added sectors (for example, pharmaceuticals), and other middle-income countries specialize in low value-added sectors (for example, apparels), within the long cycle technologies. This finding suggests that specializing in sectors with short cycle times of technology is a way to avoid direct competition with advanced countries, and to provide a niche market for latecomer countries with a certain profit rate.

Lee's study considered other variables representing various dimensions of innovation systems. These include the cycle time of technologies, originality, localization of knowledge creation, innovator concentration and technological diversification. He finds that the degree of knowledge localization and technological diversification in economies that have successfully caught up has rapidly increased over time. At the same time, such countries have specialized increasingly in short-cycle technologies. Thus, these three variables seem to hold the key to the question of the mechanism of economic catch-up. As discussed above, they also appear to occur together and to complement each other. Statistically, there is very high degree of correlation (as high as 0.7) between knowledge localization and technological diversification. In contrast, the variable of cycle time does not show such a high correlation with either of the two variables. Also, while advanced countries tend to show high degrees of knowledge localization and technological diversification, they all seem to have more patents in long-cycle technologies, which is exactly the opposite of the case with successful catching-up economies. Although the variable of knowledge localization shows rapid increases over time in catching-up economies, the variable is significant in the performance equation only in advanced economies and their firms, whereas it is too low to be significant in middle income countries. The nature of technological diversification appears similar to that of knowledge localization. Based on this information, we take both diversification and localization as the end-state variables, and the cycle time as an effective transition variable that guides us to the end-state (Lee, 2013, pp. 213–214).

Before the mid-1980s, South Korea and Taiwan specialized in sectors with low-end, long cycle times of technology such as textiles or clothing. Since the mid-1980s, however, they started to enter industries with short cycle times of technology such as electronics, semiconductors, signal equipment and digital TVs. As a result, they accomplished technological diversification by entering a variety of industries, and at the same time, the degree of localization of knowledge creation continued to rise. To sum up, consecutive entry into sectors with short cycle times of technology resulted in technological diversification, and specializing in sectors with short cycle times of technology also made firms rely less on the technology of advanced countries, enabling them to achieve fast and successful localization of knowledge creation.

So far, we have been discussing catching-up NIS. Successful catching-up countries such as South Korea and Taiwan accomplished the desired level of catching up by specializing in sectors associated with short cycle times of technology. In contrast, the degree of concentration and originality for those countries is not very different from other developing countries. Thus, Lee argued that the degree of concentration and originality is not the main element for catching-up growth. However, it is also established that the top-tier high-income countries all tend to have a more even distribution of inventors, or less concentration, as well as high originality in their patent portfolios. This fact could mean that South Korea may also need to improve on these aspects, or to switch to an NIS more typical for top-tier advanced countries. This issue is explored in more detail in the following section.

THE NIS IN THE 2010s IN KOREA AND FOUR EUROPEAN COUNTRIES

The results of the characterization of the NISs of Korea and four European countries are shown in Figures 3.1 to 3.5. We discuss each country's NIS using the figures.

First, the NIS of Italy has the longest cycle time as compared to the other countries. This finding implies a sound basis for high profit capability. However, the NIS of Italy also reveals a low degree of technological diversification and knowledge localization, as well as a medium level of originality. The longest cycle time of the Italian NIS apparently demonstrates consistency with the small and medium-sized enterprise (SME)-oriented nature of Italian industry, with strength in tacit knowledge-oriented sectors such as machine tools. Although this feature suggests something positive, the NIS of Italy tends to indicate a low degree of preparedness for the 4IR as indicated by low originality and less diversification.

In comparison, the NIS of the UK reveals the highest degree of originality and a relatively long cycle time of technologies compared with other European countries. However, the NIS of the UK is not significantly diversified, and also has the lowest degree of intra-national diffusion or knowledge localization. The last feature of low degree of knowledge

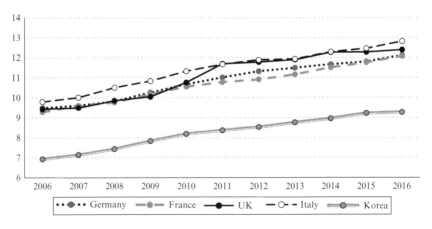

Figure 3.1   Average cycle time of technologies

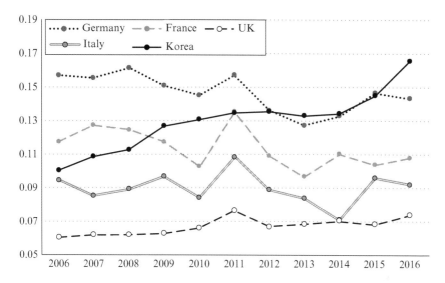

Figure 3.2   Intra-national diffusion of knowledge

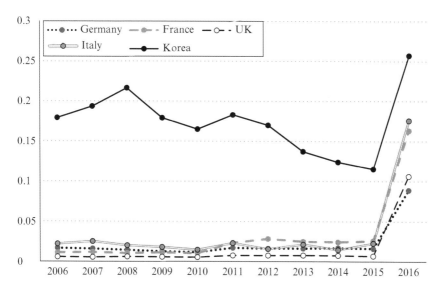

Figure 3.3   HHI Index of assignee concentration

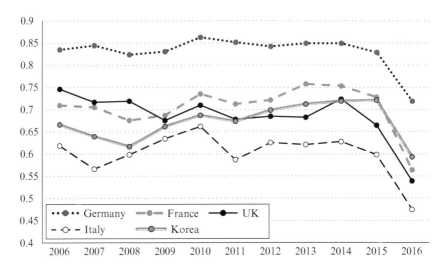

Figure 3.4   Technological diversification (number of patented sectors divided by 438)

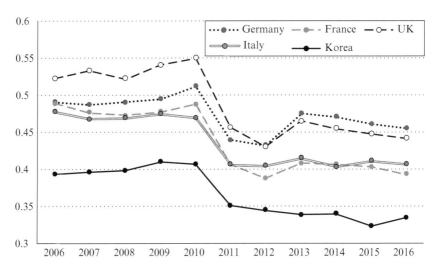

Figure 3.5   Originality

localization is not necessarily negative because it may indicate a high degree of internationalization, implying heavy reliance on international sources. In terms of preparedness for the 4IR, the UK compares well in terms of originality, but not that well in terms of technological diversification.

The NIS of Germany has the highest degree of diversification and knowledge localization. Germany also has relatively high originality and a medium cycle time of technologies. Thus, Germany can also be regarded as well prepared for the 4IR, based on its highest degree of technological diversification and relatively high level of originality. By contrast, the values for the five variables of the NIS in France all tend to be in the middle when compared with other countries. In other words, France has no clear-cut distinction in any of the five aspects of the NIS.

Finally, Korea manifests the highest degree of knowledge localization and concentration, which is regarded as a feature of the East Asian model of NIS, in the sense of a somewhat nationalistic and big-business-led NIS. A very high degree of knowledge localization is also observed in Japan. Korea must also catch up with the European countries in terms of obtaining additional patents in long cycle time-based technologies and further technological diversification. Although the short-cycle technologies and big-business-based NIS has served well as the catch-up mode of NIS, this does not bode well in terms of the long-term perspective and preparedness for the 4IR, which require more diversity. The NIS of Korea is still low in terms of originality.

Lee (2013) confirms that South Korea passed through its first technological turning point after the mid-1980s by specializing in and entering sectors with short cycle times of technology. Thus, the country has been very successful in catching up with the income level of advanced countries. Since the 2000s, the South Korean government has promoted industries such as biotechnology. Consequently, South Korea successfully passed through the second technological turning point by entering sectors with long cycle times of technology. This process is still continuing. Although this industrial promotion policy has succeeded in producing a certain number of patents (knowledge), general agreement prevails that those industries have still not achieved significant commercial success (Lee et al., 2017). Leaping into sectors with long cycle times of technology is not the only problem that South Korea faces. As the analysis in this chapter reveals, the country must also reduce the excessive degree of concentration by big businesses. However, making this transition, with the current NIS led by big businesses, will be very difficult. Instead, the participation of various agents is necessary, such as the small and medium-sized enterprises.

SUMMARY AND CONCLUDING REMARKS

This chapter analyzes and compares the national innovation systems of Korea, Italy, the UK, France and Germany. For these five economies, five aspects of the NIS are analyzed using US patent data in the last decade: originality, cycle time of technologies, knowledge localization, technological diversification and inventor-level concentration of innovation activities.

The NISs of the UK and Germany exhibit a high degree of originality and technological diversification, which is good in terms of preparedness for the fourth industrial revolution (4IR). Meanwhile, although the NIS of Italy has the longest cycle time, this feature implies a low degree of preparedness for the 4IR, as indicated by low originality and less diversification. In the meantime, the NIS in France tends to be in the middle in the five aspects of the NIS, thereby exhibiting no clear-cut distinction in any of the five aspects.

In comparison, Korea shows the highest degree of knowledge localization and concentration, which is regarded as a feature of the East Asian model of the NIS in the sense of somewhat nationalistic and big-business-led NIS. Although the short-cycle technologies and big-business-based NIS have served well as the catch-up mode of the NIS, this does not bode well in terms of long-term perspective and preparedness for the 4IR. Its NIS is still low in terms of originality.

REFERENCES

Acemoglu, Daron, and James A. Robinson, 2012. *Why Nations Fail*. New York: Crown Business.

Hall, B.H., Adam B. Jaffe and Manuel Trajtenberg, 2001. "The NBER Patent Citation Data File: Lessons, Insights and Methodological Tools," NBER Working Paper 8498.

Jaffe, Adam B., and M. Trajtenberg, 2002. *Patents, Citations, and Innovations: A Window on the Knowledge Economy*. US: MIT Press.

Jaffe, Adam B., M. Trajtenberg and M.S. Forgaty, 2000. 'Knowledge Spillovers and Patent Citations: Evidence from a Survey of Inventors', *American Economic Review* 90(2): 215–218.

Jaffe, Adam B., M. Trajtenberg and R. Henderson, 1993. "Geographic Localization of Knowledge Spillovers as Evidenced by Patent Citations," *Quarterly Journal of Economics* 108(3): 577–598.

Lee, Keun, 2013. *Schumpeterian Analysis of Economic Catch-up: Knowledge, Path Creation, and the Middle-income Trap*. Cambridge: Cambridge University Press.

Lee, Keun, Buru Im and Junhee Han, 2017. "The National Innovation System (NIS) for the Catch-up and Post-Catchup Stages in South Korea." In Choi, J. et al. (eds), *The Korean Government and Public Policy in Development Nexus: Sustaining Development and Tackling Policy Challenges*. Cham, Switzerand: Springer.

Lee, K., and B.Y. Kim, 2009. "Both Institutions and Policies Matter but Differently at Different Income Groups of Countries: Determinants of Long Run Economic Growth Revisited," *World Development* 37(3): 533–549.

Lee, K., and Minho Yoon, 2010. "International, Intra-national and Inter-firm Knowledge Diffusion and Technological Catch-Up: The USA, Japan, Korea and Taiwan in the Memory Chip Industry," *Technology Analysis and Strategic Management* 22(5): 553–570.

Lundvall, Bengt-Ake, 1992. *National System of Innovation: Toward a Theory of Innovation and Interactive Learning.* London: Pinter Publishers.

Schwab, Klaus, 2016. *The Forth Industrial Revolution.* Geneva: World Econ Forum.

Trajtenberg, Manuel, Rebecca Henderson and Adam B. Jaffe, 1997. "University vs. Corporate Patents: A Window on the Basicness of Innovations," *Economics of Innovation and New Technology* 5(1): 19–50.

APPENDIX ON DATA SOURCES AND FIGURES

Data Sources

The data used in this study were collected from the United States Patent and Trademark Office (USPTO) Grant Red Book (http://patents.reedtech.com/pgrbft.php). Patent Grant Full Text contains the full text, including tables, sequence data, and "in-line" mathematical expressions of each patent grant issued weekly from January 1976 to the present. The file format is SGML (Standard Generalized Markup Language) or ASCII text. These text data include patent number, series code and application number, type of patent, filing date, title, issue date, inventor information, assignee name at time of issue, foreign priority information, related US patent documents, classification information, US and foreign references, attorney, agent or firm/legal representative, Patent Cooperation Treaty (PCT) information, abstract, specification and claims. Approximately 4000 patent grants are issued per week. From these text data, we construct a new database through the data extraction process using SAS text mining. We have then analyzed these data to construct the values for the five measures of the NIS discussed in the text.

Definitions of the Five NIS Variables

Using granted patents DB and citation DB, we calculated localization, HHI (Hirschman–Herfindahl Index: concentration of assignees), originality, technological diversification, and the cycle time of technologies.

Localization (Jaffe et al., 1993; Lee and Yoon, 2010; Lee, 2013)

$$Localization_{xt} = \frac{n_{xxt}}{n_{xt}} - \frac{n_{cxt}}{n_{ct}}$$

n_{xxt}: the number of citations made to country x's patents by country x's granted in year t

n_{xt}: the number of all citations made by country x's patents granted in year t

n_{cxt}: the number of citations made to country x's patents by all patents, except country x's patents filed in year t

n_{ct}: the number of all citations made by all patents filed in year t, except country x's patents

Hirschman–Herfindahl index: concentration of assignees (Lee, 2013)

$$HHI_{xt} = \sum_{i \in I_x} \left(\frac{N_{it}}{N_{xt}^*} \right)^2,$$

where I_x is the set of assignees, N_{it} is the number of patents filed by assignee i in year t, and N_{xt}^* is the total number of patents filed by country x in year t, excluding unassigned patents.

Originality (Hall et al., 2001; Trajtenberg et al., 1997)

$$Originality_i = 1 - \sum_{k=1}^{N_i} \left(\frac{NCITED_{ik}}{NCITED_i} \right)^2,$$

where k is the technological sector (especially patent class k), $NCITED_{ik}$ is the number of citations made by the patent i to patents belonging to patent class k, and $NCITED_i$ is the total number of citations made by patent i.

Technological diversification (Lee, 2013)
This number pertains to the quantity of technological sectors in which a country has registered patents out of a 438 three-digit sector in the US patent classification system.

$$Diversification_i = \frac{N_i}{total\ number\ of\ sectors}$$

where N_i is the number of technological sectors of patent i. The total number of sectors is 438 until 2016.

Cycle time of technologies = backward lag (Jaffe et al., 1993)
For any publication Patent A, Publications 1, 2, 3 cited in A are backward citations of A:

Cycle time of technologies = application (grant) year of Patent A–application (grant) year of citations of Patent A

In this case, the windows of opportunity are 25 years.

PART II

Lessons from past industrial policy

4. Industry and government in the long run: on the true story of the American model

Marco R. Di Tommaso, Mattia Tassinari and Andrea Ferrannini

INTRODUCTION

This chapter aims at analyzing the long history of the industry–government relationship in the United States (US) and interpreting it with regard to the promotion of an American model of economy. Dealing with the debate on the government role in the US economy, it is immediately clear that industrial policy has been a contentious issue over American history. Strong arguments have always been raised supporting the idea that economic development must rely on government guidance (Chang and Grabel, 2014), and equally persistent arguments have claimed that interference in markets would only lead to failures and inefficiencies (Krueger, 1990; Le Grand, 1991; Chang, 1994; Lerner, 2009). Throughout American history, rhetoric has tended to emphasize the strengths of a free market in guiding the country's destiny, despite government policies actually taking a far more interventionist tack (Cowling and Tomlinson, 2011; Bianchi and Labory, 2011; Wade, 2012; Stiglitz and Lin, 2013; Di Tommaso and Schweitzer, 2013; Tassinari, 2014; Di Tommaso and Tassinari, 2014; Tassinari, 2019). Therefore, this chapter highlights the conflict between rhetoric and reality, by going beyond an ideological perspective in the debate about government intervention. We discuss the policy practices of the US government and provide a long-run interpretation of the American model of industry–government relationship.

In particular, the following research questions underlie this chapter:

1. Has the federal government actually played an active role in the historical experience of American industrialization, and more broadly for the promotion of an American model of economy?
2. When did these interventions take place, and for what purpose?

3. What were the goals and tools of government intervention?

These questions might appear surprising if one thinks of the United States as having a consistent political rhetoric and economic history character-ized by an unconditional confidence in the market, and by a tradition of opposition to government interference. Here, we suggest that the true story of the American model is different.

Our inquiry begins with the days following political independence, when the US also wanted to gain industrial and economic independence. America's first proponent of industrial policy was Alexander Hamilton, who expressed cogent ideas about the country's need to catch up to leading industrialized countries. From this starting point, we trace the development of government intervention through the various stages of the country's industrialization, up to the present days of the first 18 months of Trump administration.

AMERICA'S INDUSTRIAL POLICIES OVER THE YEARS FROM INDEPENDENCE TO THE COLD WAR

The Hamilton Approach to Support US Industrialization

In 1791 the Secretary of the Treasury, Alexander Hamilton, presented to the United States Congress his *Report on the Subject of Manufactures*, which proposed an economic policy program for the industrial develop-ment of the country. The document clearly defined interventions that were consistent with a strategic vision on the future of the US economy, based on the promotion of the American infant industry: tariffs on imported products, a prohibition on exporting innovative machinery, direct subsidies to those industries considered to be strategic, tax exemp-tions for production of raw materials, and support for improving national infrastructures (Hamilton, 1791 [2007]).

In concrete, the strategy suggested in the Report found practical appli-cation, and the interventionist approach inspired by the ideas of Hamilton characterized the first phase of growth of American industry (Chang, 2002). For example, under this scenario the railway industry was one of the first to catch crucial attention by the government (Cochran, 1950; Hill, 1951; Carter, 1968; Lloyd, 1982; Dobbin, 1994). In the early decades of the nineteenth century the government played an important role in the planning, financing and regulation of this industry. Initially, the state and local governments – in partnership with the private sector – played the main role. Later, from 1860, the federal government became a central actor: firstly, offering land, guarantees and loans for the construction of four transcontinental lines, and then regulating the entire rail system (Dobbin, 1994). Federal regulation began in 1887, with the Interstate Commerce Act and the creation of the first federal regulatory agency: the Interstate Commerce Commission (Bingham and Sharpe, 1998). Although regulation and antitrust policy were becoming important for promoting competition in the US economy,[1] at the same time a number of "special cases" were identified in areas considered strategic for the national interest.

For instance, the iron and steel industry, which had benefited from high protectionist tariffs since the years of independence, was clearly favored in the late nineteenth century by the creation of cartels and strategic alliances, thus leading to the formation of an important national oligopoly (Nester, 1997; Wilson, 2006). Similarly, at that time the automotive industry attracted the attention of the federal government, which ensured that tariffs on imported goods fluctuated between 25% and 50% from 1913 until 1934, then stabilized at a level of about 10% in subsequent years. More generally, over a period of 30 years, the duties on foreign industrial products grew progressively, reaching 40%, and they were then maintained at this high level until the first half of the twentieth century. Overall, this was a long period in which the domestic industry took advantage of protection from foreign competition, strong and continuing public demand, and massive government investments in equipment, technology and infrastructure (Nester, 1997; Di Tommaso and Schweitzer, 2013).

The Great Depression and the Preparation for the Second World War

Focusing on the years between the two World Wars, there was another "special moment" that characterized the relationship between industry and the federal government in the United States: the Great Depression. During those years, the American government intervened substantially in the national industrial system. Within the New Deal, one of the most important actions promoted by President Roosevelt was the National Industrial Recovery Act of 1933, through which the government promoted employment, both as a direct employer as well as through contracts for public goods and services in the private sector. Furthermore, the Buy American Act of 1933 supported a wide variety of domestic industries, by placing limits on the purchase of foreign products for public procurement. Some firms were also exempted

---

[1]   In those years the institutional structure underlying the American antitrust policy started to be set up, in particular with the Sherman Antitrust Act of 1890 and the Clayton Antitrust Act of 1914.

from the antitrust regulation, fostering the creation of cartels and monopolies when conceived to pursue a national strategic interest (Dobbin, 1993). In this scenario a central role was played by the Reconstruction Finance Corporation (RFC), which was a national development bank created few decades earlier by the government for directly financing businesses and industries that needed capital: from 1932 to 1935 the RFC distributed more than $2 billion to companies unable to obtain credit from the private sector (Bingham and Sharpe, 1998). Finally, the Roosevelt administration also decided to promote an ambitious reform of the banking system through the Banking Acts of 1933 and 1935, which provided a series of actions to support and protect banks from bankruptcy (Bingham and Sharpe, 1998). In those years the federal banking system – that is, the Federal Reserve System – was also reformed, and the Federal Open Market Committee was created for defining the stance of monetary policy.

In the aftermath of the Great Depression, the attention of President Roosevelt gradually turned to reorganizing the entire American economy to make it ready to meet the looming World War.[2] In a few years the whole domestic industrial sector was incentivized and converted to meet the military needs. The government architecture of domestic industry of the First World War was immediately recharged and strengthened with the set-up of different boards, councils and offices – involving government officials, military leaders and managers of private industry – in order to coordinate and convert the entire national industrial sector to respond to the military needs.[3]

In those years, the government expenditure managed by the War Department, the Navy Department and their subcontractors reached $315.8 billion. The growing public demand for goods and services in the civilian sector and the government funds to conduct research and development (R&D) for military purposes resulted in a significant boost to the development of economies of scale and learning in a selected number of private enterprises. In this regard, the concentration of firms involved in military production was striking: only 100 firms received about two-thirds of the contracts (Di Tommaso and Schweitzer, 2013).

---

[2] Since the First World War, the military capabilities of the nation were consistently maintained, with an important government involvement in the development of weapons, machinery, military technology and R&D funding. A nearly continuous line assuring the strength of the US military sector can be identified over the long run, taking into account the years of preparation for conflicts, the war times themselves (ranging from the First World War to the recent conflicts in Iraq and Afghanistan) and the post-war "inertia." For more details, see McNeill (1982) and Weiss, L. (2014).

[3] In this regard, the Berry Amendment of 1941 excluded foreign competitors from the provision of goods and services in the field of defense (Weiss and Thurbon, 2006).

The Years of the Cold War

The Second World War had de facto created a policy scenario characterized by a well-established habit of supporting particular industries, tolerance for oligopolies and cartels in strategic sectors, and a strong presence of the public hand in the management of national industries. After the Second World War the threat coming from the Soviet Union emerged, further reinforcing the "special relationship" between the government and many domestic industries. In the context of the Cold War, the Vannevar Bush Report (Bush, 1945) highlighted that scientific progress had to be promoted through important public programs. In 1948, with the creation of the National Security Council and the Central Intelligence Agency, the institutional framework in the field of national security was strengthened. Within this setting four decades of massive public investment in the defense industry began, and about $16 trillion was spent by the government in those years, including $4 trillion on nuclear weapons (Nester, 1997; Schwartz, 1998; Mowery, 1998). Undoubtedly, a turning point was the Soviet launch of *Sputnik*, that is, the first satellite in orbit around the Earth, in 1957. This event highlighted the close relationship between technological superiority and national defense, causing a series of (emotional and political) reactions in the US and stimulating measures aimed at filling the perceived technological gap with the Soviets (Weiss, 2014). Government funds for research were thus increased, and education in science was explicitly encouraged. In 1958 the Advanced Research Projects Agency (ARPA),[4] the National Aeronautics and Space Administration (NASA) and the Small Business Investment Corporation (SBIC) were established, with the specific goal of putting constant efforts toward increasing technological innovation in the military and civil fields (Block, 2008; Fuchs, 2010; Weiss, 2014). Over just a decade, the expenditure in research and development increased from 1.5% of US gross domestic product (GDP) to more than 3% (Weiss, 2014; Block, 2008; Block and Keller, 2011; Mazzucato, 2013).

Support to the military sector played an important role in the development of infant industries in those years. For example, the information and communication technology (ICT) industry benefited enormously from the investments in the military field (Markusen et al., 1991; Abbate, 1999; Fong, 2001; Mazzucato, 2013), thanks to the growing demand for computers commissioned during the 1950s and 1960s by the Department of Defense, the Air Force, the Army Signal Corps, the Atomic Energy

---

[4]   Later renamed the Defense Advanced Research Projects Agency (DARPA).

Commission, NASA, the US Weather Bureau (now the National Center for Atmospheric Research), the National Institutes of Health and the Social Security Administration.[5]

Similar dynamics concerned the development of nuclear energy used for civilian purposes. Already at the end of the 1930s, the Manhattan Project had funded research for the development of atomic weapons that were eventually used in 1945 against Hiroshima and Nagasaki. At the end of the Second World War, the federal government instituted a number of research centers and national laboratories on applications of nuclear energy for civilian purposes, and in 1954, President Eisenhower approved the Atomic Energy Act, which encouraged technological advancements in the production of nuclear energy in the subsequent decades (Di Tommaso and Schweitzer, 2013).

The biotechnology sector was another infant industry in those days that strongly benefited from government support. A series of actions were promoted by the Nixon administration (Hurt, 2011), which in 1969 decided to convert the national research program for the construction of biological weapons to civilian purposes, in order to promote the development of the biomedical industry. Government intervention in this area was motivated primarily by the competitive challenge from Europe, Japan and the Soviet Union in an industry explicitly considered to be strategic. For instance, in those years the National Science Foundation and the National Institutes of Health financed a project with crucial implications: recombinant DNA. Many of today's successes in the American biotech industry can be traced back to this early research program (Hurt, 2011; Di Tommaso and Schweitzer, 2013).

RECENT TIMES: FROM REAGAN TO BUSH JR

Rhetoric and Practice of Industrial Policy during the Reagan Administration

By the end of the 1970s, European and Japanese manufacturing had been catching up since the Second World War and was making serious inroads into previously strong American markets. In a context of strong political and economic turmoil both at the domestic and the international

---

[5]   In this context, for instance, during the 1960s the Department of Defense also funded the research that then led to the birth and development of the Internet. For discussions on the role of the US government in the development of computer technology, see Mazzucato (2013), Adner (2012), Ceruzzi (2003), Audretsch (1995), Abbate (1999) and Kenney (2003).

level, President Carter established an Economic Policy Group explicitly instructed to formulate a proposal for a national industrial policy (ERP, 1981; Bingham and Sharpe, 1998). For the first time these words entered the American political discussion, stimulating a wide debate inside and outside academic circles.[6]

However, when President Reagan was elected in 1980, he immediately declared his opposition to any kind of industrial policy plan, and the Carter's program was never implemented. The economic strategy of the new Republican administration was based on a thriving academic literature concerning government failures,[7] which was supported by a strong political rhetoric that emphasized the freedom of markets and individual initiative as mantras of the American economic model. "Reaganomics" – as Reagan's approach was soon named – claimed to use other levers of economic policy, promoting interventions aimed to increase the level of investment and to reduce the amount of currency in circulation (ERP, 1984, 1990).

Nonetheless, these positions soon became unworkable. The high US trade deficit of those years created an increasing consensus favoring protectionist policies as a quick solution to economic problems and saving jobs (ERP, 1986). Protectionist interventions were promoted in all those sectors that appeared to be in strong difficulty: among others, automotive, textiles and clothing, steel and semiconductors (Baldwin and Richardson, 1987; Richman, 1988; Niskanen, 1988).

In the automotive sector, imports into the American market had reached 30%, and Chrysler in particular had already lost 40% of its workers, being at risk of bankruptcy. In 1979, President Carter had already begun to take action to save the companies considered "too big to fail": with the Chrysler Corporation Loan Guarantee Act, the company received $1.5 billion from the federal government as a guarantee on loans and $3.5 billion as additional capital and concessions from labor unions. After 1981, the Reagan administration decided on a program of general protection of the entire automotive industry (Graham, 1992; Di Tommaso and Schweitzer, 2013). In March 1982, a Voluntary Export Restraint was negotiated with the Japanese government, limiting the volume of imports of cars from Japan to 1.68 million cars. In the subsequent years the limit gradually rose, but still remained in place until 1985, with 2.3 million cars imported (Niskanen, 1988; Richman, 1988; Bingham and Sharpe, 1998).

---

[6] See Reich (1982, 1984), Etzioni (1983), Schultze (1983), DiLorenzo (1984), Dorn (1984), Dumke (1984), Johnson (1984), Niskanen (1984), Norton (1986), Eisinger (1990) and White (2007).

[7] See Krueger (1990), Le Grand (1991), Chang (1994), Buigues and Sekkat (2009) and Di Tommaso and Schweitzer (2013).

Similarly, in the steel sector the administration negotiated restrictions on European exports as anti-dumping penalties in 1982, setting a general limit of a 5.5% share in the American market, regardless of the amount of the subsidy European goods had received (Niskanen, 1988). In the semi-conductor industry, in 1986 the Reagan administration exerted pressure on the Japanese government to set a higher market price on memory chips and apply it even in third-country markets, in order to increase sales of American chips internationally. However, these conditions were not fully accepted by the Japanese government, and the United States responded by imposing a tariff of 100% on $300 million worth of imports from Japan (Niskanen, 1988; Richman, 1988). The same measures arose in the textile industries, leading to the renewal of the Multi-Fiber Agreement as a system of quotas on exports adopted by the industrialized countries to regulate imports (Niskanen, 1988).

At the same time, other measures continued to play an even more focused role in terms of protection and support to American industry. In particular, the Department of Defense (DoD) was called upon to play a central role by actively supporting various industries (Reich, 1982; Weiss, 2014). For instance, two consortia for the development of new technologies were created in the machinery tools and semiconductors industry, both of whicvh were being strongly threatened by foreign competition: the National Center for Manufacturing Sciences (NCMS) in 1986 and the SEMATECH (Semiconductor Manufacturing Technology Initiatives) in 1987, with the latter receiving support of about $100 million from the DoD in 1989 (ERP, 1989; Irwin and Klenow, 1996; Block, 2008; Wade, 2010).

Other federal departments and agencies continued to exercise an important influence on technological advancements and industrial development, including in particular the Department of Energy, NASA, the National Science Foundation and the National Institutes of Health. In this context, policies for technology transfer from government agencies to the private sector became particularly relevant. The University and Small Business Patent Procedures Act of 1980 (commonly known as the Bayh–Dole Act) gave the opportunity for private universities, small businesses and non-profit private institutions to own, as exclusive property rights, the patents emanating from research funded by the government. In subsequent years, these rights were also extended to private companies of all sizes and public universities. Unsurprisingly, the number of university patents increased from 230 in 1976 to 900 in 1987 (ERP, 1989).[8]

---

[8] Further important laws to encourage technology transfer were the Technology Innovation Act of 1980 and the Federal Technology Transfer Act of 1986, which enabled

In addition, during the 1980s other important programs were implemented to encourage local development and small business. The Small Business Innovation Research program (SBIR) launched in 1982 was particularly important because it established a consortium between the Small Business Administration (of the Department of Commerce) and other government agencies for the development of new start-ups (Lerner, 1999; Audretsch, 2003; Mazzucato, 2013). The program was crucial for creating a new innovation system based on a network of institutions and organizations at local, state and federal level, able to provide assistance and financial capital to innovative enterprises (Block and Keller, 2011; Mazzucato, 2013).[9] Another relevant program was the Manufacturing Extension Partnership (MEP), which was launched in 1988 to improve industrial productivity, competitiveness and the technological capacity of American small businesses. In particular, this was accomplished through the creation of state and local government centers to provide managerial services and technical assistance to enterprises (see, e.g., Shapira, 2001).

The 1990s and the Acceleration of the Globalization Processes

In the early 1990s the international political and economic order was changing radically, fostering an important acceleration of the globalization process. In the United States the establishment of a number of multilateral and bilateral trade agreements was at the center of the political agenda (ERP, 1990). First of all, there were the negotiations in the Uruguay Round, which led in 1994 to the creation of the World Trade Organization (WTO). In this context, one of the main goals pursued by the American government was the reduction of tariffs and non-tariff trade barriers in order to better access international markets (ERP, 1995). Even if the negotiations for the establishment of economic rules under the WTO were formally carried out at multilateral level, the United States was able to exploit an undisputed political and economic leadership (Panitch and Gindin, 2012). Indeed, the WTO coincided with a historical period characterized by a substantial identity of goals between the American government and international institutions (see, e.g., ERP, 1995, pp. 212–213). In this framework, for example, the regulation of public procurement at the international level provided a clear example of the US ability to exploit the international rules to favor its industry. The WTO Government

---

federal laboratories to engage in cooperation with private companies and to retain a portion of the royalties paid to the private sector (ERP, 1989).

[9] See also Whitford (2005), Block (2008), Weiss (2014), Buigues and Sekkat (2009), Schrank and Whitford (2009), Wade (2012) and Di Tommaso and Schweitzer (2013).

Procurement Agreement was signed in 1994 with the aim of liberalizing public procurement markets (Trionfetti, 2000; Hoekman and Mavroidis, 1997). As argued by Weiss and Thurbon (2006), the United States was able to manage this new regulatory framework in a strategic way: on the one hand, by opening public procurement markets abroad through international regulation; and on the other hand, by trying to close domestic markets to foreign companies, claiming justification according to national laws (such as the Buy American Act) or through legal loopholes or other types of informal barriers. This strategy favored American businesses and national industrial development, thanks to the overall growth in domestic and foreign demand for US products.

With a similar goal, during these years many other trade initiatives were launched by the US in order to foster access to foreign markets for American products: the North American Free Trade Agreement (NAFTA) in 1992 (ERP, 1992, 1993, 1995), the Asia-Pacific Economic Cooperation (APEC) program in 1989, the Free Trade Area of the Americas (FTAA), the Trade Enhancement Initiative, the Andean Trade Preference Initiative and the Enterprise for the Americas Initiative (EAI). Overall, the trade policy initiatives undertaken by the American government during the 1990s show how the involvement and the bargaining power of the US government in the definition of the "rules of the international economic game" had an almost global reach (Stiglitz, 2002; Phillips, 2005; Katzenstain, 2005; Panitch and Gindin, 2012).[10]

In addition, policies to support technological innovation were particularly prominent in this period. Changing international political conditions and increased stability resulting from the end of the Cold War enabled (and even required) the United States to reduce its military expenditures. Concerns about the possible negative impact from this retrenchment on the technological and industrial development of the entire American economy led the government to look for alternative ways to promote innovation (ERP, 1991, 1993, 1994). In this context, the ICT industry was considered one of the priorities (ERP, 2001).[11] Among the initiatives promoted by the Clinton administration to encourage the development of this sector, it is worth mentioning: the Information Technology for the Twenty

---

[10]   In the last decades signals for important changes in this setting have become clear, in particular considering the rising of the bargaining power of China in international institutions (see Chin and Thakur, 2010; Chin, 2012; Hopewell, 2015). On the effective influence of the Washington Consensus in more recent years see, for example, Kirshner (2008), Babb (2013), Ban and Blyth (2013), Grabel (2013) and Johnson and Barnes (2014).

[11]   Between 1990 and 2000 the contribution of this industry to GDP rose from 5.8% to 8.3%. Between 1995 and 2001, private investment in the sector was growing by 28% per annum (ERP, 2001).

First Century Initiative (which aimed at increasing scientific research in the field of software and network infrastructures), the Internet Tax Freedom Act (which suspended taxes on the Internet), the ratification of the WTO's Information Technology Agreement and of the WTO's Basic Telecommunication Agreement (to encourage the opening of markets for high-tech goods and services). Finally, the Telecommunications Act of 1996 represented a relevant attempt to reform the telecommunications sector through increasing competition in local telephone markets (ERP, 2000).

Among the policies for science and technology, the Clinton administration was also committed to improve the partnership between government and the private sector. The launch of the Advanced Technology Program (ATP), directed by the National Institute of Standards and Technology, was particularly important. In 1993 the Partnership for a New Generation of Vehicles (PNGV) was also founded. With the participation of American auto manufacturers, along with suppliers operating in the sector and universities, the PNGV had the goal of developing environmentally friendly technologies for vehicles (ERP, 2001). In addition, in those years the National Cooperative Research and Production Act further liberalized cooperation in the field of research. As a result, almost 740 joint ventures were registered in 1998 (ERP, 2001).

Beyond these programs and initiatives, the Clinton administration increased funds for research conducted by the National Science Foundation and by the National Institutes of Health by more than 60% and 80%, respectively, in eight years. It also maintained tax credits for expenditures on research and development carried out by private firms (equal to 20% in 1999) (ERP, 2001). Finally, the Antitrust Guidelines for the Licensing of Intellectual Property of 1995 provided better control of intellectual property rights protection (ERP, 1999).

The Bush Jr Administration between the Wars and the Outbreak of the Financial Crisis

During the Bush Jr administration (2001–2009), the demands of the military sector regained an important role in the American economy due to the beginning of the wars in Afghanistan in 2001 and Iraq in 2003 (Ketels, 2007; Weiss, 2014; Buigues and Sekkat, 2009). In these years, the budget for the Department of Defense grew from 15.6% of total federal government budget in 2001, to 19.9% in 2008.[12]

---

[12] See *Budget of the United States Government: Historical Tables, Fiscal Year 2010.*

In the context of policies to promote technological progress, in 2006 the Bush administration launched the American Competitiveness Initiative (ACI). The plan, prepared by the Office of Science and Technology Policy, proposed several actions, including a doubling of public investment in R&D in ten years through the increase in funds destined to some of the major federal agencies involved in research (OSTP, 2006; Ketels, 2007). However, the initiative did not find enough support in Congress to be fully implemented (Buigues and Sekkat, 2009). Nonetheless, some of the major programs already activated in the 1980s and 1990s remained in place, such as the Advanced Technology Program (ATP), the Manufacturing Extension Partnership (MEP), the Small Business Innovation Research Program (SBIR) and Small Business Technology Transfer program (STTR). However, in some cases the budget allocated to these programs was even reduced. Nevertheless, support for R&D conducted at universities remained high. In 2003, for example, the Bush administration covered 62% of the expenditure in this area, compared to 58% in 2000 (Ketels, 2007).

In terms of trade policy, interventions had goals that were consistent with the approach that characterized the United States in the previous decade: on the one hand, to liberalize foreign markets; and on the other, to relieve American businesses from foreign competitive pressure (Ketels, 2007). In particular, the Bush administration was able to conclude a number of trade agreements at both bilateral and multilateral levels as part of the WTO Doha Round in 2001. Data published in the Economic Report of the President (ERP) in 2009 revealed that, in 2007, 41% of US exports were directed to countries with which America had a trade agreement, while only 31% of imports came from these countries (ERP, 2009).

Alongside the commitment to liberalize international commerce, other measures were important to protect the American industry. For example, in the agricultural sector the need for subsidies to compete with foreign production – often protected by the foreign governments – was particularly pronounced (ERP, 2009). Similarly, the government applied protectionist tariffs on imports in other sectors, such as textiles, wood and steel. Despite justifications by the American government that these measures were merely a response to unfair trade practices, the line held by the United States was challenged at the international level (Gallagher, 2007). In 2003 and 2004, for example, the WTO removed the American tariffs on steel. In 2007, under increasing international pressure, Congress abolished the Continued Dumping and Subsidy Offset Act of 2000 (known as the Byrd Amendment), according to which the funds obtained from duties on imported products were distributed to firms in difficulty (about $840 million for the period 2001–2003). In 2002, the WTO also forced the United

States to remove the Foreign Sales Corporation, which reduced federal taxation on profits from exports, as it represented an implicit export subsidy internationally perceived as unfair (Ketels, 2007).

INDUSTRIAL POLICY DURING THE OBAMA ADMINISTRATION

The Strategy to Address the World Financial Crisis during Obama's First Term

At the outset of the Obama presidential administration (approximately a year after the financial crisis began), the government's main aim was to foster the recovery of almost the entire American economy from the threat of a truly catastrophic economic recession. To achieve this goal, the American Recovery and Reinvestment Act (ARRA) enacted in early 2009 was undoubtedly the central action. This massive government intervention – a stimulus package worth a total of $787 billion – was oriented not only to address short-run social and economic emergencies, but also to foster a more radical change within the American productive structure, economy and society with a long-term perspective (ERP, 2010). Unsurprisingly, most of Obama's rhetoric regarding government interventions in all spheres was linked to the pursuit of broad societal goals.

About a third of the total resources available through the ARRA were earmarked for financing particular segments of the economy: primarily the financial sector, with the aim of preventing an even more severe collapse, but also other industries and targets considered to be "strategic" for the country. Other actions were also directed to education and life-long learning, science and technology, trade policy, as well as regional and small businesses development (ERP, 2010; Di Tommaso and Schweitzer, 2013).

The financial sector, having been the epicenter of the economic crisis, was one of the first to receive attention from the Obama administration. After the bankruptcy of Lehman Brothers in September 2008, the American government intervened to prevent the collapse of the entire banking system, through the bailout of numerous banks (ERP, 2010). The first actions in this direction were already implemented by the Bush administration through the Troubled Asset Relief Program (TARP), which was established by the Emergency Economic Stabilization Act of 2008. In particular, the government gave authority to the US Treasury to purchase $700 billion worth of mortgage-backed securities. The Obama administration promoted subsequent interventions to support the financial sector with the Financial Stability Plan, which was approved by Congress in February 2009. In this context, the government allocated $2 trillion to buy mortgages from banks in order to supplement liquidity in the banking system (Di Tommaso and Schweitzer, 2013).

Similarly, the automotive industry was the target of bailout policies since the beginning of the financial crisis. In 2008, Chrysler and General Motors (GM) were clearly risking bankruptcy. The industry bailout, regulated by the Loan and Security Agreement, initially started with funds provided by the Bush administration under the TARP, which allocated a total of $17.4 billion for the two companies (that is, $13.4 billion for GM and $4 billion for Chrysler).

During Obama's first term, another intervention that had great visibility in the American public opinion and at international level was surely the health reform, through the Patient Protection and Affordable Care Act (PPACA) (more generally known as the Affordable Care Act – ACA) and the Health Care and Education Reconciliation Act, both approved in Congress in 2010. These interventions substantially extended health insurance coverage. In particular, the ACA made health insurance coverage not simply available but even mandatory for most employers and individuals. This health reform – most commonly known as "Obamacare" – was expected, on the one hand, to foster the development of the whole health care industry, and on the other hand, to improve social equity, thanks to the universality of health care coverage (Di Tommaso and Schweitzer, 2005, 2010).

The American Recovery and Reinvestment Act (ARRA) of 2009 also had a major impact on the energy sector and on diffusion of "green" industries. Reduction in the dependence on foreign oil and in energy costs, improvement of industrial efficiency, creation of quality jobs and a decrease in pollution levels were the main goals pursued by the government in this field. With regard to renewable energy (for example, solar, wind and geothermal), the investment amounted to $23 billion. In the transport sector, including plug-in hybrid vehicles, electric vehicles and the infrastructure necessary for their operation, the Obama administration invested $16 billion, while another $300 million was invested through the General Services Administration for purchasing energy-efficient vehicles produced in America. In addition, in order to reduce the national consumption of electrical energy, the government promoted the construction of a modern "smart grid," with an overall investment amounting to $4 billion. Furthermore, $400 million was used for the establishment of the Advanced Research Projects Agency – Energy (ARPA-E), set up as an agency in charge of carrying out scientific research in the field of advanced energy technologies (ERP, 2010; Di Tommaso and Schweitzer, 2013).

The development of the infrastructure sector was another important element of the Obama administration's response to the economic crisis, because of its inherent long-term nature. The government promoted improvements in the traditional transportation infrastructure, for example through investments in the highway and rail systems, and the development of innovative infrastructures such as those related to broadband access and to the circulation of digital information. The ARRA allocated approximately $7 billion for investment in broadband (Di Tommaso and Schweitzer, 2013).

Finally, in the field of education, basic research and, more generally, the enhancement of science and technology, the ARRA of 2009 allocated a total of about $100 billion (ERP, 2010). Similarly, the America Invents Act of 2011 was important in promoting basic research with public funding, in order to support the creation and commercialization of innovative products through support of start-ups, and to provide greater protection of intellectual property rights (ERP, 2012).

Relaunching Growth and Economic Opportunities over Obama's Second Term

Obama declared that his second term, which began in January 2013, was aimed at addressing three main challenges: (1) to enable the American economy to use its full potential by reducing long-term unemployment; (2) to expand the economic potential of the labor force; and (3) to facilitate improved economic opportunities by reducing social inequalities (ERP, 2014).

In promoting these goals, the Obama administration repeatedly highlighted the central role that back-shoring policies had to play. Therefore, several interventions were oriented toward encouraging the return of profits earned from overseas production, especially in the manufacturing sector (ERP, 2014).

Under this scenario, one of the major initiatives included in the budget for fiscal year 2015 was the Opportunity, Growth and Security Initiative (ERP, 2014). The funds of this initiative – $56 billion – were equally shared between the civilian and the military area, in order to finance mainly: education, work training, basic research in the health field, applied research in technologies for energy efficiency and renewable energy (including electric motors, batteries and ultra-light materials for electric vehicles), creation of a national network for innovation in the manufacturing sector (with the goal of launching 45 new centers in the country), modernization of the state electricity grids, modernization of the national aviation system, and improvement in the efficiency and effectiveness of public administration.

In general, the administration assigned particular relevance to the science and technology policies, increasing federal spending in R&D for 2015 by approximately 1.2% as compared to 2014. Overall, in 2015 the federal budget included about $135 billion for research, with $2.2 billion for advanced manufacturing (12% more than in 2014), $325 million for the transition to clean energy (as part of the $5.2 billion allocated for the clean energy technology programs), $2.5 billion for the US Global Change Research Program in response to climate change, $30.2 billion for the National Institutes of Health (including research against cancer and Alzheimer's disease, as part of the BRAIN Initiative) and $7.3 billion for the National Science Foundation.

In 2013 the government also proposed expanding the Select USA initiative, launched in 2011, which aimed at encouraging foreign direct investment in the United States (ERP, 2014). This program formed global teams, led by American ambassadors, in 32 key countries, in charge of leading a coordinated process for networking potential investors. The initiative offered a number of tools, including a list of various federal and state programs available to foreign investors, in order to facilitate increased investment in the United States (Jackson, 2013).

Particular attention also was devoted to trade policy. Several initiatives were undertaken by the Obama administration with the aim of promoting trade and investment with Europe and Asia. Specifically, the administration continued the negotiations within two main regional trade initiatives: the Trans-Pacific Partnership Agreement (TPP), which included 12 countries in Asia, and the Transatlantic Trade and Investment Partnership (TTIP) with the European Union (EU) (ERP, 2014). The TPP, in particular, appeared to be very promising, in order to carry out trade relations with Asia within a single regulatory framework. In fact, such relations are nowadays characterized by a high number of individual preferential trade agreements, while TTP was expected to facilitate the entry of the United States into Asian markets (Capling and Ravenhill, 2011; Williams, 2013; Fergusson et al., 2013).

THE IRRUPTION OF DONALD TRUMP IN US POLITICS AND THE FIRST ACTIONS OF HIS ADMINISTRATION

In a general climate of surprise, Donald J. Trump won the 2016 presidential elections. the rhetoric of "Trump-Economics" during the electoral campaign can be summarized as a hybrid mix of the following elements: (1) extreme laissez-fair proposals on the business sector at the domestic level;

(2) the relaunching of significant investment in physical infrastructure; and (3) strict trade protectionism.

In this regard, the Trump presidential campaign appeared as something unique in American political history. The first distinctive element was the simplification of the rhetoric discourse, instrumented by the use of social media, in particular Twitter, leading to a process of political disintermediation and to the centralization of the decision-making. This dynamic was effective in polarizing the consensus around a few big economic and societal questions (for example, employment, taxation, migration, security) and providing immediate and all-embracing answers based on the identification of scapegoats for each policy topic.

In particular, Trump's electoral economic agenda seemed to have interpreted the protection demands, expressed by a large strata of the population, from the challenges of globalization (that is, in terms of the threat of foreign investments to domestic saving, the threat of external competition to domestic industry, the threat of migration to domestic employment) as well as from the constraints imposed by the international agreements (that is, NAFTA, TPP). In this perspective, the two main slogans adopted by Trump – namely, "America First" and "Make America Great Again" (MAGA) – should be interpreted as a rather successful attempt to meet the rising demand for economic closing by the losers of globalization (Di Tommaso, 2017).

The first 18 months of Trump's administration have been characterized by a combination of controversial declarations and some substantial actions consistent with the announcements of the electoral campaign. It seems that the application of "Trump-Economics" has been so far partially constrained by the forces in support of American capitalism, whose financial interests are likely to seek long-term continuity, thus repudiating the radical attacks by the new President on the globalization system that they themselves contributed to shape. However, by investigating the first concrete steps of the new administration it is possible to highlight a series of shifts, mainly in terms of state budget administration, fiscal measures, support to manufacturing and trade policy.

In this context, the Budget of the US Government, *A New Foundation for American Greatness*, for fiscal year 2018 (White House, 2018a) – followed and confirmed by the Budget of the US Government *Efficient, Effective, Accountable: An American Budget* for fiscal year 2019 (White House, 2018b) – stresses the need to design and implement new policies for jobs and growth based on new spending priorities. In the first instance, the proposal highlights the need to cut the federal budget in order to then move on with fiscal reforms. In this regard, it calls for a strict control over federal spending, planning a reduction by $3.6 trillion over the next ten years and the subsequent containment of the debt:GDP ratio at 60%. The main areas of spending control concern the repeal of Obamacare and the substitution of Medicaid through realignment of the related financial incentives to both federal and state budgets. At the same time, the document proposes to implement a reform of the welfare system aimed at encouraging unemployed individuals to exit their dependence on government subsidies.

The 2018 US federal budget also promotes a simplification of the tax codes along with the reduction of both income taxes (for example, lower individual income tax rates, repeal Obamacare surcharge on capital gains and dividends, abolition of the death tax) and business taxes (for example, reduction of the business tax rates, introduction of the repatriation tax for American businesses that accumulated overseas income) (Budget of the US Government, 2018, p. 13).

Overall, Trump's administration aspires to reprioritize all the sources of the federal discretionary spending, forecasting a systematic 2% decrease per year. In this framework, increasing national safety and security funds is ensured by relying on budget compensations on non-defense spending (that will be reduced by $4.3 trillion). Among the top budget priorities of the new US government, it is fundamental to highlight the invest-ment in defense, mostly based on discretionary budget authority for the Department of Defense (DoD): up to a total of $639 billion with a $52 bil-lion increase above the 2017 annualized continuing resolution. Moreover, the budget increases the Research, Development, Test and Evaluation (RDT&E) account of the Pentagon by $17.8 billion, leading the DoD to receive 45.4% of total federal R&D funding.

The relaunch of domestic infrastructures represents another top prior-ity of the US government through an announced plan of $200 billion in federal funds over ten years, in order to spur at least $1.5 trillion in infrastructure investments on surface transportation, airports, water-ways, ports, broadband and other facilities with partners at the State, local, tribal, and private level. This plan is fully explained in the official "Building a Stronger America: President Donald J. Trump's American Infrastructure Initiative" (White House, 2018c), and its long and contin-ued rhetoric was clearly illustrated during Trump's State of the Union address in January 2018: "We will build gleaming new roads, bridges, highways, railways, and waterways across our land. And we will do it with American heart, and American hands, and American grit." Nevertheless, this rhetoric illustrates the way Trump makes continuous use of declara-tions to raise expectations (in this case for infrastructure development) to shape the business environment, even before – or in some cases without – implementing concrete actions.

This is surely central in the strategy to bring back manufacturing (and thus jobs) to the US by promoting re-shoring in three ways (complementing the above-mentioned infrastructure initiative): (1) publicly blaming and threatening those manufacturers which have moved – or were planning to move – production abroad; (2) influencing expectations and gaining enhanced support from American manufacturers, mainly through a wide use of announcements and declarations; and (3) ensuring a drastic decrease in the corporate income tax. Concerning the latter point, in December 2017 the Senate approved the $1.5 trillion tax bill, which mainly includes – along with other actions – permanent tax breaks for corporations, falling drastically from 35% to 21%, although at lower levels than was promised during the electoral campaign (that is, reduction to 15%).

Focusing on Trump's stylized facts concerning trade and industrial policy, it appears clear that the neo-protectionism propaganda is increasingly coupled with concrete actions against the main US trade partners, namely the European Union, Canada, Mexico and China. Among those actions on trade policy in line with the electoral campaign there is Trump's repeal of TPP in January 2017, which suggest a switch from Obama's multilateral approach to a bilateral conception in trade relations with Asian partners. On the other side, the new administration is pushing for a withdrawal of NAFTA to favor bilateral agreements, despite political and trade relations with Mexico and Canada having been so far controversial.

Nonetheless, it is interesting to mention the diffusion of a series of neo-protectionism initiatives, which have been only partially implemented so far in concrete policy actions. In February 2017, for example, the Trump administration suggested the idea of implementing a border adjustment tax targeted at imported goods sold domestically, in order to eliminate the corporations' incentive to offshore profits, but the proposal was abandoned in July of the same year (Thomas, 2017).

In January 2018 Trump approved the Office of the United States Trade Representative (USTR) recommendations to impose safeguard tariffs on imported large residential washing machines and imported solar cells and modules – whose increased foreign imports are conceived as a serious injury to domestic manufacturers – as follows: 20% tariff on the first 1.2 million imported large residential washers in the first year, and a 50% tariff on machines above that number, with tariffs declining to 16% and 40% respectively in the third year; 30% tariff on imported solar cells and modules in the first year, with the tariffs declining to 15% by the fourth year.

Similarly, in April 2017 Trump ordered the Department of Commerce to initiate an investigation under Section 232 of the 1962 Trade Expansion Act, which would potentially allow the executive branch to place import restrictions on steel for national security reasons (Lowrey, 2017). This led to the official "Presidential Proclamation on Adjusting Imports of Steel into the United States" in March 2018, which imposed a 25% *ad valorem* tariff on steel articles imported from all countries (initially excluding Canada and Mexico, but then also extending to them through the Section 323 Tariff Modifications in May 2018). This proclamation was illustratively presented within the "America First" rhetoric: "We must protect our country and our workers. Our steel industry is in bad shape. IF YOU DON'T HAVE STEEL, YOU DON'T HAVE A COUNTRY!" (as tweeted by Trump in March 2018).

All in all, these neo-protectionist actions have undoubtedly activated a spiral of reactions from the main trade partners, boosting trade wars, whose global effects – not only on trade, but also on production, consumption, and in monetary terms – are not yet evident and will need to be comprehensively analyzed. Among the main reactions to the US tariffs on steel and aluminum it is worth mentioning:

- the European Commission adopted rebalancing measures targeting a list of US products worth €2.8 billion (June 2018);
- Canada introduced surtax provisions against C$16.6 billion in imports of steel, aluminum and other products from the US, representing the value of 2017 Canadian exports affected by the US tariffs (July 2018);
- Mexico introduced tariffs ranging between 15% and 25% against US exports to its market, valued at $3 billion (June 2018);[13]
- India decided to suspend concessions to the US on 30 products, equal to the amount of trade affected by US measures (June 2018).

A more pragmatic approach on foreign policy has been so far undertaken with regards to the controversial relations with Russia; in this case the economic issues (that is, the removal of sanctions) have been subordinated to the pursuit of a constructive engagement in the Middle East (in particular, dealing with the Syrian crisis). This was also the case of the early relations with China, where trade disputes were initially subordinated to the joint management of the North Korean crisis. For instance, during his official visit to China in November 2017, President Trump uttered words of praise for Xi Jinping, imputing the trade current deficit to the previous administrations, and putting emphasis on the complementarity of the two economies and the need for a mutually

---

[13]   Political and trade relations with Mexico seem to have improved after the presidential election of Andrés Manuel López Obrador in July 2018, which led to the signature of a new preliminary trade deal with Mexico in August 2018.

beneficial cooperation.[14] This rapidly changed only few months later with the exacerbation of a trade war concerning technology and intellectual property. Here again, an even quicker spiral of neo-protectionist actions and reactions between the US and China was boosted between January and July 2018:

- US tariffs imposed on more than 1300 categories of Chinese imports, for a value of US$50 billion (March 2018);
- Chinese tariffs imposed on 128 products imported from America (April 2018);
- a 25% tariff imposed by the US on $50 billion of Chinese exports ($34 billion from July 2018, with a further $16 billion from August 2018);
- Chinese reaction of further tariffs imposed on $50 billion of US goods (July 2018);
- US 10% tariff imposed on $200 billion worth of Chinese goods (September 2018);
- Chinese 10% tariffs imposed on $60 billion of US imports (September 2018).

Concerning industrial policy, Trump's actual initiatives seem to fluctuate between continuity and change with respect to the Obama administration. On one hand, the new President continues to pursue an approach directed to attribute a new centrality to the manufacturing sector; on the other hand, differently from Obama's interest in the upgrading of the advanced manufacturing industries, the concerns of the current government have been revealed to prioritize a return to traditional manufacturing sectors requiring more workers and less skills, such as coal mining, steel, textiles and cars.

Regarding this, it is also worth analyzing Trump's rhetoric–practices binomial regarding the automotive sector, which has always played a key role in the economic and political history of the US. In particular, the following four elements have so far characterized Trump's strategy for the sector:

1. Recognition as a strategic sector deserving selective policies, which has been made concrete so far simply through meetings with big players anticipated and/or followed by the usual rhetorical claims and announcements.
2. Explicitly threatening automakers and/or implicitly incentivizing automakers to re-shore in the US, by use of public blaming (as in

---

[14] "Donald Trump blames US predecessors for China trade deficit," *Financial Times*, November 9, 2017.

the case of Toyota and GM), or conversely by openly rewarding companies (for example, Ford, Fiat-Chrysler, GM, Toyota, Mazda) when they announced investment plants in US plants.

3. Raising expectations for protectionism, again through both public attacks via Twitter against "big trade imbalances" and "stupid trade" with the EU and China, and investigation for potential tariffs.[15]

4. Raising expectations for changing regulatory mechanisms, in particular by rolling back the efficiency rules and eliminating a regulatory burden on automakers – that is, Corporate Average Fuel Economy (CAFE) – in exchange for more car production and hiring in the US.

Finally, the new administration exhibits a clear willingness to downsize the previous government's efforts towards the development of green industry. Since the first months of his presidency, Trump has promoted several actions to dismantle the system of incentives provided by Obama in support of the reduction of carbon emissions, and the promotion of renewable energy. The most evident initiative was his announcement of the US withdrawal from the Paris Agreement on global warming in June 2017. In parallel, he announced the intention to repeal the 2015 Clean Water Role regulation, aimed at improving water resource management in the country, and signed an executive order to review the application of Obama's Clean Power Plan concerning the restriction of greenhouse gas emissions and the identification of emissions' social costs. In addition, another executive order deactivated the temporary ban on mining coal and steam protection promoted by the previous administration. Finally, the launch of the America First Energy Plan aims at undoing the Obama administration's climate policies and ending the Climate Action Plan. In this regard, it prescribes a reduction in the regulations on domestic fossil fuel extraction, and the introduction of incentives to revitalize the creation of jobs in oil, gas and coal production (Vakhshouri, 2017).

FINAL REMARKS

By recalling the real historical experience of American industrialization, this chapter has discussed to what extent the federal government has been effectively playing an active role, by going beyond an ideological

---

[15] An official investigation started in May 2018 (again under Section 232 of the Trade Expansion Act of 1962, as in the case of steel) concerning whether vehicle and parts imports were threatening the industry's health and ability to research and develop new, advanced technologies.

perspective and studying the past and contemporary industry–government relationship. In particular, we have shown how, under what circumstances, and in what way, the US federal government has intervened in domestic industry, consolidating a specific American model for the industry–government relationship.

As we have seen, the term "industrial policy" entered the American academic and political debate only recently – that is, at the end of 1970s – though its reality can be traced back to 1791. Since the early days of Hamilton and American independence, the US government in Washington has played a central role in America's economic growth and in the process of industrial upgrading. This role has been actively exercised in many historical moments coinciding with social and economic turning-points (both domestically and internationally), with surprising continuity until the present day, marked by the current tentative recovery from the last economic crisis. Indeed, comparing present practices to the country's historical policy precedents allows highlighting specific circumstances and actions that would also help to better focus the current debate on today's industrial policy options.

In other words, since the days of America's independence, public intervention has assumed a strategic role to foster the creation, the development and the consolidation of national industry, and more broadly the promotion of an American model of economy. In particular, the following recurrent practices of the US industry–government relationship can be identified over time:

● funding, protecting and supporting infant industries and strategic sectors;
● promoting the enlargement of the extent of the market;
● consolidating a continuous "special relationship" between government and some selected industries (for example, steel, automotive);
● extensively using public procurement and public works;
● continuously investing in infrastructure development;
● exploiting and maintaining the central relationship with the defense and military industries;
● advancing science and technology, by constantly encouraging the advancement of the frontier in both new and advanced sectors;
● using bailouts and "too big to fail" special interventions;
● actively shaping the definition of supranational, international and bilateral trade agreements beneficial to domestic industries.

At specific times, these interventions have surely been driven by the need to address short-term socio-economic emergencies and crises, but they can also be seen in some cases as attempts to implicitly promote a strategic change and structural adjustment of the American economy in the long run (Di Tommaso and Schweitzer, 2013; Di Tommaso and Tassinari, 2017; Tassinari, 2019).[16]

It is thus clear that American industry has been continuously supported, protected, encouraged and saved by the government throughout the country's history. In more recent times this model has been confirmed, as the government has continued without much hesitation to intervene in American industry. Even in the Trump era, the continuity in the special relationship between industry and government cannot be denied and should be emphasized. This is clearly the case, for instance, in: (1) the unique attention given to demands from the military complex; (2) the special relationships with selected industries (for example, steel, automotive); and (3) investments for infrastructure development.

Nevertheless, the Trump administration has so far been characterized by certain elements of discontinuity compared to the last 30 years concerning trade and – more broadly – foreign policy, with a recent change in rhetoric that is increasingly accompanied by concrete neo-protectionist actions. The extent to which this will represent an exception within a scenario of long-run continuity, or a new structural change in the nature of the American model, is something that cannot be judged yet.

REFERENCES

Abbate, J. (1999) *Inventing the Internet*, Cambridge, MA: MIT Press.

Adner, R. (2012) *The Wide Lens: A New Strategy for Innovation*, New York: Portfolio/Penguin.

Audretsch, D.B. (1995) *Innovation and Industry Evolution*, Cambridge, MA: MIT Press.

Audretsch, D.B. (2003) Standing on the shoulders of midgets: the US Small Business Innovation Research Program (SBIR). *Small Business Economics*, 20 (2): 129–135.

Babb, S. (2013) The Washington Consensus as transnational policy paradigm: its origins, trajectory and likely successor. *Review of International Political Economy*, 20 (2): 268–297

Baldwin, R., and D. Richardson (1987) Recent US trade policy and its global implications. In C.I. Bradford Jr and H.W. Branson (eds), *Trade and Structural Change in Pacific Asia*, Chicago, IL: University of Chicago Press, pp. 121–156.

Ban, C., and M. Blyth (2013) The BRICs and the Washington Consensus: an introduction. *Review of International Political Economy*, 20 (2): 241–255.

---

[16] For the sake of comparison, see Chapter 5 on Chinese industrialization in this book, as well as Barbieri et al. (2010), Barbieri et al. (2015) and Di Tommaso et al. (2013).

Barbieri, E., Di Tommaso, M.R., and M. Huang (2010) Industrial development policy and innovation in Southern China: government targets and firms' behavior. *European Planning Studies*, 18 (1): 83–105.

Barbieri, E., Di Tommaso, M.R., and M. Tassinari (2015) Politiche industriali selettive e settori strategici. Lo scenario e le scelte di Pechino. *L'industria. Rivista di economia e politica industriale*, 3: 403–434.

Bianchi, P., and S. Labory (2011) *Industrial Policies after the Crisis: Seizing the Future*, Cheltenham, UK and Northampton, MA, USA: Edward Elgar Publishing.

Bingham, R.D., and M.E. Sharpe (1998) *Industrial Policy American Style: From Hamilton to HDTV*, New York: Armonk.

Block, F. (2008) Swimming against the current: the rise of a hidden developmental state in the United States. *Politics and Society*, 36 (2): 169–206.

Block, F., and M. Keller (eds) (2011) *State of Innovation: The US Government's Role in Technology Development*, Boulder, CO: Paradigm Publishers.

Buigues, P.A., and K. Sekkat (2009) *Industrial Policy in Europe, Japan and the US: Amounts, Mechanisms and Effectiveness*, London: Palgrave Macmillan.

Bush, V. (1945) *Science, the Endless Frontier: A Report to the President*, Washington, DC: US Government Printing Office.

Capling, A., and J. Ravenhill (2011) Multilateralising regionalism: what role for the Trans-Pacific Partnership Agreement? *Pacific Review*, 24 (5): 553–575.

Carter, G. (1968) State in, state out: a pattern of development policy. *Journal of Economic Issues*, 2 (4): 365–383.

Ceruzzi, P. (2003) *A History of Modern Computing*, Cambridge, MA: MIT Press.

Chang, H-J. (1994) *The Political Economy of Industrial Policy*, New York: St Martin's Press.

Chang, H-J. (2002) *Kicking Away the Ladder: Development Strategy in Historical Perspective*, London: Anthem Press.

Chang, H-J., and I. Grabel (2014) *Reclaiming Development: An Alternative Economic Policy Manual*, 2nd edition, London: Zed Books.

Chin, G. (2012) Two-way socialization: China, the World Bank, and hegemonic weakening. *Brown Journal of International Affairs*, 19 (1): 211–230.

Chin, G., and R. Thakur (2010) Will China change the rules of global order? *Washington Quarterly*, 33 (4): 119–138.

Cochran, T.C. (1950) North American railroads: land grants and railroad entrepreneurship. *Journal of Economic History*, 10 (S1): 53–67.

Cowling, K., and P.R. Tomlinson (2011) Post the "Washington Consensus": economic governance and industrial strategies for the twenty-first century. *Cambridge Journal of Economics*, 35(5): 831–852.

Di Tommaso, M.R. (2017) La Trump Economics non esiste (ma ha il futuro segnato). *Il Mulino – Rivista bimestrale di cultura e di politica*, 5: 851–859.

Di Tommaso, M.R., Rubini L., and E. Barbieri (2013) *Southern China: Industry, Development and Industrial Policy*, Abingdon: Routledge.

Di Tommaso, M.R., and S.O. Schweitzer (eds) (2005) *Health Policy and High-Tech Industrial Development: Learning from Innovation in the Health Industry*, Cheltenham, UK and Northampton, MA, USA: Edward Elgar Publishing.

Di Tommaso, M.R., and S.O. Schweitzer (2010) Academic knowledge production and transfer: policy targets and implications for the health industry. *International Journal Healthcare Technology and Management*, 11 (4): 227–240.

Di Tommaso, M.R., and S.O. Schweitzer (2013) *Industrial Policy in America.*

Breaking the Taboo, Cheltenham, UK and Northampton, MA, USA: Edward Elgar Publishing.

Di Tommaso, M.R., and M. Tassinari (2014) Government and industry in the United States: past practices and the debate on the present policies. *L'Industria. Rivista di Economia e Politica Industriale*, 35 (3): 369–408.

Di Tommaso, M.R., and Tassinari, M. (2017) *Industria governo e mercato: Lezioni americane*, Bologna: Il Mulino.

Di Tommaso, M.R., Tassinari, M., Bonnini, S., and M. Marozzi (2017) Industrial policy and manufacturing targeting in the US: new methodological tools for strategic policy-making. *International Review of Applied Economics*, 31 (5): 681–703.

DiLorenzo, J.T. (1984) The political economy of national industrial policy. *Cato Journal*, 4 (2): 587–607.

Dobbin, F. (1993) The social construction of the Great Depression: industrial policy during the 1930s in the United States, Britain and France. *Theory and Society*, 22 (1): 1–56.

Dobbin, F. (1994) *Forging Industrial Policy*, Cambridge: Cambridge University Press.

Dorn, J.A. (1984) Planning America: government or the market? Introduction, *Cato Journal*, 4 (2): 365–380.

Dumke, G. (1984) Preface. In C. Johnson (ed.), *The Industrial Policy Debate*, San Francisco, CA: Institute for Contemporary Studies, pp. ix–x.

Eisinger, P. (1990) Do the American states do industrial policy? *British Journal of Political Science*, 20 (4): 509–535.

ERP (various years) *Economic Report of the President* (ERP), Washington DC: United States Government Printing Office. Years: 1984, 1986, 1989, 1990, 1991, 1992, 1993, 1994, 1995, 1999, 2000, 2001, 2009, 2010, 2012, 2014.

Etzioni, A. (1983) The MITIzation of America? *Public Interest*, 72: 44–51.

Fergusson, I.F., Cooper, W.H., Jurenas R., and B.R. Williams (2013) *The Trans-Pacific Partnership Negotiations and Issues for Congress*, Washington DC: Congressional Research Service.

Fong, G. (2001) ARPA does Windows: the defense underpinning of the PC revolution. *Business and Politics*, 3 (3): 213–237.

Fuchs, E.R.H. (2010) Rethinking the role of the state in technology development: DARPA and the case for embedded network governance. *Research Policy*, 39 (9): 1133–1147.

Gallagher, K.P. (2007) Understanding developing country resistance to the Doha Round. *Review of International Political Economy*, 15 (1): 62–85.

Grabel, I. (2013) Global financial governance and development finance in the wake of the 2008 financial crisis. *Feminist Economics*, 19 (3): 32–54.

Graham, O.L. (1992) *Losing Time: The Industrial Policy Debate*, Cambridge, MA: Harvard University Press.

Hamilton, A. (1791 [2007]) *Report on the Subject of Manufactures*, republished 2007, New York: Cosimo.

Herrera, G. and Friedman, J. (2017) *Unpacking the Trump Budget's Tax and Spending Plans and Unrealistic Assumptions*, Washington, DC: Center on Budget and Policy Priorities.

Hill, G.F. (1951) Government engineering aid to railroad before the Civil War. *Journal of Economic History*, 11 (3): 235–246.

Hoekman, B.M., and P.C. Mavroidis (1997) *Law and Policy in Public Purchasing*, Ann Arbor, MI: University of Michigan Press.

Hopewell, K. (2015) Different paths to power: the rise of Brazil, India and China at the World Trade Organization. *Review of International Political Economy*, 22 (2): 311–338.

Hurt, S.L. (2011) The military's hidden hand: examining the dual-use origins of biotechnology in the American context, 1969–1972. In F. Block and M.R. Keller (eds), *State of Innovation: The US Government's Role in Technology Development*, Boulder, CO: Paradigm Publishers, pp. 31–56.

Irwin, D.A., and P.J. Klenow (1996) Sematech: purpose and performance. *Proceedings of the National Academy of Sciences of the United States of America*, 93 (23): 12739–12742.

Jackson, J.K. (2013) *Foreign Direct Investment in the United States: An Economic Analysis*, Washington DC: Congressional Research Service.

Johnson, C. (1984) *The Industrial Policy Debate*, San Francisco, CA: Institute for Contemporary Studies.

Johnson, J., and A. Barnes (2014) Financial nationalism and its international enablers: the Hungarian experience. *Review of International Political Economy*. http://dx.doi.org/10.1080/09692290.2014.919336.

Katzenstain, P.J. (2005) *A World of Regions: Asia and Europe in the American Imperium*, New York: Cornell University Press.

Kenney, M. (2003) The growth and development of the Internet in the United States. In B. Kogut (ed.), *The Global Internet Economy*, Cambridge, MA: MIT Press, pp. 69–108.

Ketels, C.H.M. (2007) Industrial policy in the United States. *Journal of Industry, Competition and Trade*, 7: 147–167.

Kirshner, J. (2008) Dollar primacy and American power: what's at stake? *Review of International Political Economy*, 15 (3): 418–438.

Krueger, A.O. (1990) Government failures in development. *Journal of Economic Perspectives*, 4 (3): 9–23.

Le Grand, J. (1991) The theory of government failure. *British Journal of Political Science*, 21(4): 423–442.

Lerner, J. (1999) The government as venture capitalist: the long run impact of the SBIR program. *Journal of Business*, 72 (3): 285–318.

Lerner, J. (2009) *Boulevard of Broken Dreams, Why Public Efforts to Boost Entrepreneurship and Venture Capital Have Failed and What to Do About It*, Princeton, NJ: Princeton University Press.

Lloyd, J.M. (1982) *Railroads and Land Grant Policy: A Study in Government Intervention*, New York: Academic Press.

Lowrey, A. (2017) The limits of "Made in America" economics. *Atlantic*. https://www.thetlantic.com/business/archive/2017/07/made-in-america/534399/.

Markusen, A., Hall, P., Campbell, S., and S. Deitrick (1991) *The Rise of the Gunbelt: The Military Remapping of Industrial America*, New York: Oxford University Press.

Mazzucato, M. (2013) *The Entrepreneurial State. Debunking Public vs. Private Sector Myths*, London, UK and New York, USA: Anthem Press.

McNeill, W. (1982) *The Pursuit of Power: Technology, Armed Force, and Society since A.D. 1000*, Chicago, IL: University of Chicago Press.

Mowery, D.C. (1998) The changing structure of the US National innovation system: implications for international conflict and cooperation in R&D policy. *Research Policy*, 27 (6): 639–654.

Nester, W.R. (1997) *American Industrial Policy*, London: Macmillan.

Niskanen, W.A. (1984) A "supply-side" industrial policy. *Cato Journal*, 4 (2): 387–406.

Niskanen, W.A. (1988) US trade policy. *Cato Review of Business and Government*. https://www.cato.org.

Norton, R. D. (1986) Industrial policy and American renewal. *Journal of Economic Literature*, 24: 1–40.

Office of Science and Technology Policy (OSTP) (2006) *American Competitiveness Initiative: Leading the World in Innovation*, Washington, DC: Domestic Policy Council.

Panitch, L., and S. Gindin (2012) *The Making of Global Capitalism: The Political Economy of American Empire*, London: Verso.

Phillips, N. (2005) US power and the politics of economic governance in the Americas. *Latin American Politics and Society*, 47 (4): 1–25.

Reich, R.B. (1982) Why the US needs an industrial policy. *Harvard Business Review*, 60 (1): 74–81.

Reich, R.B. (1984) *The Next American Frontier*, New York: Penguin Books.

Richman, S.L. (1988) The Reagan record on trade: rhetoric vs. reality. Cato Policy Analysis Working Paper no. 107.

Schrank, A.J., and J. Whitford (2009) Industrial policy in the United States: a neo-Polanyian interpretation. *Politics and Society*, 37 (4): 521–53.

Schultze, C.L. (1983) Industrial policy: a dissent. *Brookings Review*, 2 (1): 3–12.

Schwartz, S.I. (1998) *Atomic Audit: The Costs and Consequences of US Nuclear Weapons Since 1940*, Washington DC: Brooking Institute Press.

Shapira, P. (2001) US Manufacturing Extension Partnership: technology policy reinvented? *Research Policy*, 30 (6): 977–992.

Stiglitz, J. (2002) *Globalization and its Discontents*, New York: W.W. Norton & Co.

Stiglitz, J.E., and J.Y. Lin (2013) *The Industrial Policy Revolution I: The Role of Government Beyond Ideology*, New York: Palgrave Macmillan.

Tassinari, M. (2014) Industrial policy in the United States: the theoretical debate, the rhetoric, and practices in the era of the Washington Consensus. *L'Industria. Rivista di Economia e Politica Industriale*, 35(1): 69–100.

Tassinari, M. (2019) *Capitalizing Economic Power in the US. Industrial Strategy in the Neoliberal Era*. Cham: Springer. https://doi.org/10.1007/978-3-319-76648-5.

Thomas, L. (2017) Retailers cheer the death of the border adjustment tax. CNBC. https://cnbc.com/2017/07/27/retailers-cheer-the-death-of-the-border-adjustment-tax.html.

Trionfetti, F. (2000) *Discriminatory Public Procurement and International Trade*, Oxford: Blackwell Publishers.

Vakhshouri, S. (2017) The America First Energy Plan: renewing the confidence of American energy producers. Issue Brief, August, Atlantic Council.

Wade, R.H. (2010) After the crisis: industrial policy and the developmental state in low-income countries. *Global Policy*, 1 (2): 150–161.

Wade, R.H. (2012) Return of industrial policy? *International Review of Applied Economics*, 26 (2): 223–239.

Weiss, L. (2014) *America Inc.? Innovation and Enterprise in the National Security State*, New York: Cornell University Press.

Weiss, L., and E. Thurbon (2006) The business of buying American: government procurement as trade strategy. *Review of International Political Economy*, 13 (5): 701–724.

White, L.J. (2007) Antitrust policy and industrial policy: a view from the US. Presented at the Second Lisbon Conference on Competition Law and Economics, Lisbon.

White House (2018a) *A New Foundation For American Greatness*, Budget of the US Government for fiscal year 2018, Office of Management and Budget, Washington, DC. https://www.whitehouse.gov.

White House (2018b) *Efficient, Effective, Accountable: An American Budget*, Budget of the US Government for fiscal year 2019, Office of Management and Budget, Washington, DC. https://www.whitehouse.gov.

White House (2018c) *Legislative Outline for Rebuilding Infrastructure in America*, Washington, DC. https://www.whitehouse.gov.

Whitford, J. (2005) *The New Old Economy. Networks, Institutions, and Organizational Transformation of American Manufacturing*, Oxford: Oxford University Press.

Williams, B.R. (2013) *Trans-Pacific Partnership (TPP) Countries: Comparative Trade and Economic Analysis*, Washington DC: Congressional Research Service.

Wilson, M.R. (2006) *The Business of Civil War: Military Mobilization and the State, 1861–1865*, Baltimore, MD: Johns Hopkins University Press.

5. Chinese industrialization, planning and policies: local growth and global equilibria

Marco R. Di Tommaso, Chiara Pollio, Elisa Barbieri and Lauretta Rubini

INTRODUCTION

China has acquired a core role in global manufacturing, becoming the center of global networks of production. On the one hand, this position is the result of the planning and policy efforts of the national government to promote growth and structural change. On the other hand, to achieve such results, the Chinese policy actors have deeply interacted with overseas capital and interests that entered the country and made use of its social, human, economic, policy and environmental resources to build some of the most important hubs of production worldwide. In this scenario, the interplay between the Chinese (national, regional and local) governments and international interests has shaped the national mode of production of contemporary China.

A special example of such a dynamic is represented by the growth trajectory of Southern China, particularly Guangdong. Half as large as Germany but with 20 million more people, Guangdong has acquired a central role in the national economy and, in the last decades, also in the international context. This province is the first in terms of contribution to national gross domestic product (GDP) (10%) and exports (nearly 30%) and the second for foreign direct investment (FDI) attraction (about 15%) (NBS, 2015). Nowadays its economic performance is comparable to those of some important Organisation for Economic Co-operation and Development (OECD) countries: for instance, its export value is not far from that of Japan, its import value is between that of India and Belgium, and the GDP figures are comparable to those of Poland or Australia[1]

---

[1] The data on Guangdong are from NBS (2017), while those on countries are from UNCOMTRADE.com and OECD.com, retrieved on May 4, 2018.

(Barbieri et al., forthcoming-b). The path of industrialization of this province is characterized by an intense spatial agglomeration of firms and industries, in both rural and urban areas. Impressive data refer to the sectoral specialization of these agglomerations, to their "volume" (in terms of number of both industries and workers), and finally to their capacity to attract foreign investors, initially from Hong Kong and Taiwan, and subsequently from all over the industrialized world. This geography is the result of different and interlinked dynamics; some of these clusters in fact relate to explicit and planned choices, others to a spontaneous flourishing of the private sector or to the complex processes of transformation of public and collective ownership (Bellandi and Di Tommaso, 2005; Barbieri et al., 2015).

There is little doubt that Guangdong's economic performance is deeply linked to the joint action of governments, at both national and local level. The national authorities selected this area to experiment with the opening to foreign market forces and with the geography of production since the beginning of the open door policy, assigning to provincial policy-makers a growing level of autonomy (Di Tommaso et al., 2013a). The local authorities have gone ahead with the experimentation path designed by national policies to promote industrialization and growth in specific policy frameworks, which in many cases have become pioneers at the national level. Spatially targeted policies are a large part of this story (Zheng et al., 2016; Barbieri et al., forthcoming-b): since its targeting as one of the key regions of the open door policy, Guangdong has fully and deeply experimented with a variety of these tools (Barbieri et al., 2012).

In this chapter, we focus on one particular initiative: the "specialized towns" program. Since the launch of the program in 2000, the number of specialized towns (STs) has constantly grown, reaching a total of 416 in 2016 and becoming the backbone of Guangdong's industrial growth according to its policy-makers (Su and Sun, 2016). In 2015, they accounted for 37% of the provincial industrial output and 32% of the total export of the province, but in some prefectures (for example, Foshan, Dongguan, Zhongshan) their contribution was close to 100% of the output; taken together, they produce nearly US$384 billion a year (GDASS, 2017). A high number of the manufacturing towns included in the program are examples of places where the alliance between Chinese and global goals has clearly been successful in incentivizing growth and industrialization. Indeed, some of them have become global production hubs, where huge quantities of manufactured goods are realized to respond to the international demand. Such towns have historically seen a strong intervention of overseas capital and actors. The national and local governments' actions have largely interacted with this production framework to plan and enhance industrial and economic performance, contributing to production efficiency, innovation, competitiveness and structural change.

Our aim in this chapter is to offer detailed and unique analyzes on the experience of STs. After having framed it in the literature debate, we focus on the description of the policy, on its tools and evolution in time, and then on the trends of its spatial and sectoral distribution. To better describe the STs phenomenon in terms of economic and social achievements and limits, we concentrate on three cities (Dongguan, Foshan and Zhongshan) whose economic activity is dominated by STs. We conclude with some remarks about the challenges and perspectives of the program, that also set the future research agenda on the topic.

The analysis in this chapter is largely the result of lengthy research carried out by the authors on this topic, developed through a repeated series of fieldwork in Guangdong and in its STs, the last of which was held in July–September 2017. The fieldwork has allowed the authors to collect data and policy documents on-site, but also and above all to interview and discuss with several policy actors at various levels (provincial, city and townships), scholars and company managers, and to see first-hand, the results and the evolution of the STs program. These areas strongly contribute to national GDP, and exports and in some specific products (smartphones, suitcases, toys only to name some) they cover a large portion of global production. It is therefore crucial to study the development trajectory of such territories to better understand the global consumption–production equilibria and the extent to which they trigger either inclusive innovation processes or mere exploitation of places.

THE RELATED LITERATURE DEBATE

The experience of STs reflects policies and practices to some extent inspired by, or related to, different streams of international literature. We can identify at least three types of contributions that should be taken into account in this sense. The first is the literature on industrial agglomerations (starting from Marshall, 1890 [1961]). A key role in this respect is played by the analyzes of the historical evolution and features of Italian districts, that have highlighted the role of joint actions and collaborations in industrial agglomeration that produced the "industrial atmosphere" constituting their source of competitiveness (Becattini, 1998; Becattini et al., 2009; Sforzi and Lorenzini, 2002; Bianchi, 2017). The literature on Italian districts has been then transposed in the international debate and has become an ideal-type for the analysis of industrial agglomerations (Pyke and Sengenberger, 1992), also with respect to developing countries

(Nadvi and Schmitz, 1994). More recent contributions start from the literature on clusters and agglomerations to develop new insights, such as those coming from the new economic geography and the related variety literature (Boschma et al., 2012; Content and Frenken, 2016; Fujita and Krugman, 2004; Ottaviano and Puga, 1998). These authors have focused on industrial agglomerations to analyze the linkages between inter-industrial spillover, knowledge flows and division of labor at the regional level. Although ST policy initiatives explicitly take into account these contributions, and in particular that of the Italian school of districts, an important difference needs to be considered while analysing this phenom-enon. Indeed, STs are generated as an *ex post* initiative promoted by the central provincial government, where local policy-makers are explicitly requested to participate in the program and to demonstrate that they fulfill the requirements (for example, a minimum degree of specialization). However, these townships appear to miss many other features of the dis-trict experience, that relate in particular to the existence of a community of firms and people that gives rise to the industrial atmosphere. On the contrary, Guangdong clusters are often the result of the joint action of planned policies on one hand, and on the other hand of external forces such as foreign capital and migrations, that make these agglomerations very far both from the Italian real experiences of districts and from the ideal-type that has been developed by the international literature.

A second stream of the international debate that seems to be very useful in the interpretation of the STs experience is that related to industrial poli-cies, intended as the set of tools and initiatives able to interact with market forces to pursue the structural transformation and upgrading of the economy and the promotion of general industrial, economic and societal objectives (Chang, 1994; Cimoli et al., 2009; Di Tommaso et al., 2013a; Di Tommaso and Schweitzer, 2013; Rodrik, 2004). Indeed, China and, as we shall see, the STs initiative, are among the clearest examples of the role that industrial policies can play in order to achieve various societal targets. However, it should be also underlined that the relationship between market and state that is typical of capitalistic societies holds to only a limited extent in the Chinese experience, since this is largely characterized by an economic organization based at all levels upon the Five-Year Plan long-term strategy.

Thirdly, the bottom-up relationship between policy actors, typical of the STs, together with the recent trend of tailored policies that we will analyze later in the chapter, recall the literature about place-based policies that has recently emerged in the international debate (Bailey et al., 2015; Barca et al., 2012; Hildreth and Bailey, 2013; Kline and Moretti, 2013; Neumark and Simpson, 2015). However, as far as we know, the extent to which a true process of participation of local forces takes place in the process of production, and in the definition of objectives of local industrial growth, needs to be further investigated. A bottom-up relation in the context of STs is mainly limited to policy actors and government institutions, and while some degree of participation may be observed for firms and universities, for example, a large portion of the population contributing to the economic environment of these townships (primarily, the workers) seems to be excluded.

Apart from the references to international literature, international scholars approaching the Chinese industrialization experience should be aware that a large part of the debate on these topics takes place among Chinese scholars and policy-makers and is largely unintelligible to external analysts. We refer to a number of Chinese-written books, scientific journals and policy documents that are the backbone of the elaboration of "capitalism with Chinese characteristics." These contributions are difficult to explore by an international audience not only because of the language, but also because they refer to a literature corpus that is rooted in the history of the national debate and has elaborated its own concepts and tools (GDASS, 2017; Di Tommaso et al., 2013a; Nolan, 2012).

STs have experienced a constant and remarkable growth in terms of industrial development and GDP, but in many cases they have brought about problems in terms of social, economic and environmental sustainability. In this framework, the future research efforts studying this kind of agglomeration should concentrate on connecting this reality with two streams of the literature that have so far been largely neglected. The first is related to the contributions on human development: many of these agglomerations have been surprisingly effective in promoting the economic growth of localities, but still little is known about their (potential) capacity to encourage the human and social development of the communities living in the same localities. In this regard, we believe it is a priority to build a bridge between the contributions about human development (Anand and Sen, 2000; Démurger et al., 2002; Gillis et al., 1992; Sen, 2005) and those regarding industrialization processes, and in particular the particular industrial policy measures implemented by the Chinese government in the Guangdong province. Much has still to be done in this regard, although some first contributions have started to emerge with respect to specific case studies (Barbieri et al., forthcoming-a; Biggeri, 2017) and categories of populations (Chan and Pun, 2010).

Lastly, a stream of literature that should be taken into account while studying the STs phenomenon is that of political economy studies (Cohen, 2017; Frieden and Martin, 2003; Gilpin, 2011, 2016). This would allow a better understanding of the dynamics of consensus creation, political stability and relations between groups and interests. Furthermore, these types of clusters play a core role in global production dynamics and global consumption networks and therefore require careful analysis of their impact on international equilibria between actors and interests.

THE EXPERIENCE OF SOUTHERN CHINA'S SPECIALIZED TOWNS

The impressive industrial and economic growth of the Guangdong province has been centered on the prefectures of the Pearl River Delta (PRD) and, to a lesser extent, of the coastal areas. The PRD area, in fact, had several advantages that made it one of the favored areas for the first policy experimentations related to spatial concentration of production: two out of the three first national Special Economic Zones (SEZs) were located there (Zheng et al., 2016). First, the Pear River has always been a traditional commercial and communication route; second, the PRD is located right next to Hong Kong and Macao, which represented the first channels of entry of foreign capital and trade in the country. This has made the PRD area the most suitable part of mainland China for the attraction of FDI (Barbieri et al., forthcoming-b). Because of its strategic position, the PRD was the pilot area in which the first opening policies were implemented. It is also the area in which the "one city, one product" policy, aimed at supporting the agglomeration of specialized firms in some specific localities, and more in general to promote industrial development, competitiveness, innovation and technological upgrading, was launched. The rapid growth of the PRD has induced policy-makers to slightly adjust their intervention, implementing measures to shape the "geography" of its industry, trying to: (1) rationalize the dramatically fast – and often chaotic – development of the PRD area; and (2) encourage the development of the other lagging areas (Barbieri et al., 2012; Sarcina et al., 2014; Di Tommaso et al., 2013b).

The Main Features of the STs Program

The STs program consists in an *ex post* recognition of some particular features of the towns that apply to the program. Each potential ST is studied by a group of government experts that eventually awards the town with the label of "Specialized Town." Such recognition is given according to some specific criteria (Di Tommaso et al., 2013a): (1) the town has to be a "township" from an administrative point of view or, less frequently, a "county" or an "urban district"; (2) at least 30% of its industrial output (or employment) has to be concentrated in one industry (defined in specific sectoral terms to the three-digit level equivalent of international classification systems), that is called a "specialized sector"; (3) the annual value of the industrial output has to exceed 2 billion yuan (equal to about US$293 million).

Once the certification is obtained, the certified STs are entitled to receive a subsidy of 30 000 RMB from the Department of Science and Technology of Guangdong Government (DSTGG), provided that an additional a is financed by the local government in the proportion of 1 (province): 10 (city): 50 (town) (Wang, 2009; Wang and Yue, 2010). This fund has to be mainly used to establish the so-called Technology Innovation Platform, the aim of which is to help firms in the development of new technologies, in the upgrading of their production, and in favoring the establishment and consolidation of relationships among actors. The activity of the innovation centers is not only directed to the single firm, but aims to favor an improvement in the reputation of the whole productive system of the town, possibly supporting the development of a common and easily recognizable brand (Arvanitis and Qiu, 2004; DSTGG, 2003, 2006a; Wang, 2004).

These 416 townships belong to very different categories, in terms of size, degree of urbanization, period when they developed, and so on. For some of them, industrialization flourished thanks to local small and medium-sized enterprises (SMEs), and while in some cases this process can be connected to a district-like development, in others it is the result of the fast growth of private actors with no linkages among them. In other cases, industrial growth was led by a top-down process originated either by the privatization of the so-called Townships and Villages Enterprises (TVEs) or by the action of big state-owned enterprises (SOEs) or private companies that polarized the industrial growth in the area. Yet other industrial clusters were born due to their geographical localization near traditional trade routes or logistic areas. Finally, in other cases, such as Dongguan, the impressive industrial development was mainly triggered by the attraction of high-tech foreign-funded investors, often causing a chaotic growth of the town (Barbieri et al., 2009; Bellandi and Di Tommaso, 2005; Di Tommaso and Bazzucchi, 2013).

Features and Role of the Technological Innovation Platforms

The technological innovation platforms are at the center of the STs initiative. First, they are designed to help firms with services for the development of new technologies and the upgrading of production. Second, they aim at encouraging cooperation among the different economic and institutional actors of the town, building a link between private firms and public research institutions to foster innovative projects (Barbieri et al., 2010; GDASS, 2017; DSTGG, 2017). We identify three main categories of innovation platforms (Barbieri et al., 2010; DSTGG, 2008a): (1) information networks, used to disseminate technology, exchange and diffuse commercial information and carry out Internet based cooperation among actors; (2) innovation centers, directly created or supported using funding provided by the local and the provincial government; and (3) research and development (R&D) centers within leading firms.

Interviews with policy actors revealed that the DTSGG has tried in recent years to create a competitive market for innovation centers, where several service centers are created and encouraged to compete for the supply of services to the companies in the town, in order to increase efficiency. Innovation centers operate in their everyday activities and strategic choices mostly by following a market logic, but at the same time they maintain linkages with the political funding actors mainly through the board of directors, which is in charge of defining the strategic priorities and areas of intervention.

The activity of innovation platforms contributes substantially to innovation in Guangdong (Table 5.1): in 2015, for instance, they completed 620 projects and produced more than 3 million yuan of output across the whole province. More generally, the innovative effort produced in the STs is evident not only in the activity of the innovation platforms, but also in the number of innovation and research providers, although these figures vary in the different cities of the province.

The Phases of the STs Program Implementation

We can identify at least four phases in the STs policy evolution. The first can be traced back to the 1990s. Indeed, although the concept of "Specialized Town" was a new one in 2000, it stemmed from a previous government intervention for the promotion of economic development in rural areas. It was in fact based on the experience of the Spark Plan, a national program promoting technological innovation in rural areas with a double aim: on the one hand, upgrading agriculture production and, on the other, promoting a gradual structural shift towards manufacturing (Barbieri et al., 2009; DSTGG, 2006b; Zhang and Ling, 2003). The underlying idea was that strengthening the innovative capacity of the agricultural sector would have positive spillover effects on the whole economy, therefore favoring a parallel growth of industrial productions (Di Tommaso et al., 2013a).

The measures of the Spark Plan also included the creation of several investment areas, the so-called Spark Technology Investment Zones,

Table 5.1 Data on innovation of STs by city, 2015

City	Investment in science and technology (10000 RMB)	Of which public (%)	Engineering centers	No. firms with R&D centers	No. innovation service providers	No. public research centers	No. projects by innovation platforms	Output value of innovation platforms (10000 RMB)
Chaozhou	97239	11.00	19	43	239	13	6	6279
Dongguan	1222027	11.93	110	1432	521	168	24	18556
Foshan	1335283	6.54	234	832	351	110	301	102265
Guangzhou	17828	14.10	5	24	42	16	8	n/a
Heyuan	4445	53.21	n/a	0	172	9	8	998
Huizhou	98726	2.40	5	67	43	15	n/a	n/a
Jiangmen	228226	5.92	48	82	80	26	75	17334
Jieyang	36382	11.71	10	27	57	24	7	7723
Maoming	10372	24.56	2	2	67	33	13	14766
Meizhou	40320	25.78	11	13	328	68	25	13954
Qingyuan	10476	5.09	n/a	7	10	6	n/a	n/a
Shantou	62073	20.05	21	100	176	64	13	13408
Shanwei	3105	39.45	n/a	10	105	9	6	612
Shaoguan	7441	19.42	n/a	13	55	14	6	3826
Yangjiang	27348	32.62	8	39	71	12	4	4100
Yunfu	13620	32.62	8	13	60	16	10	7239
Zhangjiang	33870	14.14	5	20	196	46	11	15096
Zhaoqing	21955	19.34	7	36	109	27	18	23336
Zhongshan	639190	16.33	94	446	182	70	78	43066
Zhuhai	45157	45.20	13	38	36	23	7	8100
Total	*3955083*	*11.00*	*600*	*3244*	*2900*	*769*	*620*	*300658*

Source: Su and Sun (2016).

where firms could benefit from the availability of funds from government subsidies and bank loans (Barbieri et al., 2010). While studying these investment areas, some experts of the DSTGG realized that in most cases each area tended to specialize in a specific sector, what has been called "one city, one product" (Wang and Yue, 2010; Su and Sun, 2016), that formed the basis of the ST program.

A second phase of the pilot development of the program took place in the period 2000 to 2003, specifically through two formal policy documents named the "Plan for the ST Technological Innovation: Pilot Test" and "Managerial Methods for the ST Technological Innovation: Pilot Test" (DSTGG, 2008b). Most of the STs recognized in this phase were located in the core area of the PRD, while a smaller number were in the eastern part, where the SEZ of Shantou was also established. These cases, coupled with the recognition of some analogous international industrial agglomeration cases considered to be successful all over the world (such as industrial districts, firm clusters, local systems of innovation, and so on), have been the basis for a new strategy in which Guangdong policy-makers started to design measures to actively support these types of industrial agglomerations (Di Tommaso et al., 2013a). The guiding principles of this period can be summarized as promoting industrial growth and upgrading, while at the same time rationalizing the industrial distribution after the first accelerated industrialization wave in the province (Barbieri et al., 2009; Di Tommaso et al., 2013a).

A third phase of the program implementation can be identified from 2003 to 2008. After the establishment of the first specialized towns, the program extended to some other cities in the province such as Meizhou, Foshan, Shantou and Jiangmen. The recognition of specialized towns was then viewed by policy-makers as a tool to upgrade production and at the same time to promote marginal areas of the province. This double path of policy implementation clearly appeared in the documents issued, such as "Thoughts and Strategies for the Development of Clusters in Guangdong and for Brands Creation" (2005), the "Coordinated Promotion Plan between Province and (Prefecture) City" (2005) and the "Guangdong Province Government's Suggestion on the Promotion of the Development of Specialized Towns" (2006), that recognize the strategic value that STs had in the overall development of Guangdong (Barbieri et al., 2010; Di Tommaso et al., 2013a; Lin, 2006; Su and Sun, 2016). These documents have several features in common. First, provincial and local institutions start to work together to regulate the clustering processes to avoid sectoral overlapping and to orientate the territory towards the construction of a coordinated and integrated regional innovation system; unsurprisingly, the Guangdong Provincial Specialized Towns Development Promotion

Association (POTIC) was established in these years (Su and Sun, 2016). Second, many of these documents mainly point to the diffusion of good practices, such as a better use of knowledge, of patenting and intellectual property rights (IPR) practices, and the diffusion of territorial branding strategies. Third, emphasis is given to collaboration between universities and research institutions and the local innovative public and private environment, as well as to the establishment of "demonstration towns" where all such processes are put in place with positive results.

After 2008, a fourth phase started and can be considered to be still ongoing. Both the official documents and the sectoral and geographical transition of the ST policy from 2008 on seems to be in line with the whole change of Chinese policy towards endogenous growth and innovation. The most important policy line in the framework of the ST program is the "One Town, One Policy" issued in 2010 (DSTC, 2011a, 2011b). With this measure, provincial policy-makers aimed at incentivizing each town to find and implement its own development path, while simultaneously supporting the overall economic development of the Guangdong province. This implies the following actions: (1) to simplify the political administration of STs by further decentralizing the town's economic management to local authorities; (2) to optimize and strengthen the industrial structure of STs and to manage urban development; (3) to restore public accounts to good order so as to have the resources for the renewal of old infrastructures and the construction of new ones; (4) to promote quality enhancement, especially in traditional industries; and (5) to help STs increase their share of GDP, their innovation potential and, more generally, their competitive capacity (Tsai, 2013). On the same lines, the "One Institute, One Town" initiative of 2012 aimed at creating a university or technical tertiary education institution in each town (Su and Sun, 2016). Finally, two more elements of empowerment of local sources can be found in the initiatives and plans produced by the DSTGG and Guangdong governments in this period. On the one hand, there is a great emphasis on the promotion of micro, small and medium-sized enterprises and on building public innovation services to suit their specific needs; on the other hand, a few official governments and initiatives are focused on enhancing the quality and the innovative performances of those towns specialized in production with strong local features, traditional sectors and those that are in more remote areas (Di Tommaso et al., 2013a; DSTGG, 2017; Su and Sun, 2016). Figure 5.1 illustrates the location of Guangdong's specialized towns up to the end of 2015, following the four phases described above.

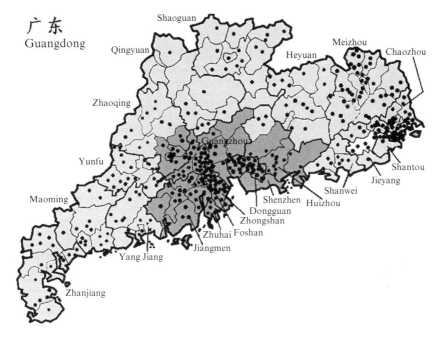

Note: * The 17 new towns recognized from 2015 to 2018 are not included in the map due to unavailability of data.

Source: Authors' elaborations on data from Guangdong Provincial ST Development Promotion Association.

Figure 5.1 STs in Guangdong

THE EVOLUTION AND RECENT TRENDS IN LOCALIZATION, SECTORAL DISTRIBUTION AND LOCAL BASED ACTIVITIES

This section is based on the result of fieldwork and data collection at the ST level in Guangdong. The continuous evolution of the phenomenon of STs, along with the heterogeneity of available data, has induced us to continuously compare and verify information, using several official sources when possible. In particular, data were initially directly gathered from the official statistics provided by representatives of the DSTGG. These data were useful in sketching a general framework and in identifying some required context variables (such as temporary and permanent population, output, GDP, and so on). We then integrated the information with more specific sources. First, we consulted several other official documents, publications and websites. Other relevant data sources were the Research Development Center of Guangdong Province, POTIC and the South China University of Technology. Additionally, we collected data and information from local governmental bodies. When possible, we also relied on field case studies and interviews with relevant stakeholders (mayors, town chiefs, party representatives, entrepreneurs, policy-makers in charge of the innovation centers, and so on). Finally, we promoted an extensive phase of cross-checks, in order to minimize the risk of mistakes, inconsistencies and non-reliable information. At present, our dataset covers the 399 STs officially recognized at the end of 2015.[2]

General Trend

At the end of 2015, more than 25% of Guangdong township-level entities were recognized as specialized towns. The number of STs has grown year by year since the beginning of the program in 2000. While in the first period (2000–2003) the launching of the program concerned a relatively small number of towns (69 at the end of 2003), a strong boom occurred over the period 2004–2008: in five years, the total number grew to 277, with two peaks of new recognized STs in 2005 (58) and 2008 (48). After 2008, the number of new STs – for obvious reasons – decreased at the pace of 15–20 a year (Figure 5.2).

In 2015 this group of towns represented 40% of total GDP in Guangdong

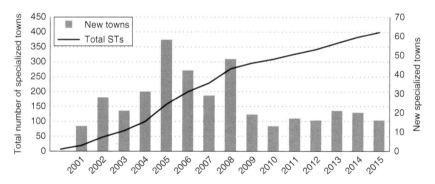

Sources: Based on POTIC data.

Figure 5.2   Temporal evolution of STs

2   From fieldwork talks with DSTGG officials, we know that as of July 2017 the officially recognized STs stand at 413. However, at that date there was no official available source and statistics about the 14 new towns.

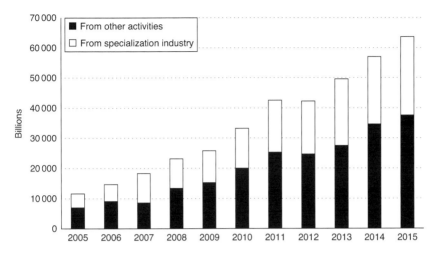

Source: Based on Guangdong Academy of Social Sciences data.

Figure 5.3   Output of specialized towns (yuan)

(NBS, 2015). Their gross domestic output grew steadily over a decade, with a small reduction only between 2011 and 2012. Between 2005 and 2015 the output coming from specialized industries was on average above the required threshold of 30% and was stable at around 40% of total output (Figure 5.3).

Geographical and Sectoral Trends

The growth in the number of STs has not been evenly distributed across the areas of Guangdong (Figure 5.4). The launching phase started in the PRD's towns and, to a lesser extent, in other areas of the coast (Figure 5.4a). In the boom period, a far larger number of counties hosted new STs: in the first years (up to 2006), the program extended mainly to the so-called intermediate area, that is, the prefecture of the "Great" PRD and other counties in the coast (Figure 5.4b). From 2006 to 2009, we see instead a surge of STs in more peripheral areas, with rural bases and mainly mountainous territory (Figure 5.4c). Finally, the most up-to-date picture shows a very small number of counties without STs. Specialized towns continue to be mainly concentrated in some counties and prefectures of the PRD (particularly in Dongguan, which is a one-county prefecture). However, a large portion of them are now also localized in the north-eastern prefectures of Meizhou and Chaozhou (Figure 5.4d).

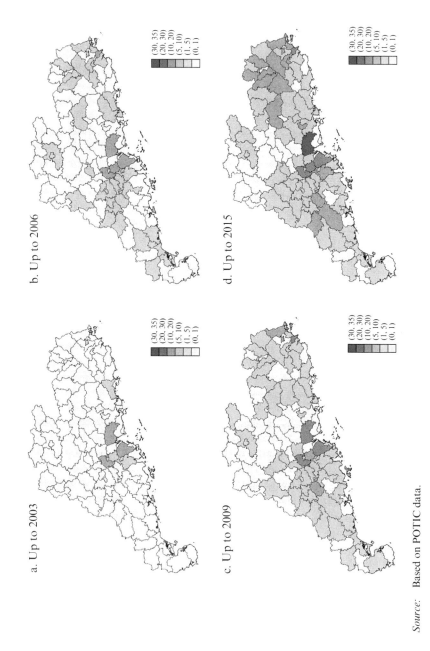

b. Up to 2006

a. Up to 2003

d. Up to 2015

c. Up to 2009

Source: Based on POTIC data.

Figure 5.4   Geographical distribution of STs

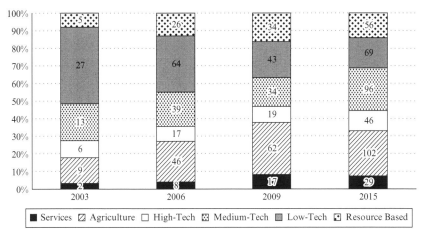

Sources: Based on various sources.

Figure 5.5 Sectoral distribution of STs

The sectoral distribution of the specialization of the towns has changed over time and reflects the shift in the aims of the STs policy (Figure 5.5). The first group of specialized towns in 2003 was predominantly specialized in low-tech production, which at that time characterized the core of Guangdong manufacturing system, particularly in the PRD. It is clear, then, that in the first period of development this tool was used to rationalize the geography of the already existing production. Gradually, however, the weight of low-tech specialized towns diminished in favor of agriculture, resource based activities and services up to 2009, and then high-tech and medium-tech in the aftermath of the global financial crisis. This double trend is due to the new aims of the policy after the experimentation period: (1) the specialization of resource based and agricultural towns, which follows the necessity to upgrade traditional productions and promote such upgrading in areas that were less involved in the development of manufacturing in the region; and (2) the promotion of technological upgrading and the growth of innovative activities in those areas that represent core clusters of Guangdong's manufacturing.

The promotion of agriculture-related activities and of medium- and high-tech sectors has been carried out differently in different areas. A clear division of labour of specialized towns exists between those located in the PRD prefectures and those outside (Figure 5.6). The STs in the PRD area (Figure 5.6a) are predominantly focused on manufacturing, with the

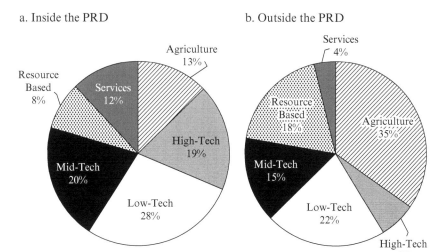

a. Inside the PRD   b. Outside the PRD

Sources: Based on various sources.

*Figure 5.6   Sectoral distribution of STs according to PRD and non-PRD
                areas, 2015*

sum of mid- and high-tech STs exceeding the number of low-tech ones. Agriculture, services and resource based activities play a marginal role, with the service STs group specialized in activities in many cases strictly connected to the manufacturing sector (such as logistics). A completely different situation is found outside the PRD (Figure 5.6b), where it is clear that the policy has been used with the aim of promoting specialization activities relatively less connected with manufacturing. Indeed, this group of STs is far more concentrated on more traditional productions related to the agriculture and resource based sector, and even in the manufacturing group the number of low-tech STs exceeds the sum of mid- and high-tech ones.

"Local Source" Based Townships

Finally, the analysis of the trajectory of the policy has allowed us to acknowledge that the initiative has gradually shifted towards the need to follow the path of endogenous growth and endogenous sources. Based on their history of economic development, the literature identifies two main categories of specialized towns (Bellandi and Di Tommaso, 2005; Wang, 2009; Wang and Yue, 2010):

- exogenous clusters, whose growth and economic development has mainly been triggered by the attraction of FDI and where the policy has been mainly aimed at favoring the relationships between foreign firms and existing enterprises;
- endogenous clusters, whose birth is mainly due to local factors; for example, some of them result from the evolution of ancient productive systems, while others have been pushed by the privatization of town TVEs.

In accordance with this classification, looking into the history and the features of each township, we find that some of them have followed an economic and industrial development that is rooted in their economic and cultural history (which we will call "local source" based); on the other hand, there is another group of towns that has undergone a process of growth triggered by external forces, such as foreign capitals but also exogenous political actors ("non-local source" based).

Following this line, we analyzed the context of each township to distinguish between these two groups and to observe whether a change in the policy towards one group or the other has happened. We worked through a content analysis on the various local and regional sources and isolated the group of "local source" townships. The criteria that we used to identify them recall Becattini's contribution on industrial districts as originated by the historical profile of the production atmosphere of the hosting areas (Becattini, 2015). Based on this, we included each township in the "local source" group if its specialized production has at least one of these features:

- it is rooted in the history of the town;
- it is based on local resources (for example, aquaculture in townships next to water);
- it is a traditional or typical production of the region, or mainly oriented towards national markets (such as for example rice cookers or pottery);
- it is a non-typical production derived from production rooted in the history of the town (such as machinery for stone processing in areas previously used as quarries);
- it is strictly linked to physical characteristics of the territory (such as port logistics in coastal areas).

It is true that some specific productions, such as information and communication technology (ICT), are *per se* to be considered exogenous as they have been introduced in these townships as a product of the process of opening and internationalization. In addition, some activities that are

Table 5.2   Sectoral distribution of "local source" and "non-local source" based STs

	Sectors					
	Agriculture	High-tech	Low-tech	Mid-tech	Resource based	Services
"Local source" based townships	102	3	37	8	41	18
"Non-local source" based townships	0	43	32	88	15	11

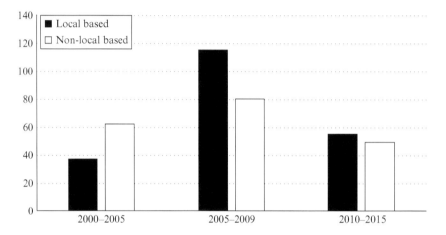

Figure 5.7   Distribution of STs according to their local or non-local origin, 2000–2015

by their nature oriented to serve local or national markets (such as in the agriculture sector to a large extent) tend to be naturally collocated in the group of "local source" based activities. Nonetheless, the distinction between these two groups is only partially overlapping with a sectoral distribution of township: within the manufacturing sector (independently of the level of technology) and in services both types of specialization coexist (Table 5.2).

The group of local based STs corresponds to more than half of the total (209 out of 399 towns). What emerges from the analysis of the time trend is that the relative weight of local based towns has grown from the mid-2000s on, and specifically in correspondence with the shift of policy orientation towards endogenous sources and growth (Figure 5.7).

Regarding the geographical distribution of local based versus non-local based townships (Figure 5.8), we can confirm that there is a qualitative difference between the path of specialization in the PRD and non-PRD areas. Local based townships are mainly concentrated in the inner and mountainous areas of the non-PRD, which require a larger public investment and a focus on their role for the local markets and on the existing sources of production. However, the predominance of non-local specialization among the PRD prefecture is a clear sign of the exogenous nature of their economic growth path, which has largely been based on foreign capital and migrations.

ACHIEVEMENTS AND LIMITS OF THE SPECIALIZED TOWNS BASED GROWTH: A TALE OF THREE CITIES

The ST initiative has been a core instrument for the industrial development of the whole province. Nowadays, specialized towns are spread all over Guangdong and substantially contribute to its economic performance. Indeed, the ST program has been, and still is, particularly relevant to some cities of the province located in the PRD. This is the case of three cities, Dongguan, Foshan and Zhongshan, which in many regards represent core territories of industrial production, both in general and in relation to specific manufacturing products. In these three prefectures, the whole industrial production has been organized around the STs system: nowadays, specialized towns represent 75% (Zhongshan) to more than 90% (Dongguan and Foshan) of their total townships and subdistricts. Some townships are specialized in more than one, often interlinked, product or sector (Dongguan and Foshan). Therefore, the economic performance and evolution of these three townships is representative of the achievements that the program generated.[3]

According to the latest data (from 2016),[4] these three cities are among the best-performing ones in terms of GDP in the whole region, ranking second (Foshan), third (Dongguan) and fifth (Zhongshan). Since the beginning of the program (in 2000), their GDP growth has been some points higher than both the provincial average and the PRD average. These three territories represent the core of the provincial industrial

---

[3] We exclude Shenzhen in the following calculations and comparison, given its status of Special Economic Zone and its substantially independent economic trajectory with respect to the rest of the province.

[4] If not specified otherwise, all the data in this section are taken from NBS (2017, 2006, 2005, 2001).

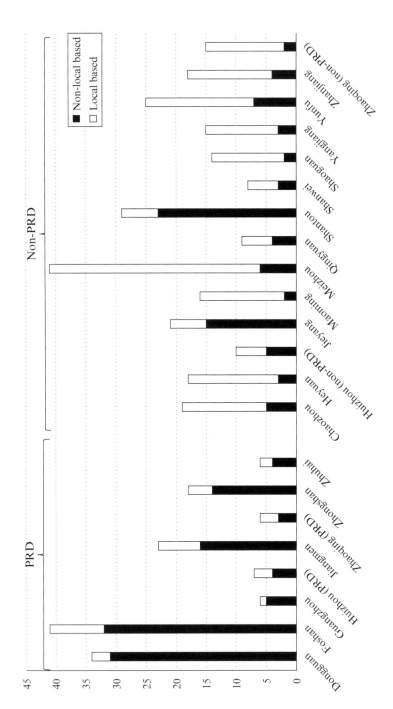

Figure 5.8   Geographical distribution of local based and non-local based STs, 2015

production, accounting for 35% of Guangdong industrial GDP, and are indeed industrial based areas, since 40–55% of their total value-added comes from the industrial sector. Equally impressive is their performance on foreign markets: Dongguan is the first exporter in the whole province, while Foshan and Zhongshan rank third and sixth, respectively. Together they represent 30% of the provincial export value. While the export propensity of Dongguan was clear even before the take-off of the STs program, the export growth rate of Foshan and Zhongshan became higher than the provincial average over the period 2000–2016.

One of the core areas of intervention of the ST program is innovation and, more in general, the upgrading of the industrial system. The three ST based cities also perform very well from this point of view. In terms of inputs, Dongguan, Foshan and Zhongshan are the areas, after the capital city, where private firms invest the most and employ the largest amount of people in R&D. This might indicate that the ST program was successful in stimulating private initiatives in the fields of innovation and upgrading. The situation is more blurred in terms of public R&D investments (very high in Dongguan, moderate in Foshan and low in Zhongshan), suggesting that the composition of the innovation activities in the three cities is heterogeneous and that the public–private mix may vary greatly according to the local features of the industrial environment. The output of this innovation process, which we proxy with the new products sold in 2016, seems to be very high: the three cities together account for almost half of the total value, and more than half of the exports of the whole province. Their growth in this area from 2003 is particularly impressive compared to the other cities: approximately 20 percentage points more than the provincial average.

There is little doubt that as far as the industrial, export and innovation levels are concerned, the performance and growth of these three STs based cities have been impressive and above the already high provincial average. However, there are also some social, environmental and quality-of-life related costs of the ST experience that need to be taken into account when evaluating the social desirability of this model.

First, the economic performance of the cities is not equally mirrored in the remuneration that goes to workers: average wages in Foshan and Zhongshan are still relatively high compared to the average of the region – ranking fourth and sixth – but the situation is far worse in Dongguan, which is twelfth out of 21 cities. Additionally, the growth rates of nominal wages from 2000 to 2016 are among the lowest in the whole province. Moreover, the high economic performance only partially corresponds to improvements in workers' conditions. Taking the average death rate on duty by 100 million RMB of output, while Foshan has one of the lowest figures and was able to substantially reduce it in the period 2000–2016, Zhongshan and Dongguan perform worse than the provincial average, regarding both 2016 levels and the trend over the whole period. Poor workers' conditions are also reflected in the social unrest existing in these areas: according to the China Labour Bulletin, 40% of the strikes and workers' protests in the province over the period 2011–2016 were concentrated in Dongguan (235 cases), Foshan (75) and Zhongshan (33).[5]

Second, the results in terms of education are poor relative to the strong economic performance of the area, with very heterogeneous results for the three cities. Against a provincial average of 0.9 graduates and 1.2 new enrollments in regular secondary school in 2016, Zhongshan performs far better (1.8 graduates and 2.5 enrolled), Dongguan is around the average (1 and 1.3), while Foshan is largely below it as far as the number of graduates is concerned (0.6 and 1.8). Data on the number of teachers per student show analogous results. However, the three cities have undergone a similar positive change in terms of growth of secondary education: while from 2000 to 2016 the overall provincial average of both newly enrolled and new graduates every 100 persons diminished by 96%, all the figures related to the three cities grew, although at different rates.

Lastly, Foshan, Dongguan and Zhongshan are among the most polluted cities of Guangdong: they are responsible for 30% of the provincial amount of industrial wastewater and 23% of industrial gas emissions. We do not have data to assess whether processes of pollution reduction and environment-friendly initiatives are being implemented in these cities. What we can do is to highlight the difference among the three cities in terms of attitude towards the environment, by using as a broad indicator the per capita park area. While in 2016 at the provincial level each citizen has 17.9 square metres of green areas, in Dongguan this figure peaks at 23 (first city in the province), in Zhongshan it is 18.4, while Foshan is far below the provincial average with 13.9. Overall, while the ST program has undoubtedly produced positive results on economic and innovation performance, it also hides huge social and environmental downsides that negatively affect the life of those living and working in these areas.

FINAL REMARKS

The ST program has had a core role in the economic development path of Guangdong and has recently inspired other national programs. There is

---

[5] Data are available at http://www.clb.org.hk/.

little doubt that the initiatives related to STs were successful in promoting upgrading and economic growth across Guangdong and were also able to reach more remote areas in order to encourage the rationalization of industrial agglomeration and the regional balancing.

However, there is growing concern among local scholars and policy-makers about the long-run sustainability of this model of economic development. Although there are some examples of townships that were able to combine economic growth and societal well-being and were taken as examples of new, more sustainable development by national governments – such as Beijiao, which pioneered the national initiative of the "characteristic towns" (Luo, 2016) – this chapter has shown that the territories that based their development on the ST model are underperforming in terms of quality of life, exploitation of the environment, services for daily life, education and workers' conditions. Moreover, some studies have highlighted that such townships host large numbers of migrant workers who live and work in very poor conditions and cannot access public services, such as health or education for their children (Song, 2014).

There is still a long way to go for Chinese policy-makers to improve the living conditions of these places of production. However, the responsibility of these issues should not be attributed only to the local or national context: while analysing experiences of this kind one should always keep in mind that these places play a key role in the global consumption and production equilibria: not only because these localities are world manufacturing hubs for some specific products,[6] but also because widespread production and consumption habits in the world would not be possible without these Chinese localities. For these reasons, while there is no doubt that local governments need to tackle these sustainability issues directly, no change is plausibly possible if the international community is not able to rethink its consumption model and its worldwide consequences.

Future research should therefore be devoted to explore the connections between the successful industrial policy model of specialized towns and a series of issues that are still wide open, such as the difficulties of these systems to generate indigenous innovation; the increasing competition coming from other localities of the Global South of the world, increasing the trend of multinationals to relocate in places able to guarantee lower production costs; the fragility of this export-oriented model, which has been dramatically highlighted by the 2008 Great Recession; and, last but not least, the need for an improvement in the working conditions and in

---

[6] For example: the ST of Shilling supplies 70% of the production of bags and suitcases for the European Union and United States markets, while the ST of Tangxia accounts for 40% of the global production of golf products (Jankowiak, 2017).

the quality of life of these "company-towns," which have become global production hubs at the expense of social conditions, to such an extent that they might be the place of the future explosion of the Chinese "social bomb."

REFERENCES

Anand, S., and Sen, A. (2000). The income component of the Human Development Index. *Journal of Human Development*, 1(1), 83–106. https://doi.org/10.1080/1464 9880050008782.

Arvanitis, R., and Qiu, H. (2010). R&D in universities and different institutional settings in South China: research for policy. Final research report for IDRC.

Bailey, D., Hildreth, P., and De Propris, L. (2015). Mind the gap! What might a place-based industrial and regional policy look like? In D. Bailey, K. Cowling, and P. Tomlinson (eds), *New Perspectives on Industrial Policy for a Modern Economy* (pp. 287–308). Oxford: Oxford University Press.

Barbieri, E., Di Tommaso, M.R., and Bonnini, S. (2012). Industrial development policies and performances in Southern China: Beyond the specialised industrial cluster program. *China Economic Review*, 23(3), 613–625. https://doi.org/10.1016/j. chieco.2010.12.005.

Barbieri, E., Di Tommaso, M.R., and Huang, M. (2010). Industrial development policy and innovation in Southern China: government targets and firms' behaviour. *European Planning Studies*, 18(April), 83–105. https://doi.org/10.1080/096543 10903343542.

Barbieri, E., Di Tommaso, M.R., Pollio, C., and Rubini, L. (forthcoming-a). ICT clusters promoting innovation and social change: the case of Dongguan, China.

Barbieri, E., Di Tommaso, M.R., and Rubini, L. (2009). *Industria contemporanea nella Cina Meridionale: governi, imprese e territori*. Rome: Carocci.

Barbieri, E., Di Tommaso, M.R., and Tassinari, M. (2015). Selective industrial policy and strategic sectors: the choices of Beijing, *L'industria*, 36(3), 403–434, doi: 10.1430/81869.

Barbieri, E., Pollio, C., and Prota, F. (forthcoming-b). The heterogeneous effects of spatially targeted programs: evidence from counties and districts in Guangdong.

Barca, F., McCann, P., and Rodríguez-Pose, A. (2012). The case for regional development intervention: place-based versus place-neutral approaches. *Journal of Regional Science*, 52(1), 134–152. https://doi.org/10.1111/j.1467-9787.2011.00756.x.

Becattini, G. (1998). *Distretti industriali e "Made in Italy". Le basi socioculturali del nostro sviluppo economico*. Torino: Bollati Boringhieri.

Becattini, G. (2015). *La coscienza dei luoghi*. Rome: Donzelli.

Becattini, G., Bellandi, M., and De Propris, L. (eds) (2009). *A Handbook of Industrial Districts*. Cheltenham, UK and Northampton, MA, USA: Edward Elgar Publishing.

Bellandi, M., and Di Tommaso, M.R. (2005). The case of specialized towns in Guangdong, China. *European Planning Studies*, 13(March), 707–729. https://doi. org/10.1080/09654310500139244.

Bianchi, P. (2017). Giacomo Becattini, the science and the consciousness of places. *L'industria*, 38(2), 139–156. doi: 10.1430/87782.

Biggeri, M. (2017). L'evoluzione dei cluster industriali nei paesi BRICS: una prospettiva di sviluppo umano e sostenibile. *L'industria*, 38(1), 15–48. doi: 10.1430/87137.

Boschma, R., Minondo, A., and Navarro, M. (2012). Related variety and regional growth in Spain. *Papers in Regional Science*, 91(2), 241–256. https://doi.org/10.11 11/j.1435-5957.2011.00387.x.

Chan, J., and Pun, N. (2010). Suicide as protest for the new generation of Chinese migrant workers: Foxconn, global capital, and the state. *Asia-Pacific Journal: Japan Focus*, 8(2), 1–33. https://doi.org/10.1177/0097700412447164.

Chang, H.J. (1994). *The Political Economy of Industrial Policy*. Basingstoke: Palgrave Macmillan.

Cimoli, M., Dosi, G., and Stiglitz, J.E. (2009). *Industrial Policy and Development: The Political Economy of Capabilities Accumulation*. Oxford: Oxford University Press.

Cohen, B. (2017). *International Political Economy*. London: Routledge.

Content, J., and Frenken, K. (2016). Related variety and economic development: a literature review. *European Planning Studies*, 24(12), 2097–2112. https://doi.org/ 10.1080/09654313.2016.1246517.

Démurger, S., Sachs, J.D., Woo, W.T., Bao, S., and Chang, G. (2002). The relative contributions of location and preferential policies in China's regional development: being in the right place and having the right incentives. *China Economic Review*, 13(4), 444–465. https://doi.org/10.1016/S1043-951X(02)00102-5.

Di Tommaso, M.R., and Bazzucchi, L. (2013). Cina contemporanea: un'analisi sulle politiche per la promozione della specializzazione industriale a livello territoriale. *L'industria*, 3, 417–432, doi: 10.1430/74601.

Di Tommaso, M.R., Rubini, L., and Barbieri, E. (2013a). *Southern China: Industry, Development and Industrial Policy*. London, UK and New York, USA: Routledge.

Di Tommaso, M.R., Sarcina, A., and Bonnini, S. (2013b). Industrializzazione e squilibri territoriali: un'analisi esplorativa dedicata al caso cinese. *L'industria*, 3, 449–470. doi: 10.1430/74603.

Di Tommaso, M.R., and Schweitzer, S.O. (2013). *Industrial Policy in America: Breaking the Taboo*. Cheltenham, UK and Northampton, MA, USA: Edward Elgar Publishing.

Department of Science and Technology China (DSTC) (2011a). Specialized towns: the importance of sustaining wealth in Guangdong. Report on the innovation capacity building in Guangdong specialized towns. *Science and Technology Daily* (in Chinese).

DSTC (2011b). The economy of specialized towns in Guangdong: "a third of the world"'. *Science and Technology Daily* (in Chinese).

DSTGG (Department of Science and Technology Guangdong Government) (2003). The innovation of industrial clusters in Guangdong. Internal report.

DSTGG (2006a). Report on the summary of the five-year implementation of the plan of ST technology innovation pilot test and an overview of the development of the STs. *DSTGG Magazine on Specialized Towns Technology Innovation Dynamics*, 115(6), 1–6 (in Chinese).

DSTGG (2006b). Suggestion on the promotion of the development of Specialized Towns. Retrieved from www.zhyz.gov.cn/.

DSTGG (2008a). Patterns of technology innovation platform in Specialized Town (in Chinese). Retrieved from http://www.zhyz.gov.cn/.

DSTGG (2008b). Policy and instruments on specialized town technology innovation in Guangdong. Retrieved from http://www.zhyz.gov.cn/.

DSTGG (2017). A data analysis of the development of Specialized Towns (in Chinese). Internal Report.

Frieden, J.A., and Martin, L.L. (2003). International political economy: global and domestic interactions. In Ira Katznelson and Helen V. Milner (eds), *Political Science: The State of the Discipline* (pp. 118–146). New York: W.W. Norton. https://doi.org/10.2307/3013899.

Fujita, M., and Krugman, P. (2004). The new economic geography: past, present and the future. *Papers in Regional Science*, 83(1), 139–164. https://doi.org/10.1007/s10110-003-0180-0.

Gillis, M., Perkins, D.H., Roemer, M., and Snodgrass, D.R. (1992). *Economics of Development* (3rd edn). New York: W.W. Northon & Company.

Gilpin, R. (2011). *Global Political Economy: Understanding the International Economic Order*. Princeton, NJ: Princeton University Press.

Gilpin, R. (2016). *The Political Economy of International Relations*. Princeton, NJ: Princeton University Press.

Guangdong Academy of Social Sciences (GDASS) (2017). The pattern and path of collaborative innovation of Guangdong industrial clusters. Internal report.

Hildreth, P., and Bailey, D. (2013). The economics behind the move to "localism" in England. *Cambridge Journal of Regions, Economy and Society*, 6(2), 233–249. https://doi.org/10.1093/cjres/rst004.

Jankowiak, A.H. (2017). Cluster-based development: a Chinese cluster policy. *Research Papers of Wroclaw University of Economics*, 486, 71–79.

Kline, P., and Moretti, E. (2013). Local economic development, agglomeration economies, and the big push: 100 years of evidence from the Tennessee Valley Authority. *Quarterly Journal of Economics*, 129(1), 275–331.

Lin, P. (2006). What is "coordinated promotion plan between province and (prefecture) city"? *Journal of Guangdong Science and Technology*, 14(8), 5–6 (in Chinese).

Luo, Zhanxian (2016). Beijiao township in Shunde prefecture is the first Chinese characteristic little town. *Nanfang Daily*, October 15. http://gd.qq.com/a/20161015/004010.htm (accessed July 13, 2018) (in Chinese).

Marshall, A. (1890 [1961]). *Principles of Economics* (9th Variorum edn). London: Macmillan.

Nadvi, K., and Schmitz, H. (1994). Industrial clusters in less developed countries: review of experiences and research agenda. IDS Discussion Paper, no. 339.

NBS (National Bureau of Statistics) (2001). Guangdong Statistical Yearbook. Available at: http://www.gdstats.gov.cn/tjsj/gdtjnj/.

NBS (2005). Guangdong Statistical Yearbook. Available at: http://www.gdstats.gov.cn/tjsj/gdtjnj/.

NBS (2006). Guangdong Statistical Yearbook. Available at: http://www.gdstats.gov.cn/tjsj/gdtjnj/.

NBS (2015). Guangdong Statistical Yearbook. Available at: http://www.gdstats.gov.cn/tjsj/gdtjnj/.

NBS (2017). Guangdong Statistical Yearbook. Available at: http://www.gdstats.gov.cn/tjsj/gdtjnj/.

Neumark, D., and Simpson, H. (2015). Place-based policies. *Handbook of Regional and Urban Economics*, 5(August), 1197–1287. https://doi.org/10.1016/B978-0-444-59531-7.00018-1.

Nolan, P. (2012). China and the global economy. In D. Shambaugh (ed.), *Charting China's Future* (pp. 55–64). London: Routledge.

Ottaviano, G.I.P., and Puga, D. (1998). Agglomeration in the global economic geography. *World Economy*, 21(6), 707–731.

Pyke, F., and Sengenberger, W. (eds) (1992). *Industrial Districts and Local Economic Regeneration*. Geneva: International Institute for Labour Studies. https://doi.org/10.2307/2524335.

Rodrik, D. (2004). Industrial policy for the twenty-first century. CEPR Discussion Paper no. 4767. https://ssrn.com/abstract=666808.

Sarcina, A., Di Tommaso, M.R., and Bonnini, S. (2014). China: industrialization, growth and territorial disparities. A challenge to the sustainability of the process of change and development. *L'industria*, 3, 531–548. doi: 10.1430/78328.

Sen, A. (2005). Human rights and capabilities. *Journal of Human Development*, 6(2), 151–166. https://doi.org/10.1080/14649880500120491.

Sforzi, F., and Lorenzini, F. (2002). I distretti industriali. In IPI (ed.), *L'Esperienza italiana dei distretti industriali* (pp. 20–33). Roma: IPI–Istituto per la Promozione Industriale, Ministero delle Attività Produttive.

Song, Y. (2014). What should economists know about the current Chinese hukou system? *China Economic Review*, 29, 200–212.

Su, W., and Sun, T. (eds) (2016). Development path. *Guangdong Specialized Towns*, 21, 4–5 (in Chinese).

Tsai, M. (2013). Interpretation of the "one town, one policy" – policy for Guangdong Specialized Towns. http://www.potic.org.cn 2013-01-25, url (accessed May 25, 2018) (in Chinese).

Wang, J. (2004). Developing innovation based industrial clusters: policy recommendation. *Economic Geography*, 7(433) (in Chinese).

Wang, J. (2009). Interaction and innovation in cluster development: some experiences from Guangdong province, China. In B. Ganne and Y. Lecler (eds), *Asian Industrial Clusters, Global Competitiveness and New Policy Initiatives* (pp. 325–362). Singapore: World Scientific.

Wang, J., and Yue, F. (2010). Cluster development and the role of government: the case of Xiqiao textile cluster in Guangdong. In D.Z. Zeng (ed.), *Building Engines for Growth and Competitiveness in China: Experience with Special Economic Zones and Industrial Clusters*. Washington, DC: World Bank Publications.

Zhang, M., and Ling, H. (2003). Building Specialized Town technology innovation platform with rich content: a interview with Mr Ma Xianmin, Vice Director of Department of Science and Technology of Guangdong. *Journal of Guangdong Science and Technology*, 2, 15–18 (in Chinese).

Zheng, G., Barbieri, E., Di Tommaso, M.R., and Zhang, L. (2016). Development zones and local economic growth: zooming in on the Chinese case. *China Economic Review*, 38(59), 238–249. https://doi.org/10.1016/j.chieco.2016.01.001.

6. Long-term challenges of industrial development in Latin America and the Caribbean[1]

Jorge Máttar

INTRODUCTION

The purpose of this chapter is to identify and characterize the main structural challenges facing industrial development in Latin America and the Caribbean from the perspective of both the state and the entrepreneurs. Industrial policy is normally understood in the region as a task of almost exclusive responsibility of the government; in this chapter we argue that the private sector must play a principal role in the design, implementation and evaluation of industrial policy, together with the state and civil society. Special consideration is given to the effects of digitalization on manufacturing employment and output in the region – with emphasis in Mexico – and the ways in which policies can respond to that challenge.

Development policies in Latin America and the Caribbean since the end of World War II gave the industrial sector a strategic role, led by manufacturing, which was supposed to spearhead the growth of the entire economy. This strategy followed the experiences of other regions of the world that managed to industrialize their economies in the late nineteenth and early twentieth centuries, and other recent industrialization processes such as those of South Korea, the Republic of Taiwan and China; to the best of our knowledge, there are no relevant development experiences that have not been sustained in a dynamic, productive, innovative and diversified manufacturing sector.[2]

After nearly 70 years a successful national development experience (understood as the attainment of a higher stage of development), lasting in economic, social and environmental terms, cannot be found in Latin

---

[1] Revised version of a paper presented at the International Conference: Globalization, Regional Growth and the 4th Industrial Revolution, October 19–20, 2017, Bologna, Italy.
[2] Except in very small economies, or those with very particular circumstances (Luxembourg, Monaco, Singapore).

America and the Caribbean. The region has experienced periods of relatively high economic growth and rising social welfare, for example in the 1950s and 1960s, thanks to the so-called import substitution policies with industrial protection; or the short period from 2002 to 2008, fuelled by the boom in commodity prices, mainly in South America. However, most of these periods only lasted a few years and very few lessons were learned, thus insufficient and localized growth prevails. In the 1950s and 1960s, the dynamism of the economy was due in large part to the rapid transformation of the industrial sector of that period; in 2002–2008 it was rather the high prices and international demand for commodities (primary goods and natural resources-based manufacturing products) that brought about growth.

The region has not been able to establish an industrial development strategy that reaps in a sustainable way the benefits promised by the manufacturing sector due to its multiplier effects in the rest of the economy: manufacturing can boost the largest technological spillovers, is the main carrier of technical progress, and is responsible for greater scaling in employment skills, as has happened in today's developed economies. There are multiple attempts to explain why the region continues with a truncated industrialization, as Fernando Fajnzylber affirmed since the late 1980s (Fajnzylber, 1983). The lack of a strategy with a long-term vision, the absence of an "entrepreneurial" state (in the sense of Mazzucato, 2013), events in the external order that have motivated important oscillations in policy decisions, dominated by an aspiration of immediacy of profits and lack of innovation culture in the business sector, and a macroeconomic policy that in the last 30 years has prioritized the nominal equilibria over the real ones, are all factors that contribute to explain the incomplete and defective industrialization of the region. With this background, this chapter attempts to establish the challenges facing the development of the industrial sector today, to discuss the current industrial policy proposals in contemporary Latin America, and concludes with policy suggestions to face the identified challenges, one of which is dealt with in more detail: the impact of automation on employment.

The chapter begins with a brief account of the evolution of industrial policy and development in Latin America; some characteristics of the current situation of the economies of the region are identified, in order to emphasize the importance of incorporating the long-term vision into the work of public affairs, without which the necessary changes to move towards a sustainable, inclusive and equitable development would not be forthcoming. With this background, a characterization and identification of the challenges facing Latin American development is proposed and, therefore, the relevant industrial policies, starting from the assumption that to move to a sustainable development path a strategic action of the state is necessary; we identify central policies that would be indispensable to face that fundamental challenge of progressive structural change. Special consideration is given to the irruption of the so-called fourth industrial revolution as a new challenge for manufacturing in Latin America, mainly with regard to its effects on employment (Schwab, 2016). Finally, in the last section, we discuss the conditions that should prevail for the implementation of an industrial policy addressed to that purpose. A long-term vision and a strategy in which the state and the private sector concur are key for the structural changes necessary to take place for the sustainable development of the region. The experience of the last 25 years shows that privileging market action to the detriment of public policies has not brought about the path towards the future that we all want for the region.[3]

POLICY AND INDUSTRIAL DEVELOPMENT IN LATIN AMERICA AND THE CARIBBEAN: HISTORICAL PERSPECTIVE.

The current situation of the Latin America and the Caribbean (LAC) region's industrial development and the challenges it faces are linked to the historical performance of the industry, the policies (or lack thereof) that the region has suffered since the mid-1950s, as well as the corresponding responses of economic agents. Before identifying and discussing the challenges of industrial development in the region, it is useful to review briefly the long-term evolution of both the policies and the performance and development of the industrial sector (the manufacturing sector, unless otherwise indicated).

The Golden Period of Growth: From the Late 1940s to the 1970s

In the first period, covering approximately the period from the 1940s to the beginning of the 1970s, active policies of industrialization with tariff protection, subsidies and financing were in force in most countries of the region, including tax and financial incentives to infant industries. This period coincided with the expansion of the world economy and trade after

---

[3]   While admitting a variety of ways to achieve it, the common vision of the "future we want for the region" stems from the result of discussions regarding the Post 2015 Development Agenda, which eventually gave rise to the world agreement of the Sustainable Development Goals. See United Nations (2012, 2015).

the end of World War II. Optimism in the region was high, since a long period of prosperity with social welfare was envisioned. In the 1960s, the whole continent of the Americas, at the initiative of the United States government, agreed on a strategy called the Alliance for Progress, consisting of large infrastructure investment projects that sought to promote a long period of development (see Kennedy, 1961; Máttar and Perrotti, 2014).

The industrialization scheme was aimed at advancing the local production of light manufactures of low-technological complexity and labor-intensive processes, replacing imports, mainly of generalized final consumer goods, and maintaining a quota of imports of capital goods that, at a later stage, would also be replaced by the development of the capital goods industry. The model worked at the beginning mainly in the larger economies, that is, Argentina, Brazil and Mexico. It was based on the abundance of natural resources and low-skill labor and a "competitive" exchange rate (stable, with a tendency to devalue), configuring what authors such as Fajnzylber termed the spurious factors of competitiveness, since no attention was paid to the incorporation of technical progress, innovation and technology (see Fajnzylber, 1983, 1992; CEPAL, 1990).

At the end of this period attempts were made – generally unsuccessfully – to develop sophisticated manufactures and some capital goods, mainly in Argentina, Brazil and Mexico. Brazil was the only country that advanced in the endogenous development of sophisticated manufactured goods, such as the aircraft industry (with the state-supported firm Embraer). In the case of Mexico, perhaps the most successful experience was the strategy for the automotive sector and the auto parts industry, in partnership with leading transnational corporations that took advantage of attractive conditions created by foreign direct investment (FDI) legislation. In Argentina a successful example is provided by the steel industry, which later became transnational and is still internationally competitive (see Bielschowsky and Stumpo, 1995; CEPAL, 1993).

At the beginning of the 1970s, institutions such as the United Nations Economic Commission for Latin America and the Caribbean (ECLAC) underscored the need to give impulse to manufacturing exports; among other reasons due to the persistence of imbalances in the trade balance account, which prevented a faster growth of the economy as a whole, as it translated into substantial increases in imports (see Lahera et al., 1995; Bielschowsky, 2010).

There were also relatively successful but sporadic attempts at regional integration, which at one time had a manifestation in the industrial sector, with the so-called integration industries, which had an ephemeral success in Central America, a region composed of small economies pioneering the integration process. The idea was especially relevant for economies with small markets, insufficient to sustain national industries in activities with considerable scale economies. A few projects were discussed in industries such as chemicals, cement and paper during the 1960s, but they were not implemented due to a lack of financing, long-term vision and political will. There are no successful experiences of integration of industrial development projects that can be highlighted, with the exception of infrastructure development (basically, energy and transportation) in South America and the Central American isthmus (CEPAL, 2013).

Despite the shallow depth and diversification and reduced technical progress of the industry, from the 1940s to the mid-1970s the region achieved gross domestic product (GDP) growth rates of around 6% per annum, but the impact of rising oil prices in the mid-1970s and the subsequent increase in international interest rates in the early 1980s, under conditions of high indebtedness, abruptly ended this period and inaugurated the so-called "lost decade" of Latin America and the Caribbean.

Recession, Adjustment and Change of Model: the 1980s and 1990s

The 1980s were characterized by a virtual stagnation of per capita GDP growth, high inflation and fiscal, financial and exchange rate important imbalances in LAC. In the field of industry, promotion of development mechanisms was dismantled and policy became reactive in the face of the need to stabilize macroeconomic indicators and to reduce balance-of-payments disequilibrium.

Structural reforms aimed at market predominance – to the detriment of the state – were undertaken in the second half of the 1980s with the objective of achieving a more active participation of the private sector in production and exports that, according to the scheme, should become a lever for economic growth. Many public enterprises were privatized or divested; goods, services and financial markets were deregulated; and opening up to the external sector was undertaken. The stimulus programs for the industrial sector were significantly reduced, both for budgetary reasons and the need to balance the fiscal accounts, as well as for ideological and political economy reasons, which raised arguments about the inefficiency, lack of vision, lack of ability and corruption in the management of public resources by the state. In some countries, however, some sectoral policies prevailed, particularly in the automotive industries of Brazil and Mexico.

The Washington Consensus permeated the entire region in the 1990s, anchored in the notion of the private sector as the growth lever (in lieu of the state) and the export sector as the engine for growth. The motto for development was "export-led growth" by "levelling the playing field" to compete on an equal footing with international players, thereby opening the economy, lowering import tariffs, privatizing or divesting public enterprises, and putting reliance on market action ("industrial policy" was almost exclusively reduced to competitiveness policies). In effect, international players were treated the same nationally and the field of play was levelled, but the national players did not possess the same skills, strategy, training or knowledge as the international ones. Latin American players were less equipped than outsiders and, therefore, the game remained very uneven. More precisely, the opening of the economy and the idea of the outward growth model required accompanying policies for domestic firms to be in a position to compete with international companies. Only sectors with a dominant presence of transnational corporations were in a position to face international competition and, to that extent, they were relatively unscathed by the dismantling of protection, and economic, financial and commercial opening and deregulation.

The results of the Washington Consensus neoliberal policies in the 1990s were mixed: inflation was reduced and stabilized at one-digit levels in most countries, fiscal imbalances receded, balance-of-payments disequilibria were reduced and exchange rate volatility diminished. This is what structuralists called "nominal equilibria" of the economy. The problem was that the growth of exports did not bring about a comparative dynamism in domestic production. The basic reason was low value-added in products exported, with small linkages with the rest of the economy; and, in the case of manufacturing in Mexico and Central America, the export surge was explained by the *maquiladora* industry, by definition with no linkages to domestic productive chains. Thus "real equilibria" was neglected by the mainstream; growth, income and welfare advanced at a slow pace in the 1990s, far from the dynamism needed to recover from the lost decade of the 1980s (see ECLAC, 2002). This structural characteristic of LAC industrialization is the basis of the risks that are faced today, and will be in the near future, by industry as a consequence of digitalization.[4]

Three Sub-regions, Three Styles of Latin American Development in the Twenty-first Century

The poor results of neoliberal policies led structuralists, neo-structuralists and other critics of the Washington Consensus to coin the phrase "export led but no growth." Adjustments to the strategy were needed according to some scholars, and radical changes acoording to others. At the beginning of the new century the emergence of three different development style trends

---

[4] In this chapter we use the terms "automation," "digitalization" and "robotization" interchangeably.

in three geographical areas of Latin America became clear. Thus, a model of industrial development with three different styles was consolidating:

- The South America model, based on the exploitation of natural resources, their nil or very low industrial transformation, using low and medium technologies, and exports mainly directed to Asian and European markets.
- The model of the North America sub-region of Mexico, Central America and the Dominican Republic, dominated by the production of manufactured goods with very little industrial transformation, almost nil innovation and technical progress, with the main destination of exports being the United States.
- The model based in the tertiary sector, mainly financial services and tourism, typical of the small economies of the Caribbean region and of Panama.

This three-style model of Latin American and Caribbean development was well identified at the beginning of the new century. The favourable cycle of commodity prices led to an unprecedented boom in the production and exports of commodities in all South American countries, which in the period 2002–2008 boosted LAC GDP growth at an annual average rate of more than 5%, the highest for a similar span of years in more than four decades. Analysts and some government officials talked about the "great decade" of Latin America, with Brazil as the finest example of this boom; however, a strategy of greater industrial transformation of raw materials was not in place, and the end of the boom found the South American countries without an alternative plan to face the end of the super-cycle of raw materials.

The Northern Region of Latin America and the Caribbean (RNALC), formed by Mexico, the Central American countries and the Dominican Republic in the Caribbean, deepened its model of basic assembly of imported parts and components of manufacturing goods, and its shipments predominantly to the United States, with little innovation and technological spillovers, and limited learning. The signing of free trade agreements between Central America, the Dominican Republic and the United States in the mid-2000s, together with the full operation of the North American Free Trade Agreement (NAFTA) between Canada, the United States (US) and Mexico, provided an additional push to the productive and export orientation of the RNALC model towards the North American market. Mexico also tried to diversify its external insertion through the signing of free trade agreements with more than 40 countries, but the United States prevailed as the main export destination (about 80%

of the total), although Mexican imports of Chinese products grew significantly, reaching 18% of total imports in 2016, compared to 47% of the US.

The Caribbean area maintained its orientation towards economic development based on services, mainly tourism and financial, and a precarious development of manufactures; in a very few cases the export of raw materials is relevant, as is the case of oil in Trinidad and Tobago. The small size of the Caribbean economies motivated their need to export, although without achieving diversification or a successful international insertion "Caribbean brand." Currently the Caribbean economies are looking for an external insertion that is more conducive to their long-term development, but face external financing constraints due to the high levels of their external debt (Hendrickson, 2017).

The Twenty-first Century: More of the Same or Virtuous Structural Change?

The deepening of the pattern of development of the three sub-regions of Latin America and the Caribbean in the last decade shows the vulnerability of the scheme, which is not conducive to regional prosperity, sustainability or equity in its development. The pending issues in terms of inclusion, equity and poverty alleviation are evidence of the insufficiency of the model, which does not generate enough economic growth; such growth, in addition to being low, is both concentrated and unequal, mainly in terms of wages, technological intensity and technical progress.

The so-called structural heterogeneity underlines the fundamental reasons for insufficient, uneven and concentrated development. The productive sector, in particular manufacturing, is characterized by structures in which establishments of very different levels of economic performance coexist. On the one hand, there are dynamic sectors of high productivity, comparable to those of the developed economies, in which medium-sized and large companies, many of them foreign-owned, prevail; on the other hand, there are sectors where the presence of smaller enterprises is high and the scales of productivity are several times smaller than those of the larger sizes. This heterogeneity is reflected in the general conditions of employment and, in particular, in wages, identifying here the primary source of income inequality at the level of the whole economy. Given the characteristics of public expenditure and tax collection in the region (very low progressiveness), the distribution of income is practically unaltered by the intervention of state policies, which are often regressive, as opposed to the European case, in which taxes and transfers reduce the Gini coefficient by 20–40 percentage points (ECLAC, 1998, 2017).

In the second decade of the twenty-first century, the region retains very similar challenges to those it has faced since the period of import substitution; other challenges aggravate the urgency of structural changes to the model to be undertaken jointly by the state and the entrepreneurs. For instance, the impact of the so-called robotization of production in employment is expected to affect especially repetitive and low-skilled jobs, which are precisely those that abound in the region (see Frey and Osborne, 2013; Krull, 2016; World Economic Forum, 2016; McKinsey Global Institute, 2017, among others). Likewise, the effects of exponential technological change mean that the technological gap (currently considerable) between the leading countries and the region will increase.

The experience and lessons of what are now developed economies in which the manufacturing sector has played a very important role remains an enigma for the region, despite having shown benefits in North America, Europe and East Asia, for example. Indeed, the widespread implementation of policies in certain sectors of the economy was considered unnecessary by policy-makers for a long period, approximately from the late 1980s to the beginning of the second decade of the twenty-first century, with the exception of horizontal support such as competitiveness or science and technology policies, but even these had very limited scale and scope.

In Latin America today there is a greater openness and readiness of economic policy to undertake actions deliberately aimed at promoting certain sectors of industry or, if not, to strengthen horizontal policies more systematically. Policy-makers in some countries have reached the conviction that actions are needed from the state to promote growth, competitiveness and the strengthening of industry, and also to encourage or stimulate specific sectors. The challenge is enormous, because the regions of Southeast Asia, China, India and the so-called "countries in transition" have advanced in industrial development at a faster pace than Latin America.

Long-term Approach to Industrial Development

One of the factors that has not been extensively studied as an explanation for the region's reluctance to establish sustained industrial policy programs is related to the absence of medium- and long-term policies (state policies) that extend beyond the government periods, which in the region's countries last between four and five years (except Mexico: six years). Numerous cases of international experience show that the creation, development and consolidation of an industrial sector that is capable of acting as an engine of the economy requires a sustained effort, with short-, medium- and long-term objectives and with state leadership, private sector commitment and with an increasingly participatory citizenship, not only in decision-making but also in monitoring and evaluation[5] (see, e.g., Chang, 2003; ECLAC, 2014).

The development of Latin America and the Caribbean has lacked long-term planning and vision, which, to some extent, has influenced growth and the perpetuation of a scheme that does not end up by contributing to sustainable development. This is the background to show the importance of the identification of the long-term challenges of industrial development in the region. This is precisely the case of the impact of automation on employment in LAC countries, which we will deal with below.

The world in general, and Latin America and the Caribbean in particular, is experiencing a period of instability, low growth and increased uncertainty about the future. In the short and medium term, a moderate trend of world output and trade is expected, which will lead to a continuous slowdown in economic dynamism in the region. To the extent that these tendencies are verified, government agendas in Latin America prioritize the management of the very short term, especially where the impact is more noticeable and in those countries that go through presidential electoral processes (17 countries in 2017–2019).[6] On the other hand, the situation imposes additional challenges to the work of national states that, in the last two decades, have advanced in the institutionalization of public policies trying to integrate the simultaneous realization of social, economic and environmental development visions.

The question that arises in the context of the objectives of this chapter is how to maintain and promote an agenda of progressive structural transformations in the economy with job creation, particularly in industry, in a context of low economic dynamism; and how to give medium- and long-term industrial policies a significant role in the policy mix, without ignoring the need to address short-term urgencies. In short, the issue is how to articulate the management of short-term and long-term policies, in order to maintain the essence of inclusive and sustainable development.[7]

The region faces the challenge of maintaining growth at levels compatible with the creation of productive jobs, preserving social and environmental priorities, in order to protect the sustainability of the process in

---

[5]   In the experiences of industrialization in countries such as South Korea and Taiwan, active citizen participation in the significant decisions of public policy was not the rule. In contrast, 50 years later, in Latin America, the present times demand a more participatory role for society in the fundamental decisions that affect the development of the countries.

[6]   Haiti, Ecuador, Honduras and Chile in 2017; Costa Rica, Cuba, Paraguay, Colombia, Mexico, Brazil and Venezuela in 2018; El Salvador, Panama, Guatemala, Argentina, Bolivia and Uruguay in 2019.

[7]   Ruiz Duran (2017), for instance, considers global megatrends and identifies and analyses the implications for the future of industrial policy or, rather, for the industrial policy for the future.

the long term. Latin American countries should prevail in pursuing an integral approach to development, even in the context of this unfavorable global environment, which, in the case of the labor market, threatens the continuity of actual jobs, not to mention future jobs, due to robotization processes in the economy.

The proposal of progressive structural change for the inclusive and sustainable development of the region refers to prospective thinking to shape and influence the future, which in turn requires ruptures in institutions, productive apparatus, public management and in the non-functional state–market–society equation (ECLAC, 2010). The present relationship between the state, the market and society is non-functional in the sense that conspires against the path of inclusive, equitable and sustainable development. The region has given up opportunities to push forward an industrial development agenda to generate transformative change processes when conditions were more propitious, the last of which occurred during the commodity boom period (2002–2008), particularly in South America. An industrial development strategy is a fundamental condition for prosperity and social welfare, which must be the ultimate goals of development.

A medium-term scenario of mediocre growth, and the opportunities offered by the 2030 Agenda for Sustainable Development (United Nations, 2015), are factors that compel governments of the region to explore alternatives to the path and style of development and the engines of growth followed by the region in the last 20 years. The complexity of the international scenario highlights, once again, the need for structural transformations spearheaded by manufacturing to systematically and permanently raise the productivity of the economy and boost competitiveness.

THE CONTEMPORARY CHALLENGES: INDUSTRY AND POLICIES

The challenges of industrial development in Latin America depend, to a greater or lesser extent, on the objectives of the development model and the mix of policies and instruments necessary to achieve those objectives. This chapter argues that the "future that we all want" in Latin America and the Caribbean (see United Nations, 2012) is one of prosperity, justice, inclusiveness, sustainability and equality; that is, the Latin American societies aspire to a scenario such as that laid out in the 2030 Agenda for Sustainable Development (United Nations, 2015). We argue that achieving sustainable development is the result of deliberate actions, agreed between the state, the private sector and society, implicitly and through processes of dialogue and consultation, with the coordination and leadership of the state and citizen participation; this is a policy for successful industrial development, which we now define for the purposes of this chapter.

Industrial policy is defined as the state intervention to stimulate specific economic activities and promote structural change (this is especially relevant for Latin America and the Caribbean). It should be a dynamic, democratic and participatory process in which a series of actions are applied to pursue or achieve certain objectives based on national development priorities. In a broad sense, industrial policy includes services and primary activities, in addition to manufacturing. It has a wide variety of instruments at its disposal, which can be classified into six types of policies: (1) commercial; (2) support for small enterprises; (3) science, technology and innovation; (4) sectoral and territorial; (5) education and training; and (6) competition and competitiveness (Alvarado and Padilla Pérez, 2017).[8]

Recognizing the progress made by industrial development policies in the region over the last decade, it should be noted that, in general, there has been no continuity or consistency in the implementation of policies or long-term industrial development strategies. This requires the identification of long-term objectives associated with the challenges facing both the whole economy and the industrial sector.

Progressive Structural Change (PSC): The Biggest Challenge?

Given the above considerations, we propose that progressive structural change (PSC) is the key challenge of industrial development in the region; that is, a virtuous change in the composition of output and employment towards dynamic activities of increasing productivity that incorporate more technical progress, quality and well-paid employment and, in addition, implies fundamental changes in the conception of the public policy task, which gives the state the role of leader and coordinator of the process of strengthening the industrial sector (ECLAC, 2014).

Progressive structural change is the only strategy capable of altering the long-standing low productivity and growth rates, and the inequality and poverty trajectories that have affected the region in the last 50 years. As experience in developed countries shows, economic and social progress

---

[8] Over the last 15 years industrial policy actions in the region have been characterized by increasing international trade competitiveness; legitimacy of horizontal or neutral instruments; support for small businesses and micro-enterprises, basically for their job creation capacity; science, technology and innovation policies aimed at advancing towards knowledge-based economies; and focus on subnational and local economic areas (Peres, 2011).

requires deliberate policies to boost and strengthen the productive sectors. The LAC region has not found a development strategy to make the qualitative leap that will lead it along a virtuous path of high growth, high productivity, decent wages and, consequently, a reduction of poverty and inequality. This is precisely what progressive structural change pretends to take care of; but it requires industrial policies that take the lead in the public agenda, in which real balances (growth, investment, employment) are the fundamental objectives, while nominal balances (inflation, interest rate, exchange rate) – central in LAC public policy over the last 25 years – become instruments to support the achievement of the real balances. Other tasks should be articulated and fed back to contribute to progressive structural change and be undertaken both by the private sector (output and investment decisions) and by the government and state (industrial policy actions). These are described below.

Challenges to be faced by the private sector

1. Increase competitiveness and productivity through more investment in research, development and innovation; discover, exploit, develop and consolidate competitive advantages such as innovation, technical progress, training, in lieu of comparative advantages such as exchange rate, wages and exploitation of the abundant and varied natural resources of the region.

2. Reduce the magnitude of structural heterogeneity by means of a strategy to lessen the considerable differences in productivity, both across sectors and between firm sizes, in order to lower the dispersion of wages and, therefore, of income inequality.

3. Create and develop new sectors, which are dynamic and bearers of technical progress; integrate more and better the national and regional productive apparatuses: selective substitution of imports, inclusion of depressed territories, projects of regional productive integration, among others.

4. Turn the manufacturing sector into the engine of economic growth: selective substitution of imports, exports with added value, incorporation of technical progress, strategic associations with exporting world leaders.

5. Make the best use of the impact of robotization of production, particularly concerning its effects on employment. Well-known analyses indicate that the jobs most likely to disappear are those that require the lowest qualification and the most basic skills, exactly the characteristics that abound in the labor force in the region. Therefore, it is necessary to launch retraining programs, re-engineering of skilled and unskilled workers, as well as managerial cadres (see Box 6.1).

BOX 6.1   IMPACT OF ROBOTIZATION ON EMPLOYMENT IN LATIN AMERICA

One of the consequences of accelerated technological development and innovation is the automation of very diverse and numerous productive processes that are rapidly substituting labor. In the developed world it is a phenomenon that will affect millions of jobs, but it is estimated that in developing countries the impact could be higher, given that the effect will be greater in those routine, repetitive activities that demand less education, skills and dexterity; precisely the characteristics that abound in the labor force of the region.

In one way or another, technological change has effects on all states, markets and societies, both advanced and developing, but challenges differ across countries, due to their varied economic structures. In Latin America, the infrastructure necessary to take advantage of new technologies is deficient: many people in the region use the Internet, and it is part of the digital revolution, but there is a part of the population that does not have access to technology or uses it in a superficial and basic way, which is associated with the different expressions of inequality in the region.

There is a certain consensus that the future prospects of the manufacturing industry are not good in the region, although the service sector can be an opportunity for development, within the framework of a growth strategy based on services, in which it is foreseen that robotization would have a less forceful impact than in the typical manufacturing of countries in the region. For this purpose, it is necessary to move from the use of the Internet for consumption to a productive use, taking advantage of its growing penetration in the region, and also to create opportunities for employment growth. However, the generation of new precarious, low-quality jobs must be avoided, even at the expense of the number of jobs.

Therefore, the policy has to take account of these processes and adapt the institutional framework to new situations and new problems, both with respect to the incorporation of new technologies into the structures of the economy, and in terms of employment creation. National and regional plans can help the region by harmonizing technological developments within and between countries. The regional single market, which was proposed by ECLAC at the Fourth Latin American Telecommunications Congress, is an idea in that direction (CLT16, 2016). Therefore, it is necessary that societies have an awareness of the impacts of new technologies in the labor market and that they know how to incorporate the new circumstances in an institutional framework so that the effects of technology are beneficial for all.

Source: Based on Krull (2016).

Challenges to be faced by the industrial policy stakeholders[9]

1. An industrial development strategy has to be agreed upon at the highest level among representatives of the state, the market and the

---

[9]   Based on Peres (2011).

society (a social pact), containing a long-term vision, compatible with state policies and objectives agreed in an open, transparent and participatory manner.

2. Policy design should be accompanied, not followed, by explicit consideration of the institutions that will have to implement them. This means involving industrial policy stakeholders, and creating institutions which allow this participation on a continuous basis (for example, a national innovation system, competitiveness and productivity programs, retraining of the labor force, especially to face the impact of automation, and so on).

3. Training programs should be strengthened to increase the quantity and the quality of human resources specialized in policy design, implementation and evaluation. These capabilities were diminished or lost during the years of the Washington Consensus and have not fully recovered.

4. The institutions and the individuals that link policy design and implementation should be developed, through strengthening of public institutions, search for leaders in the private sector and intermediate implementation agents, such as business associations.

5. Better policy evaluation systems should be created, to improve design, focus and implementation; some assessments exist of specific or more general programs, but overall knowledge about the impact of policies is scarce. Instruments seldom establish the criteria and mechanisms for follow-up and evaluation. There is a lack of consensus on how to evaluate complex policies with multiple targets, objectives and lines of action.

As for the implementation of industrial policy, the current international context imposes certain restrictions, mainly derived from the difficulty of applying protection measures to domestic production, within the framework of changes in the rules of international trade of the last two decades. This fact has important implications for the promotion of potential enterprises in new sectors or products, whose profitability would probably be greater if the possibility of protection existed. In other words, the selection of winning sectors must take the lack of protection and the importance of promoting new activities into account, with stimuli that do not violate the rules of international trade (Peres, 2011).

ADDRESSING THE CHALLENGES OF PROGRESSIVE STRUCTURAL CHANGE FOR DEVELOPMENT[10]

Progressive structural change is at the heart of a process of growth with decent employment and equity in the long run. This change is not the result of spontaneous forces, but of active policies to stimulate sectors of high productivity with greater intensity of knowledge (Schumpeterian efficiency) and strong dynamism of their internal and external demands (Keynesian efficiency), as corroborated by countless successful international development experiences.

Structural change requires an industrial policy that explicitly defines a direction for the effort that must be sustained, respecting the productive, scale and institutional specificities of the countries, as well as certain inherent objectives of the development stage of each state. In practice, industrial policy involves choosing sectors that will drive this process; but this effort is sterile if it is not accompanied by institutional development to ensure the effective implementation of those policies, including social consensus and political will around those goals, aspects in which much remains to be done in Latin America.

A popular consensus among Latin American industrial development scholars regarding the public policy cycle indicates that policy design in the region is made with little success: policies are half-implemented and are usually flawed, their results are not significant and their impact is rarely evaluated at all. Thus, successful implementation of policies in Latin America and the Caribbean has been historically low. Peres and Primi (2009) identify five causes of widespread failures in policy implementation, and the resulting gap between what is decided and what is implemented, which for the purposes of this chapter stand as fundamental challenges to be addressed.

Non-operational or Unattainable Objectives

The formulation of non-operational or out-of-reach objectives transfers the decision to implement policies to the resource allocation stage, where obstacles are most likely to be partially resolved. The basis of the problem is that, because of their flaws in formulation, policies tend to resemble declarations of good purpose rather than instruments for allocating resources.[11]

---

[10]   Part of this section is based on ECLAC (2014).
[11]   In recent years, management and budget results-based methods have become popular in countries of the region, still with implementation failures; when the project initiatives come

The practice in the region is usually the preparation of policy documents that lead to long lists of needs and objectives, in which a methodological guide of the policy implementation process is usually absent. While the multiplicity of objectives may be due to the action of many actors in complex societies, it also reflects the inability to prioritize and build consensus around a few that can be effectively implemented.[12]

Good practice in addressing the problem is provided, for instance by sectoral agreements in Colombia, which include an assessment of the success factors showing that: (1) a well-structured, quantifiable, time-bound agreement is easier to follow; (2) a limited number of simple commitments leads to greater achievement rates; (3) the leadership and decision-making power of the people in charge of implementing the agreements are fundamental; and (4) the production chains supported prior to the agreements achieved better results (Velasco, 2003).

Scarcity of Human and Financial Resources

The implementation of industrial development policies demands high-quality human resources and significant financial effort. Their lack of availability, especially in small economies, often requires external resources (reimbursable and non-reimbursable loans, technical assistance, horizontal cooperation) to formulate them and, moreover, to implement them, with undesirable consequences in national decision-making. For example, when donor priorities change and policy support is withdrawn, it generally disappears; if, in contrast, priorities last longer, conflicts of interest may arise between the external partner and the host country.

In addition, the announcement of policies is usually not accompanied by an implementation program, nor information on costs and funding for full implementation and evaluation. The situation is made even more complex by the fact that direct fiscal subsidies and credit with subsidized interest rates are not widely accepted in the community. A macroeconomic policy is then required, which recognizes the need to use these instruments.

In the case of technical assistance and horizontal cooperation, peer-to-peer schemes have been tried out in LAC that promote the exchange of

---

with deficiencies, the corrected result is usually partial and is far from constituting a robust investment program proposal. See, for example, CEPAL (2017).

[12]   The Global Delivery Initiative, led by the World Bank, shows the diversity of factors that can cause failures in the implementation of investment projects of very diverse types in many different countries of the world; the basis of the analysis is the information of projects executed by the Bank itself and other institutions such as the Inter-American Development Bank, the African Development Bank and the Asian Development Bank. See http://www.globaldeliveryinitiative.org/.

experiences and good practices and lessons learned among practitioners and policy-makers. Well executed, with a good identification of the issues of cooperation and relevant partners, these programs often provide learning that is multiplied within the beneficiary entities and are, therefore, usually long-lasting. In some of these experiences, the contributing partners of technical assistance have been institutions from developed countries able to pass on their experience and lessons in topics of interest to the region (Winchester, 2016).

Reduced Institutional Capacity

In general, the countries of the region lack institutional capacity to implement policies. The difficulty arises when it comes to programs that seek to reflect best international practices, rather than the needs and specificities of countries interested in implementing them. This often results in unrealistic policy formulations that, even worse, are often driven by instances with little influence in the power structure of governments or by business associations with low representativeness and little economic and political weight.

The problem is exacerbated because in the region the policy formulation and implementation instances are usually separated. While countries can increase their institutional capacity over time – and in the region some have done so – institutional creation and innovation require stability of objectives and institutional continuity for longer periods than the usual four to six years of governments in LAC, as well as financial resources that confer capacity for action.

In some countries, a young generation of practitioners, implementators, evaluators, decision-makers and policy-makers is slowly emerging, with a modern, transparent and genuine development-oriented attitude. Sometimes they are subject to frustration due to the fact that decision-making processes are altered by political reasons, ideology or, even worse, corruption. As several studies have shown, politics and corruption are frequent in policy decisions, assignment of funds for programs and investments, and implementation failure; their success and relevance are often spoiled by these negative factors (see, e.g., Warner, 2014). It is crucial to introduce fundamental changes in the public sector that promote probity, stability, sustainability and medium- to long-term vision in the formulation of plans, policies and industrial development programs in the region.

Weaknesses of Public–Private Agreements

Alliances between the government and the private sector to implement policies are precarious and often short-term, as evidenced at the time of public sector expenditure or investment commitments and private sector counterpart expenditures. Moreover, plans and programs that are only developed to respond to political pressures from economic or social actors proliferate, to request international financing, or to comply with legal or constitutional provisions. Sometimes the resources of development programs tend to reach actors who do not necessarily need them most (for example, to improve productivity, training of the labor force or preferential financing), but who have access to decision-makers over the allocation of resources.

The business sector, which strongly defended protection policies until the end of the 1970s, does not show the same strength to carry out policies of diversification and improvement of productive specialization in the countries of the region (CEPAL, 2008). Risk aversion and short-term vision in investment decisions is the norm in the private sector, with the exception of large, multinational companies that have sophisticated strategies and are fully equipped to face risks.

Weakness of Economic Signals: Evaluation of Policies and Programs

The problems of implementation of sectoral policies are amplified by the weakness and ambiguity of the economic signals of the programs. At best, the entrepreneur is offered a set of signals that are difficult to interpret and translate into concrete measures, and the effect of which on profitability is uncertain. However well formulated a policy may be, it will hardly achieve its objectives if it is not accompanied by clear signs of profitability. Implementation failures and the perception that "policies do not work" affect the legitimacy of industrial policies and the interest they may have have for their main recipients, namely entrepreneurs. This leads to a paradoxical situation: entrepreneurs believe that the resources available to implement policies are scarce and that risk is high, and at the same time do not use all of these resources.

Evaluations of the implementation and effects of industrial policies are limited not only by the available information, but also because, until very recently, these policies have rarely explicitly indicated criteria and mechanisms for their evaluation. Such an assessment would in any case be complicated by the fact that policies often have multiple objectives and lines of action, often without establishing verifiable quantitative targets. What has been done to assess the effects of industrial policies is even more limited and unsatisfactory than what has been done to evaluate the implementation of these policies. In the region, there are only evaluations of some specific programs, such as support for small enterprises or technological innovation, or general evaluations of what happened after policy implementation, without arguments clearly indicating causality between actions and results.

Executing Policies as Planned

What can be done to overcome these problems of discrepancy between what is decided and announced, and what is done and evaluated? Three lines of action should be explored further; they are not a magic solution, nor are they easy to put into practice, but they open up alternatives and deserve to be explored from perspectives that combine the economic, institutional and management dimensions.

Institutional factors
Policy formulation must be accompanied by explicit consideration of the institutions that are to implement them. This implies that those interested in industrial policy must engage with the issue of state reform. It is about transforming the state structure – strengthening executing agencies with political power, effective budgetary instruments and technical capacity – so that it is functional to the designed policies. This is especially important when implementing systems-wide or cross-sectoral policies which, by definition, will cover more than one sector or more than one executing agency. Here, again, medium- and long-term consideration of the work of institutions is crucial.

Human resources for implementation
Given the scarcity of qualified human resources in the areas of the state linked to the implementation of policies, a second line of action is to transfer highly qualified and executive staff that are working on the formulation of policies to these areas. It is essential to train and/or reallocate human resources, which must be accompanied by appropriate incentives such as economic remuneration, but also by demands for transparency, accountability and quantifiable results. The impact of digitalization on employment is a good example to develop knowledge and capacities to design strategies to avoid severe employment setbacks.

Evaluators
A third line of action is to develop and strengthen policy-makers – that is, institutions and individuals that guarantee policy execution – by combining formulation, action and funding capacities. To this end, public or private institutions can be identified and strengthened to lead and implement effectively. In addition, it is advisable to strengthen the evaluation mechanisms with a positive approach to improve the practice of the public

policy cycle, leaving behind the vision of "punishment" that is usually present in the evaluation schemes.

The region's experience shows that long-term institutional development within the state is possible, as has been done in ministries in charge of macroeconomic policy and in central banks. Private policy leadership has been effective in some cases (for example, in the formation of some productive conglomerates at the local level), but in the region it has been seen that leadership is difficult to systematize and tends to focus on a few relatively powerful sectors. Thus, economically weak sectors, which need great efforts by policy-makers, tend to have weak leadership.

THE IMPACT OF AUTOMATION ON THE LABOR MARKET IN LATIN AMERICA: THE CASE OF MEXICO[13]

In addressing progressive structural change in Latin America a new great challenge is emerging from the changing nature of employment as a result of the fourth industrial revolution. There is a tendency to automate and digitize a wide variety of processes that workers normally perform. In this new industrial stage there is a growing interaction between the cybernetic and the physical world, facilitated by computer systems, artificial intelligence and communication networks.

Although this is happening more rapidly in industrialized countries where "Industry 4.0" is moving faster, it is also happening in developing countries. The tendency is to move from producing with the lowest possible costs, to producing in the most intelligent way (Van Agtmael and Bakker, 2016). That is why it is no longer so attractive for global companies to invest in countries with an abundance of labor. A more detailed outlook, with special reference to Mexico, is addressed in what follows.

Challenges of Automation for Employment in Latin America

The productive specialization is likely to be highly automated in Latin America. For example, it is estimated that more than half of productive activities in Mexico are at risk (McKinsey Global Institute, 2017). Among the sectors that generate the most jobs, retail trade stands out (it can be automated at 51%, with a potential job loss of 5.5 million jobs); along with manufacturing (64% automatable, with a potential loss of 4.9 million jobs)

---

[13]   This section is based on Schatán (2018).

and the agricultural sector (with 59% of automatable jobs and a potential loss of 4.7 million jobs). Although this process can be slow, especially in agricultural activities, in others it will be faster and a gradual displacement of labor can be expected.

This process of automation and digitalization could aggravate the current precariousness of employment. About half of the total employment is in the informal sector in countries such as Brazil, Colombia, Mexico and Peru, without social protection, and generally with wages that are considerably lower than those in the formal sector. In addition, in Mexico this is added to the negative effect of an inadequate wage policy and a weakening of the unions and the instances of collective bargaining on wages. Salary increases do not reflect advances in productivity, and Mexico's minimum wage is one of the lowest in the world.

The state of affairs described provides a useful framework to design and implement policies to face these transformations in Latin American economies. The vulnerability of jobs should not be equated with imminent and inevitable job losses, for three reasons: (1) the introduction of new technology is a slow process because it faces economic, legal and social obstacles; (2) with adequate policies, workers can take advantage of the introduction of new technology by changing tasks and preparing for it; and (3) technological change generates new jobs linked to new technologies. The impact of technology on jobs will largely depend on the ability of human capital to adapt to the new circumstances.

In summary, automation and digitalization and the transition to a knowledge economy present challenges for Mexico and the region:

- possible displacement of unskilled labor and the greater vulnerability of jobs;
- permanence of depressed wages, and low productivity if there is no better preparation of people for the new profile of production;
- lack of coordination between job demand and supply;
- an educational system that does not respond to the new requirements of the current world in general, and the productive one in particular;
- limited access to information and communication technologies (ICTs) and underutilization of their potential;
- overall, persistent production, wage, education, technological and employment gaps.

Policies to Face the Challenges of the Fourth Industrial Revolution

Latin America needs to rethink the economic model that prevailed in recent decades. The abundance of cheap labor as an advantage has begun to be unsustainable. If a renewal capacity of the productive system does not emerge towards the generation of greater added value, internal inequality will deepen, the gap will be broadened with respect to developed countries (including with respect to other emerging economies), and unemployment and informality will increase.

In Mexico, a new strategy will have to be developed under adverse circumstances, stemming from the trade policy of the United States government, the goals of which are to recover jobs, strengthen its domestic market, reduce its trade deficit, and stimulate the repatriation and attraction of capital. Mexico faces, among other adversities, the protectionism of its main trading partner, a crisis of NAFTA, competition impossible to match with US fiscal stimuli to attract FDI (which can generate a flight of capital to the US from Mexico) and the closing of the escape valve for many young people to migrate to the United States to achieve better living standards.

The region requires a proactive stance, based on productive transformation strategies in the medium and long term. In Mexico, a consensus of this kind is needed that includes an industrial policy that stimulates new productive niches that can be developed in the country (in many of which there are already incursions, but not enough development) or promotes the greater integration and scaling up of sectors that already exist. It is essential to achieve coordination among the different agents that intervene in the training of talent in Mexico, that is, the education ministry, science and technology councils, universities, research centres, technological universities, business chambers and unions, among others.

The challenges of automation in employment require cross-cutting public policies, and other more specific ones. But they will be difficult to overcome the problems of employment, untapped talent, salaries, and mismatch between supply and demand of jobs, without a strategy of productive development in the medium and long term. In addition, for this to be a successful strategy, there must be effective feedback between companies, the education sector, innovation centres and responsible government agencies. In what follows, policy proposals are presented to face the challenges of automation in Mexico in particular, with special reference to employment, salary, education, talent development and training. These do not differ significantly from those of most LAC countries.

Education and development of new talents
The fourth industrial revolution must be accompanied by an educational revolution. This is a long-term task, for which a new form of teaching and learning is needed, from the preschool level to higher education and continuing education. The resources allocated to this enormous task are

insufficient, but experience in other countries shows that there is potential to make better use of the available resources. It requires the preparation of a new human talent that is capable of responding to new forms of production.

The Organisation for Economic Co-operation and Development (OECD) identifies educational policies that have been successful in school areas in Ontario, New York, Hong Kong, South Korea, Singapore and Shanghai (Snyder, 2013). Among the measures adopted are the hiring of a larger number of teachers (and management of smaller groups of students); tutorials for students whose learning lags behind; professional preparation and development for teachers; locating the best teachers and promoting their advice to other teachers within the school and other schools; seeking collaboration among schools, universities, technical schools and companies to grant dual degrees that allow students to obtain technical degrees to facilitate their entry in the labor market; creating databases so that the agents involved can appreciate the performance of students and teachers and evaluate the progress of efforts to improve education; greater learning based on specific projects of research and use of ICTs, in addition to multidisciplinary learning; and less use of standardized textbooks. Several of these measures are contemplated in the educational reform of Mexico, which shows that it is inspired by effective instruments. However, their resources are insufficient. The collaborative aspect of the measures proposed by the OECD study could be more strongly exploited in Mexico.

Higher education for a better future
Higher education teaching methods require changes in universities and technology institutions and, for this, there are very useful examples in educational systems in other countries. There are few Mexican higher education institutions that have adopted, for example, the problem-based learning system (PBL) or other non-traditional methods. The PBL system has revolutionized traditional education in many universities around the world, as it changes the role of the teacher, making it a guide to the learning process by which students learn through discovery.

PBL stimulates creative and innovative thinking, but it requires a profound change in the didactic preparation of teachers and study programs, as well as an infrastructure that is different from the traditional classroom, because spaces are needed for teamwork. There are some experiences of innovation in the teaching of this sort in Mexican higher education institutions, but they are rather isolated. Many of these initiatives are generated from specific projects sponsored and proposed by various international companies in order to achieve innovations in these companies, but there is no plan coordinated and supported by the university education system in Mexico.

Quality training
It is necessary to improve and expand the training of active workers in Mexico; it is estimated that only 37% of them have received training during their working life (Ricart et al., 2014). Many programs aim at training active workers, but they are fragmented, dispersed and with very little funding, so that they cannot significantly cover the training or more generalized retraining of the workforce. The coordination and strengthening of these programs is urgent. The public and private sectors must play a key role in the permanent training of the workforce.

The public sector in Mexico contributes only 0.01% of GDP for training, in contrast to 0.66% of GDP, on average, in the OECD. Mechanisms to support an improvement in the skills and knowledge of people exist in Mexico. The "Bécate" Program is the principal of four pillars of the Employment Support Program (PAE) of the Ministry of Labour and Social Security (STPS). The PAE offers support to people who: (1) seek employment and need to be trained to enter the labor market; (2) need to retrain their skills to change jobs; or (3) need to develop enough skills to create independent employment (self-employment). However, its scope is still very modest; in 2016, the funds allocated to the PAE were just 5 million pesos, that is, the equivalent of 0.1% of the budget of the STPS.

Support for scientific and technological development
Government support for the development of science, technology and innovation in Mexico is insufficient. The National Council for Science and Technology (CONACYT) performs very important work to promote the development of basic science, applied sciences and innovation, through the financing of research projects, scholarships, and incentives to academic excellence and encouragement to researchers. But the country is far from meeting its own goal, established by law, to invest 1% of GDP in the sector; the gap with the rest of the developed world in these activities is increasing. Investment in science and technology rose by 40% in real terms in 2013–2015, but stagnated in 2016 and was significantly cut in 2017, reaching 0.54% of GDP, far from the government's own plan (0.89% of GDP).

Promote research in science, technology and innovation (STI)
In Mexico, research in STI is carried out in numerous research centres, universities, in certain companies, and so on. Some of these are integrated with or have a close link to production clusters, which facilitate the transfer of technology and the application of new knowledge. CONACYT has 27 first-level research centres. However, this important effort has

not achieved a national leap in terms of technological development and production of greater added value of national scope. That is, these advances are circumscribed to certain areas and activities and, therefore, do not make a significant difference as a whole. It is essential to strengthen the networks among the different actors and ensure sufficient channels and financing so that advances in STI can be translated into more generalized and concrete results.

Accelerate advances in information and communication technologies

This is the basic mechanism for the country to enter the knowledge society and for people to be prepared for it. It is necessary to expand and improve the ICT infrastructure to guarantee their competitive performance in terms of bandwidth and speed, and service coverage; 30% of society has no access to the use of ICT. The effort must be aimed at reducing the price of services and enabling free access for the poorest sectors.

Horizontal training should be provided to workers for the management of ICTs, given that occupations in the knowledge economy need increasing interaction with digital media. The Program for the Development of the Software Industry (PROSOFT) and innovation should be strengthened, designed to promote strategic sectors, thus helping to create innovation ecosystems, without which it will be difficult to scale the productive system to the required technological and competitive levels.

Attracting talent

Despite the adverse circumstances of recent US policies for Mexico, there are possibilities that the country should take advantage of. The new policy of restricting the entry of immigrants into the United States, which includes highly qualified foreigners such as engineers, can offer opportunities in Mexico, since the companies that, in principle, would hire that talent in the US will seek support outside their borders. An example of this type of operation is provided by software engineers from Guadalajara with the Wizeline company based in San Francisco. They have 300 engineers in many parts of the world and work for numerous multinationals.

Several of these companies could take advantage of the greater facilities provided by Mexico for the entry of talent from third countries that will not be able to enter the United States. The most talented training in Mexico could create many good-quality jobs in this type of activity, and the government should take specific measures to attract such investments.

CONCLUSIONS: INDUSTRIAL POLICY CONSIDERATIONS TO MEET THE CHALLENGE OF STRUCTURAL CHANGE[14]

This chapter has identified challenges facing Latin American industrial development and discussed possible ways to overcome them, through policies that appeal to what we have considered the synthesis of the major challenges: progressive structural change. Just as industrial development faces challenges, so public action is responsible for helping to address these challenges and, in our opinion, these represent the fundamentals for a new industrial policy for the region, whose principles and characteristics have been presented in this chapter. In this last section, we address a set of considerations for the exercise of policies for industrial development: the criteria for selecting the sectors to be promoted, the available policy instruments, the constraints imposed by the size of the national markets and the accumulated capacities of the countries, the areas of action allowed by international trade agreements, and the political will to carry out such actions.

Picking Winners

The selection of sectors should start by recognizing that there are no universal criteria for deciding which activities are to be promoted. However, international experience shows that countries have chosen and continue to choose sectors, and that they do so by following a few more or less precise criteria, such as knowledge content of the activities, their dynamism in the international market due to a high elasticity with respect to the growth of world income and especially of the developed countries, and potential productivity growth. Other criteria are added related to the strategic nature of certain activities, their weight in output, exports or employment, at national, local or subnational level. The international experience broadly illustrates the use of these criteria, not always explicitly, in the countries of the region.

The technological dimension has increasingly been used to define the scope of industrial policies. Although traditionally a group of activities has been considered a "sector" when all of them produce goods or services with high cross-price elasticity, it is also possible to define activities that share a technological trajectory as a sector, such as the aerospace, biotechnology or ICT sectors. Different types of policy have been implemented

---

[14]   See ECLAC (2014) for a detailed discussion.

for this purpose, some centred on horizontal policies, and others that are directly involved at the level of companies, market segments or knowledge networks.

Instruments

Many of the instruments of industrial policies already exist in the programs of the countries of the region. They consist mainly of combining the instruments of competitiveness policies with direct instruments of public action in the area of financing, in particular of development banks, fiscal incentives and public investment, as well as the management of the state's purchasing power and their companies. The vision behind the formulation of these policies is based on temporarily granting favorable conditions of profitability to new technological activities and trajectories, such as mass access to broadband as an Internet platform that enables Cloud computing.

The promotion of infant industries is today less accepted within the framework of open economies, and it is not possible to use instruments of generalized and permanent commercial protection. This restriction weakens the economic signal (expected return) that is sent to potential investors in new activities, and causes a significant part of the cost and risk of development activities to fall on the state. This poses problems, in terms of both determining the priorities for allocating budgetary resources, and the stability of those resources during periods of fiscal restraint. Sustaining long-term development mechanisms, even beyond a period of government, remains a challenge that many countries in the region have yet to face successfully.

Another powerful instrument of sectoral policy could be the direct investment of the state that can be executed through its companies or government plans and programs, which are very important in key areas in several countries of the region, for example economic infrastructure. Although the degrees of freedom in this area are large, as shown by various cases, particularly at the local or subnational level, their use in the region is limited. Experience suggests that the instruments that have been applied so far, whose cumulative effects have not yet been evaluated, have not had the necessary inductive force. An important limitation today is the access to investment financing and, in some countries, the high indebtedness coefficients.

Size Limitation of Markets

It has been argued that small countries with less institutional capacities should not and cannot establish sector-wide policies. Without neglecting the importance of using the internal market to achieve economies of scale and learning, it should not be ignored that in open economies, or with regional or subregional integration possibilities, the issue loses its strength, as shown by the experience of many small countries that perform as competitive export platforms. Although institutional capacity is a significant requirement, particularly in the short term, the fact that it is limited does not require the scrapping of sectoral activities, but rather concentrates them on subsectors, segments or even products that are within reach of existing capacities. In this sense, experience in the region with policies to promote productive clusters reveals that even small countries have been able to formulate policies to improve their pattern of specialization.

Margin of Action Left by Trade Policy

With regard to the areas of action allowed by international trade agreements, the scope of industrial policy is currently limited by the growing interference of World Trade Organization (WTO) rules in areas formerly considered to be internal policies of each country (McMillan et al., 2014). In addition to the general reduction of barriers to trade, WTO rules prohibit export subsidies and quantitative restrictions on trade, except for least-developed countries. The rules also include trade-related measures regarding foreign investment (no national content or performance requirements can be applied) and intellectual property rights (standards on the subject must meet at least certain minimum standards).

However, the weight of these constraints should not be exaggerated, since, as Rodrik (2004) indicates, what governs the development of industrial policies is more the will of governments to implement them than their ability to do so, as shown the cases of the Republic of Korea and Singapore, among others. In the Latin American context, the renegotiation of the North American Free Trade Agreement (NAFTA) is a good example of how the imposition of determined restrictions by the US government might affect certain industries of Mexico, such as automotive and auto parts, for which the US government is proposing more national content, even at the expense of WTO rules.

Policy Evaluation and Political Will

Sector policies face an ambiguous situation in the region. Even in countries that do not consider sectoral policies acceptable, they are implemented ad hoc, together with specific measures to support sectors in crisis. Since these policies are necessary to advance the development of the region, it is necessary to ask what tasks are required to increase its legitimacy.

Two lines of action are at play. On the one hand, implementation capacity needs to be improved, bridging the gap between policy formulation and institutional capacity to carry them out; the persistence of this gap undermines the credibility of policy-makers, and therefore of the policies themselves. On the other hand, considerable progress must be made in assessing the impact of policies in terms of their ultimate objectives: economic growth, technological progress and productivity growth. Since public resources are scarce, only robust evaluations will allow space to reallocate resources from other policy areas, and will have the arguments to demonstrate that allocating fiscal resources to these policies is as important as investing in education, public health or public safety.

In addition to improving the implementation and evaluation of policies, it is necessary to strengthen the social actors interested in these policies, that is, those that would support with their resources economic and political initiatives of this nature. Industrial policies have had a slow return to Latin America and have been able to operate, albeit on a small scale in most countries, in open economies and with macroeconomic policies that favour nominal stability above that of real variables; *ex ante* it was expected that such macroeconomic policies would be incompatible with the implementation of industrial policies. For these policies to cease to have a marginal weight, social actors, including the state, will have to make them their own, compromise the support of their power and resources, and articulate them with macroeconomic, social and environmental policies that foster productive development.

Finally, an element which we have not referred to: corruption is a potential inhibitor of the success of an industrial development policy. Corruption, impunity, lack of transparency and poor accountability in the use of public funds are all factors that generate mistrust about the effectiveness of public policies. In both society and the private sector, interest groups appear that often take advantage of these failures of public administration; they reap the benefits that should be available to those who need them most (in the context of promoting development with a perspective of equity and justice). The region has generated a variety of mechanisms to combat corruption and reduce impunity, but they are far from having ceased to be an obstacle to the design, implementation and evaluation of a democratic, transparent, meaningful industrial development policy. The increased influence of citizenship opinion in public policy decisions provides optimism, but without the conviction, compromise and collaboration of open and democratic states it will be very difficult to consolidate these advances.

REFERENCES

Alvarado, Jennifer and Ramón Padilla Pérez (2017), "Política industrial y cambio estructural en México," in Mario Cimoli, Mario Castillo, Gabriel Porcile and Giovanni Stumpo (eds), *Políticas industriales y tecnológicas en América Latina*, LC/TS.2017/91, CEPAL, Documentos de proyectos, Santiago, Chile.

Bielschowsky, Ricardo (2010), *60 años de la CEPAL*, Siglo XXI Editores and CEPAL, Buenos Aires.

Bielschowsky, Ricardo and Giovanni Stumpo (1995), "Empresas transnacionales y cambios estructurales en la industria de Argentina, Brasil, Chile y México," *Revista de la CEPAL*, 55, 139–164.

CEPAL (1990), "Transformación productiva con equidad, la tarea prioritaria del desarrollo de América Latina y el Caribe en los años noventa," United Nations, March.

CEPAL (1993), "La industria argentina: un proceso de reestructuración desarticulada," October, Oficina de Buenos Aires.

CEPAL (2008), *La transformación productiva 20 años después. Viejos problemas, nuevas oportunidades* (LC/G.2367(SES.32/3)), United Nations, Santiago de Chile.

CEPAL (2013) "Integración eléctrica en América Latina: antecedentes, realidades y caminos por recorrer," Colección Documentos de Proyectos, Estudios e Investigaciones.

CEPAL (2017), *Panorama de la Gestión Pública, 2017*, United Nations, Santiago de Chile.

Chang, Ha-Joon (2003), *Kicking Away the Ladder: Development Strategy in Historical Perspective*, Anthem Press, London.

CLT16 (2016), "ECLAC Encourages the Creation of a Regional Digital Market in Latin America and the Caribbean," https://www.cepal.org/en/comunicados/la-cepal-impulsa-la-creacion-un-mercado-digital-regional-america-latina-caribe.

ECLAC (1998), *The Fiscal Covenant*, United Nations, Santiago, Chile.

ECLAC (2002), *Globalization and Development*, United Nations, Santiago, Chile.

ECLAC (2010), *Time for Equality: Roads to Open, Gaps to Close*, United Nations, Santiago, Chile.

ECLAC (2014), *Structural Change for Equality, an Integrated Approach*, United Nations, Santiago, Chile.

ECLAC (2017), "Social Panorama of Latin America," Summary, United Nations, Santiago, Chile.

Fajnzylber, Fernando (1983), *La Industrialización trunca de América Latina*, Editorial Nueva Imagen, Distrito Federal, México.

Fajnzylber, Fernando (1992), "Industrialización en América Latina: de la 'caja negra' al 'casillero vacío'," *Nueva sociedad*, 118 (marzo–abril), 21–28.

Frey, Carl B. and Michael A. Osborne (2013), "The Future of Employment: How Susceptible are Jobs to Computerization?," Oxford: Oxford Martin Programme on the Impacts of Future Technology.

Hendrickson, Michael (2017), "A Framework for Caribbean Medium-Term Development," CEPAL, Series Estudios y Perspectivas – ECLAC Subregional Headquarters in the Caribbean.

Kennedy, President John F. (1961), *On the Alliance for Progress. Address by President Kennedy at a White House Reception for Latin American Diplomats and Members of Congress, March 13, 1961*, Modern History Sourcebook. https://sourcebooks. fordham.edu/halsall/mod/1961kennedy-afp1.html.

Krull, Sebastián (2016), "El cambio tecnológico y el nuevo contexto del empleo: tendencias generales y en América Latina," Serie CEPAL, documento de proyecto, LC/W.725, diciembre. http://repositorio.cepal.org/bitstream/handle/11362/4085 6/1/S1601255_es.pdf.

Lahera, Eugenio, Ernesto Ottone and Osvaldo Rosales (1995), "Una síntesis de la propuesta de la CEPAL," *Revista de la CEPAL*, 55, 7–26.

Máttar, Jorge and Daniel Perrotti (2014), *Planificación, prospectiva y gestión pública: Reflexiones para la agenda de desarrollo*, number 126, June, Libros de la CEPAL, Santiago, Chile.

Mazzucato, Mariana (2013), *The Entrepreneurial State. Debunking Public vs. Private Sector Myths*, Anthem Press, London.

McKinsey Global Institute (2017), "Jobs Lost, Jobs Gained: Workforce Transitions in a Time of Automation, Executive Summary, December." file:///Users/jorge/ Downloads/MGI-Jobs-Lost-Jobs-Gained-Executive-summary-December-6-2017 .pdf.

McMillan, Margaret, Dani Rodrik and Iñigo Verduzco (2014), "Globalization, Structural Change, and Productivity Growth, with an Update on Africa," *World Development*, 63, 11–32.

Peres, Wilson (2011), "Industrial Policies in Latin America," Working Paper No. 2011/48, UNU – World Institute for Development Economics Research, September.

Peres, Wilson and A. Primi (2009), "Theory and Practice of Industrial Policy: Evidence from the Latin American Experience," serie Desarrollo productivo, N° 187 (LC/L.3013-P), CEPAL, Naciones Unidas, Santiago de Chile.

Ricart, Consuelo, Tzitzi Morán and Christina Kappaz (2014), "Building a Lifelong Learning System in Mexico," Labor Markets and Social Security Unit, Inter American Development Bank.

Rodrik, Dani (2004), "Industrial Policy for the Twenty-first Century," Background Paper, UNIDO, Vienna.

Ruiz Duran, Clemente (2017), "Future of Industrial Policies in the World: Toward a New Manufacturing Narrative," paper presented at the International Conference: Globalization, Regional Growth and the 4th Industrial Revolution, October 19–20, Bologna, Italy.

Schatán, Claudia (2018), "Retos de la automatización y digitalización para el empleo en México," Centro Tepoztlán Victor L. Urquidi. http://centrotepozt-lan.org/wp-content/uploads/2018/04/schatan-claudia.pdf.

Schwab, Klaus (2016), *The Fourth Industrial Revolution*, World Economic Forum – Crown Business, New York.

Snyder, Sean (2013), "The Simple, the Complicated, and the Complex: Educational Reform Through the Lens of Complexity Theory," OECD Education Working Papers No. 96.

United Nations (2012), *The Future We Want*, Rio+20 Conference on Sustainable Development, Rio de Janeiro, June. https://sustainabledevelopment.un.org/ content/documents/733FutureWeWant.pdf.

United Nations (2015), *Transforming our World: The 2030 Agenda for Sustainable Development*, New York, September. https://sustainabledevelopment.un.org/con tent/documents/21252030%20Agenda%20for%20Sustainable%20Developme nt%20web.pdf.

Van Agtmael, Antonie and Fred Bakker (2016), *The Smartest Places on Earth: Why Rustbelts Are the Emerging Hotspots of Global Innovation*, Public Affairs, New York.

Velasco, M.P. (2003), "Una Evaluación de las Políticas de Competitividad en Colombia," Regional Project Una Estrategia de Desarrollo de Clusters Alrededor de Recursos Naturales: Sus Implicaciones Sobre Crecimiento, Distribución y Medio ambiente, Santiago: ECLAC, DDPE.

Warner, Andrew M. (2014), "Public Investment as an Engine of Growth," IMF Working Paper, Research Department and Strategy, Policy, and Review Department.

Winchester, Lucy (2016), "Peer to Peer Collaboration," unpublished working paper, CEPAL-ILPES.

World Economic Forum (WEF) (2016), *World Economic Forum Annual Meeting 2016, Mastering the Fourth Industrial Revolution*, Davos-Klosters, Switzerland, January 20–23. http://www3.weforum.org/docs/WEF_AM16_Report.pdf.

7. The future of industrial policies in the world: towards a new manufacturing narrative

Clemente Ruiz Durán

This chapter argues that industrial policy in these times of deep structural changes has to become sustainable, in the sense of contributing to the resolution of global societal challenges. These "megatrends" are in fact linked to the ongoing deep transformations and have to be taken into account in a comprehensive vision in order for socio-economic development to become sustainable. The sustainability is here intended as both socio-political (guaranteeing rights of people, namely access to decent life, to education, and so on) and environmental. For this purpose, important institutional changes will be required.

GLOBAL SOCIETAL CHALLENGES

Getting Back to the Age of Mistrust

We thought distrust had disappeared with the end of the Cold War. Unfortunately, today we are once again facing mistrust among countries. Let us remember the words of President Reagan: "Nations don't mistrust each other because they're armed; they're armed because they mistrust each other." These words date from the end of the Cold War, which gave birth to mass destruction arms, but also to innovation, as in the case of Arpanet that later became the World Wide Web (Zimmermann and Emspak, 2017). Today the world is back to a mistrust age, military expenditure is increasing and bringing back the ghosts of the Cold War; if this prevails we will be facing a new age of military expenditure, and with it the focus of industrial policy on defense, trying to imagine the first-shot destruction strategy (Choi, 2017). An increase of military expenditure will have negative effects on public consumption, as it will force a reduction in welfare expenditures (education, health, housing, etc.), worsening income distribution.

Climate Change and Natural Disasters

The world is already facing the consequences of climate change: natural disasters have dramatically increased in number (Dawson, 2017), and have become more destructive. For example, in 2017, Hurricane Harvey damaged the Caribbean and the south of the United States, and Hurricane Maria devastated Puerto Rico in September of the same year (Kimberlain et al., 2016); while severe monsoon rains drenched much of South Asia, killing more than 1200 people, flooding more than one-third of Nepal and Bangladesh, and displacing tens of millions of people. Rising sea levels are posing a threat to most coastal cities in the world. The European heat wave of 2003, when unrelenting temperatures caused stagnant air to mix with pollutants, created a kind of toxic smog. An estimated 70 000 European city-dwellers died from the heat wave that summer (Di Liberto, 2015). Earthquakes in Japan, Italy and Mexico have been increasing the danger to cities and there is a call for urban redesign. Disasters pose a challenge to industrial policy on how to face the "Anthropocene Age," as it was named by Nobel laureate Paul Crutzen.[1]

Energy Challenge: The Transition Era

The global energy landscape is changing; fast-growing emerging markets are overtaking traditional centers of demand. The energy mix is shifting, driven by technological improvements and environmental concerns that demand a reduction of carbon emissions. The increasing demand for energy in the world will pose important choices and opportunities for industrial policy.

Mass Consumption Expansion and Aging

Population growth will feed mass consumption and it is expected that between 2017 and 2100 there will be an increase of 3.8 billion people into the world economy,[2] with uneven remunerations. What is expected is an increase of consumers who will demand new goods and services. The average consumer will be more sophisticated, responding to the information network that will enable them to have multiple choices in the marketplace. One of the most challenging questions is how aging and declining

---

[1] USGS. Significant Earthquakes 2017. Available at: https://earthquake.usgs.gov/earthquakes/browse/significant.php.

[2] UN Population Division Department of Economic and Social Affairs. Probabilistic Population Projections based on the World Population Prospects: The 2017 Revision.

population in wealthy nations will affect consumption patterns. The industrial policy challenge will be to acknowledge diversity and inclusion.

Poverty and Inequality: The Catch-up Challenge

Poverty remains at very high levels (Williams, 2017), although inequality declined over the period 1990 to 2017. Gross domestic product (GDP) per capita is still 23 times higher in high-income countries compared to low-income countries, in a sample of 144 countries (World Development Indicators, World Bank). The catching-up process will be a challenge; it was successful for Asian economies – that is, Singapore, Macao, South Korea, China, India, Vietnam, Malaysia, Thailand and Myanmar – but we are waiting for the "rise of the rest," as Alice Amsden (2001) stated in her book. Recently Irmgard Nübler defined two dimensions of catching up, "the concept which maintains that the dynamics of catching up are determined by the structural change and process dimensions of productive transformation. The structural change dimension relates to the patterns of change in the economic structure, while the process dimension relates to the pace and sustainability of this change" (Salazar-Xirinachset al., 2017). Manufacturing has been a key process for catching up, as it develops capabilities and learning processes, it organizes growth in a dynamic path and introduces the need to innovate along the process, ruling out stagnation. Industrial policy will have to address the catching-up process in a way that involves all lagging countries, resuming the progressive agenda that has been lost in the last decades. Macroeconomic policies could be used to promote technological change through government purchasing power, bringing development thinking to new territories to promote productive redefinition.

The Mobility Revolution

The success of the automobile industry in the world poses a threat to urban mobility: there are around 2 billion cars in the world, most of which are used for short distances and remained parked for long periods. However, when they get into the streets, congestion leads to traffic jams with negative effects: productivity losses and negative effects on family life. The need to reduce pollution from transport has been stressed for decades, and innovative green cars will have to diffuse in order for the problem to be resolved. The sharing economy is also emerging as a response, and multiple arrangements are being fixed, that is, Uber and cycling companies, and many others that help mobility.

The New Face of the State: The Governance Problem

In recent years and months there has been a surge of regionalism and nationalism among countries and regions and calls for disintegration have arisen all around, with the issues of Brexit, the North American Free Trade Agreement (NAFTA), Catalonia and Kurdistan. This call for nationalism and regionalism threatens collaboration, and it is clear that industrial policy will have to face this threat and at the same time address the problem with policies at all levels of government: supranational, national or regional. As Weiss (2011) states, industrial policy could help the overall vision or strategic direction the government wishes to set, or help the process whereby a dialogue is required with the key actors in the private and public sectors and design the policy instruments used to affect change. Industrial policy could help to have a sensitive response to avoid disruptions; and will help design a policy mix within regions and countries, which could bring-in again subsidiarity principle.

Financing the Manufacturing Revolution: The Threat to Make it Inclusive

One of the weakest links for transforming manufacturing is finance; it has been impossible to build a stable mechanism for financing productive activities, as it has risen as an autonomous mechanism. It has to be recognized that it has helped accumulation and mass consumption, but it has been unable to bring in the "unbanked," who according to the World Economic Forum number about 2 billion people (Asktrakhan, 2016). The challenge is how to design a stable finance mechanism that helps entrepreneurship and mass consumption.

The Dominance of Information Networks, the Prevalence of Big Data and Disruptive Change

The knowledge-based economy relies on the information networks that allow research to gain a broader perspective, taking advantage of big data networks delivering better processes and products. Innovation is the name of the game; information networks allow connectivity, bring in speed, accessibility and anchoring (Blackwell et al., 2017).

The Future of Employment and Robotization

Competitiveness is the name of the game; productivity has become the key of industrial policy. Industrial policy promotes the adoption of new technologies such as three-dimensional (3D) printing and smart factories, that create new manufacturing paradigms. The key challenge for companies will be deciding how best to harness their power (Tilley, 2017), either by using a mix of technology with human capabilities, in an employment-friendly manner, or in a highly automated way. The process of job creation has become more complex. Dynamic manufacturing is not necessarily employment-intensive, but if value chains are developed in the service sector, that is more labor-intensive, the employment process may find an answer, provided they are supplied by domestic firms.[3]

FROM MEGATRENDS TO MANUFACTURING CULTURES AND TRAJECTORIES

Megatrends give an overview of facts that will impact the world economy, but they do not define what sort of industrial policy we should address. We must recognize that in the last century different manufacturing cultures[4] have emerged, with heterogeneous characteristics. Industrial policy in the twenty-first century will have to be addressed in a multilayer scheme that could help catch-up, and at the same time keep providing support to GVC upgrading and emergence.

In this era of deep structural changes, driven by the above-mentioned megatrends, industrial policy requires to adapt to a new agenda. Old approaches such as import substitution industrialization (ISI), whereby macroeconomic policy management was the key element, or export-oriented industrialization (EOI), whereby the role of the state focused on opening the markets and banning the structures of support, are no longer appropriate. Today, as we move into a more complex world of permanent innovation and interactive spaces, industrial policy will have a guidance role for upgrading and ensuring fair competition. National government's industrial policies will need to provide prospective analysis in order to define and choose development paths (Altenburg & Lütkenhorst, 2015).

Manufacturing cultures have evolved over time in various ways. The maps in the Appendix show that China and the Asia-Pacific countries[5]

---

[3]   In IMF (2017) it is argued that the downward trend in labor income shares comes from low productivity, but the text does not go deeper into the causes of this process and how it relates to a new paradigm.

[4]   Manufacturing cultures in the twentieth and twenty-first centuries evolved with the introduction of mass production and consumption, to the era of lean production and of GVCs, creating their own momentum at regional and national levels, with a mix of industrial policies to face backwardness and inequality. Systematic analysis of the concept has been developed by Meric Gertler (2004), and recently by Kanger and Sillak (2018).

[5]   Including Japan, South Korea, Vietnam, Cambodia, Thailand, Malaysia, Singapore, Indonesia and the Philippines.

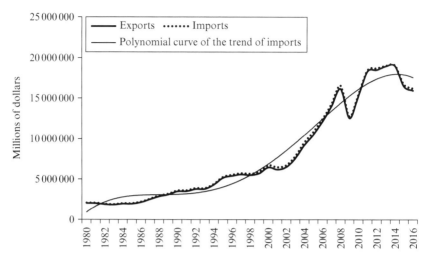

Source: Based on World Trade Organization data.

*Figure 7.1   World trade and the emergence of new manufacturing cultures,
1980–2016*

have become the manufacturing powerhouse of the world, since they
account for one-third of the global manufacturing value added (GMVA),
while the European Union share is 17.5%, and the NAFTA share is 16.8%.
The remaining third of GMVA is unevenly distributed.

The evolution of manufacturing cultures has been influenced by globalization. International trade has experienced its largest ever expansion,
starting at 2 trillion in 1980 and reaching 16 trillion in 2016 (Figure 7.1).
This growth was largely due to the renewed relations with China and transition economies after the fall of the Berlin Wall in 1989. A new geography
emerged, creating new cultures of manufacturing and helped by new trade
agreements,[6] bringing in many developing countries, as Alice Amsden
suggested in her book *The Rise of the Rest* (Amsden, 2001). Trade led the
change, but there was a remaking that brought together manufacturing
and services. As a result of these shifts, economic development now occurs
as a process of industrial upgrading within global value chains (GVCs)

---

[6]   To support trade expansion, in the last 30 years there has been an increase in trade
agreements. The World Trade Organization (WTO) reports that today the world economy
has 110 free trade agreements, 18 custom unions, 11 custom union and economic integration
agreements, 23 partial scope, 138 free trade agreement and economic integration agreements,
and 1 economic integration agreement.

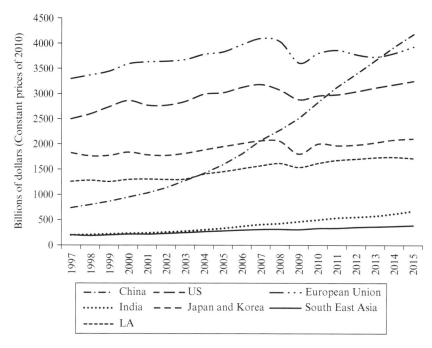

Source: Based on World Bank data.

Figure 7.2 Manufacturing trajectories, 1997–2017

(Milberg et al., 2014). GVC upgrading (Humphrey and Schmitz, 2002) will continue to be an important aspect of industrial policy in the future.

Manufacturing trajectories based on GVC upgrading (Figure 7.2) could be endangered by some political and economic factors, if protectionism emerges once again. It could lead to a stagnation of global trade and endangered catch-up processes of developing economies. Large economies could resist through their domestic markets, at a higher level of prices, as the low-cost exchange disappears. The threat will hit small economies, where industrial policy will have a larger role to compensate the negative effects of rising protection; a new era of import substitution might emerge as a result, at high costs. This scenario could happen if large countries disrupt trade agreements or believe that isolation is a better framework for their economies, such as the UK with Brexit, the US renegotiation of NAFTA, or the claim for independence of Catalonia in Spain.

Mistrust and nationalisms could enhance some manufacturing cultures based on defense systems, which interact and create a new complex reality with different paths for the different world regions. Trajectories will behave according to geo-political systems and regimes, empowering defense expenditures that in the best case would be linked to new technological development through procurement policies for the defense ministries and space projects. Large multiplier effects will derive from this process through procurement practices.

Historically, there have been examples of these interactions between the two structures. The US has been the most successful story, although it was not through a traditional platform but rather through the budget of the Department of Defense, which in 2015 represented $609 billion, or 15.9% of the Federal Budget (OMB National Priorities Project). Institutions such as the Defense Advanced Research Projects Agency (DARPA) have been remodeled over time to provide a network that could take advantage of the research network (Block and Keller, 2011). Along these lines, there has been an exercise for prospective analysis which is the report prepared by the National Intelligence Council, "Global Trends Paradox of Progress." The 2017 edition revolves around a core argument about how the changing nature of power is increasing stress, both within countries and between countries, and bearing on vexing transnational issues. The main section lays out the key trends, explores their implications, and offers three scenarios for the future. Almost all industrial countries had been able to use the military institutions to foster innovation, subsidizing business that will develop new technologies; arms producers have the capacity to satisfy more than military demands. "In fact, the US has formally reworked its military spending policy to make use of the overlap between military and civilian technologies" (Mutimer, 2000, p. 114). As part of the 1996 national security strategy, the US administration wrote, "We are structuring our defense R&D effort to place greater emphasis on dual-use technologies that allow the military to capitalize on commercial sector innovation for lower cost, higher equality and increased performance" (Mutimer, 2000, p. 114). The countries with larger defense budgets according to the Stockholm International Peace Research Institute (SIPRI) are the United States (US), China, Russia, France, India, the United Kingdom (UK), Japan, Germany, South Korea and Brazil (Table 7.1); which are at the same time the largest arm exporters. Disruptions and new arms treaties are threatening the world economy, as during the Saudi–Russia meeting in early October 2017.

THE GOVERNANCE OF INDUSTRIAL POLICY

In the last decades, with the emergence of GVCs, industrial policy requires adapting to a new agenda, due to the fact that the role of the

Table 7.1   Military expenditure as a source of industrial innovation

	US dollars in millions	% of GDP	Share of government spending (%)
US	611 186	3.3	9.3
China	215 176	1.9	6.2
Russia	69 245	5.3	15.5
France	55 745	2.3	4.0
India	55 923	2.5	8.9
UK	48 253	1.9	4.7
Japan	46 126	1.0	2.6
Germany	41 067	1.2	2.7
South Korea	36 777	2.7	12.5
Brazil	23 676	1.3	3.1
Canada	15 157	1.0	2.4
Mexico	6020	0.6	2.3

Source: SIPRI Military Expenditure Database 2017.

state has changed; all countries are adopting a mix of selective sectorial and manufacturing system policies. Financial crises of the last decade gave rise to the need to restructure large sectors of the economy; it was one of the most innovative periods for industrial policy, as a mix of measures were undertaken to prevent the collapse. As stressed by Chang and Andreoni (2017), support came from a mix of fiscal and monetary policies on a large scale, in almost all countries; old formulas were effective to avoid collapse, since "a virtuous industrialization cycle is possible only with certain macroeconomic conditions" (ibid., p. 46). These authors also highlight that the problem of macroeconomic management, and in particular demand management, opens a completely unexplored chapter in the theory of industrial policy. Macroeconomic management opens the space for restructuring productive capacities, and by setting the ceilings and floors of structural change it must not be disregarded, as they will interact and define the process of change. G20 meetings and the annual meetings of the International Monetary Fund (IMF) and the World Bank, which for many are representatives of the old regime, have been able to set the guidelines for macroeconomic behavior. These guidelines are flexible for mature economies as they can finance their deficits without problems through expansion, which is financed by the rest of the world, without restriction. As we move down in the economic cycle, macroeconomic management becomes less flexible and could become a restriction for change.

Multilayered models could be considered, combining top-down and bottom-up policy interventions, managed by different local, regional, national or federal governments. A multilayered governance model offers greater flexibility in the composition of an industrial policy package, and it often allows more selectivity in policy design, better monitoring, and policy enforcement. However, it also requires building an articulated institutional infrastructure and achieving a coherent industrial policy governance among all the government actors (Noman and Stiglitz, 2017). Macroeconomic policies will be required but they are not sufficient to manage industrial change, as we move into a more complex world of interactive spaces. Local and regional governments become key for upgrading and assuring competitive landscapes. Coordination will be required among different levels of government: supranational (European Commission), national or federal, state and local.

In the European Union, the economic integration process has aimed at building a single market and has pushed innovation in manufacturing, which accounts for two-thirds of total research and development (R&D), contributing to 50% of productivity growth, and almost two-thirds of exports and imports (Veugelers, 2017). The EU Council requested the Commission in its May 2017 meeting for a holistic EU industrial policy for the future (European Council, 2017), in order to reinforce the manufacturing culture. It has to be acknowledged that Germany was able to set the standard of the discussion, introducing "Industry 4.0" in 2015 as a guideline for developing a framework for an industrial policy of the future.

Despite the variety of industrial policy pathways, models and policy packages, a number of common focal policy domains and practices are emerging. First, all countries appear to be adopting a mix of selective sector policies and manufacturing system policies. The latter are aimed at supporting the symbiotic development (or restructuring) of complementary groups of industrial sectors. Thus, in manufacturing policies, the selectivity goes beyond sectorial boundaries and focuses on linkages across sectors.

In countries such as the US, Germany and Japan, sectorial policies tend to operate at the state, regional or municipality level, while manufacturing system policies are orchestrated at the federal or national level. In these countries, manufacturing system policies mainly consist of enabling platform technologies, as well as providing selective financial support to new ventures at the technological frontier. Multilayered industrial policy models combining top-down and bottom-up approaches offer greater flexibility in the composition and effective management of industrial policy packages. However, without strong policy enforcement and coordination at the federal or national level, multilayered policy models run the risk of incoherence, with different levels undermining one another (Andreoni, 2017). Developing economies should design industrial policy to favour GVC upgrading and emergence. This means managing the relation between foreign lead firms and domestic low-value-adding firms for the purpose of industrial upgrading and capturing more value-added in the value chain.

Techno-industrial policy has never been off the policy table, and as China continues to pursue regional industrial development strategies, the policies that emerge from central party's leading group debates and national legislative processes ensure that spatial and structural planning is to remain a critical feature of China's economy. The nexus between techno-industrial policy, banking policy and national strategic industries is not going to disappear (Kenderdine, 2017).

National governments will have a role in making prospective analysis and helping business to face the rapid change in technology that has disruptive social and economic effects. Government technological programs pushing for innovation and its translation into commercial success through R&D financing and public procurement are likely to help in orientating development towards the resolution of societal challenges.

One example of successful prospective analysis has been developed in East Asia. For instance, in the catching-up process it has been able to design adequate institutional reforms, and government guidance institutions (the Japanese Ministry of International Trade and Industry, MITI). The Ministry of Science, ICT and Future Planning in Korea has developed one of the largest prospective analyses of this kind. Prospective analysis has also been developed to analyze the Sustainable Development Goals. For this purpose, the United Nations Development Programme (UNDP) has promoted the creation of foresight centers in some emerging economies, such as Brazil, India and South Africa.

Governance problems in a multilevel government scenario are complex and have to be addressed with specific policy targets based on prospective analysis. The productive capacities will be permanently modified due to GVC upgrading, and feedback will come from innovations systems, but key factors for the flow within the matrix to work will come from macro management, acknowledging that external demand will be key for the operation of the multilevel system to work. The matrix below (Figure 7.3) illustrates how this process could take place: that is, by developing productive capacities and innovation and technology networks. Interactions could take place either way, and will stress different levels impacting specific territories. The formal supranational level might be defined not only through formal schemes such as the European institutions, but could also come from trade agreements. Either way they will affect countries

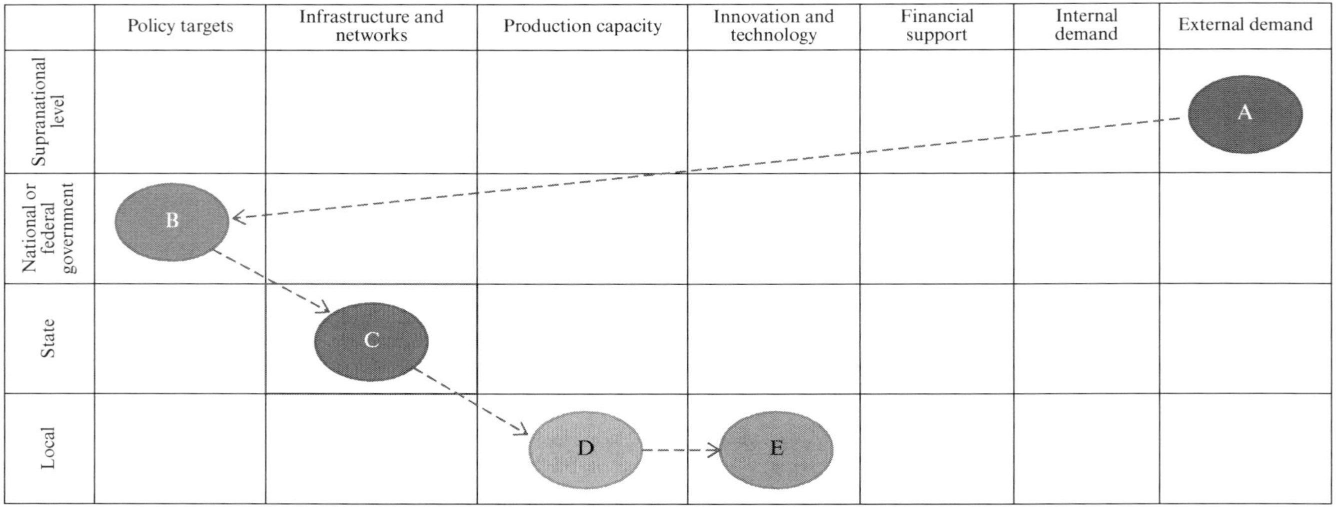

		Policy targets	Infrastructure and networks	Production capacity	Innovation and technology	Financial support	Internal demand	External demand
Supranational level								A
National or federal government		B						
State			C					
Local				D	E			

Figure 7.3   Multilevel government industrial policy packages

and territories, as has been the case with Structural Funds in the European Union, or trade decisions in NAFTA that affect regional policies and modify manufacturing systems at local level. These sorts of interactions are the ones that industrial policy should try to make coherent with long-term transformation processes.

RESILIENCE, INSTITUTIONS AND INDUSTRIAL POLICY

A big challenge for industrial policies is the need to address climate change and natural disasters. Manufacturing cultures that are environment-friendly require prevention policies that can be linked to a monitoring system. As Aoki and Rothwell (2013, p. 1) point out, "in natural disasters there have been some shortcomings: (1) decision instability that can lead to system failure after a large shock, (2) poor incentives to innovate, and (3) the lack of defense-in-depth strategies for accidents." Industrial policies might spur the development and commercialization of new technologies that could create design-monitoring mechanisms that could substantially reduce the damages caused by natural disasters. The Internet of things (IoT), for instance, could be useful to monitor large-scale transforma-tions in the environment – that is, climate and underground monitors – combined with the design of new fibers and construction materials that could be more resistant to shocks.

Industrial policy could contribute to a culture of resilience, as societies will be facing disruptive events that will require redesigning cities, to allow interactivity among medium-sized cities to reduce risks. The challenge is to redesign the whole urban spectrum, including smart houses, smart buildings that will give rise to a new urban landscape. Construction materials will be developed in smart factories with a feedback of natural disaster areas through big data, avoiding repetition of mistakes, through the analysis of materials in the disaster areas. This will require a new institutional framework that could be agile between city planners and the production facilities. Robotics will be involved in the design of cities of the future, where human beings will develop the culture of resilience.

THE ENERGY CHALLENGE: INDUSTRIAL POLICY FOR A GREEN ECONOMY

Industrial policies will have to face the energy challenge. Two stories underlie this transformation: on the one hand, we have a gradual decarbonization of the fuel mix, with rapid improvements in the competitiveness of renewable energy that, combined with nuclear and hydro energy, will provide around half of the increase in global energy out to 2035.[7] At the same time, decarbonization will affect many countries and millions of people, and will require transforming their productive capacities to face the new world of renewable energies. The global energy landscape is changing. Fast-growing emerging markets are overtaking traditional centers of demand. The energy mix is shifting, driven by technological improvements and environmental concerns. More than ever, industry needs to adapt to meet those changing energy needs.

Industrial policy will be a key mechanism to develop a soft-landing transition in the continuing adjustment of the oil market. Considerable progress has been made, but there is still a long way to go. Oil inventories are at record high levels and the impact of the significant cutbacks in investment spending on new energy projects over 2016 and 2017 has not yet been fully felt. Energy transition is being developed in the advanced economies but developing economies are lagging behind, so that decarbonization of the fuel mix will be advancing at two different speeds, which could induce some conflicts among countries.

WORLD POPULATION AND CONSUMPTION PATTERNS

Industrial policies in the twenty-first century will have to imagine new goals, as population growth will not remain stagnant: UN population projections for the year 2100 assume that it will reach 11 billion. The largest expansion in the period 2015–2100 is expected to take place in Africa (3.3 billion), followed by Asia (360 million) and North America (143 million) as shown in Figure 7.4. Manufacturing customization will have to change, as age structure will differ substantially among regions: Africa, Asia and North America will have relatively young populations, while Europe, Latin America and Oceania will have mature societies.

Emerging markets will power global growth over the next 20 years. By 2025, overall global consumption is forecast to reach $62 trillion, twice its 2013 level, and half of this increase will come from the emerging world. In 2010, the "consuming class" – people with disposable incomes of more than $10 a day – had 2.4 billion members, just over a third of the world's population. By 2025, it will rise by more than a half. Taking population

---

[7]   BP Energy Outlook 2017 Edition. Available at: https://www.bp.com/content/dam/bp/pdf/energy-economics/energy-outlook-2017/bp-energy-outlook-2017.pdf.

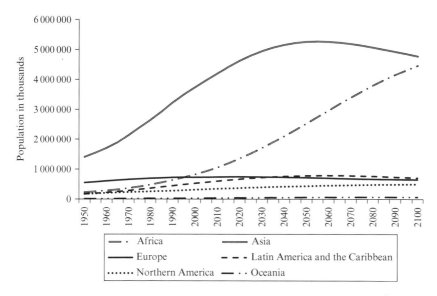

Source: Based on United Nations, Department of Economic and Social Affairs, Population Division. Probabilistic Population Projections based on the World Population Prospects: the 2017 revision.

Figure 7.4   Population evolution in the twenty-first century

growth into account, there will be an extra 1.8 billion consumers, the vast majority living in emerging regions. For manufacturers, the story is even more compelling. Mancini et al. (2017) estimate that emerging markets will be the destination of 65% of the world's manufactured goods by 2025. Consumption starts with the basics, and the purchase of capital-intensive goods (such as cars, building products and machinery) is driving the shift. By 2013, emerging markets already accounted for 59% of total demand for building materials, 57% for iron and steel, and 47% for machinery.

Population growth in Africa and Asia will help to balance the problems of aging and declining populations, mainly in Europe and Japan; this is also expected to generate large migration flows, driven by inequality between the regions.

POVERTY AND INEQUALITY: THE CATCHING-UP CHALLENGE IN THE WORLD OF GVCs

One of the aims of industrial policy in the twentieth century was to facilitate the process of convergence of low-income and developed countries.

Unfortunately, in the period 1960 to 2017, only a few countries were able to catch up, the most paradigmatic case being the East Asian economies. Formerly, the strategy was to use macroeconomic policies to alter the level of exports or imports, but today the economy is dominated by GVCs so that, as already argued, catching-up processes require managing GVCs, operating in the space of industrial organization rather than trade policies. For example, Mexico has successfully focused on the development in GVCs; however, it has failed to coherently modify its wage policy. As a result, competitiveness has relied on cheap labor, thereby threatening domestic market development. In South America, Brazil has deployed a set of policies seeking expansion of domestic demand through a combination of industrial and social policies, together with investment in innovation and infrastructure, and public financing for national firms seeking international expansion (Bresser, 2010; Gomide and Boschi, 2016; Boschi and Gaitán, 2016; Balestro, 2012). However, they have failed to address the dynamics of trade expansion. Argentina adopted a national strategy for development based on the increase in aggregate demand, in particular through small and medium-sized enterprises (SMEs) (Kulfas, 2015). South Africa has also adopted a developmental state, focusing on economic growth, industrial policies (such as the Industrial Policy Action Plan), the use of exports to drive growth, and expansion of social grants and transfers (Burger, 2014). The success of India's attempt to build a developmental state has been debated (Pingle, 1999; Kumar, 2014; Mukherji, 2016). Industrial policy has to address the change in productive capacities that could allow per capita income to grow at a more rapid pace.

Catching up has to be understood as a process of productive transformation, through a collective learning process, that is expressed in structural change patterns that help countries to achieve the development objectives and aspirations of their societies, in rapid and sustained processes of change (Figure 7.5). So defined, the catching-up concept shifts focus from growth to multiple development objectives, with the idea that synergies and trade-offs may arise between the fundamental developmental objectives of productivity increase and job creation, as well as rapid and sustained learning processes. Countries therefore need to develop patterns of productive transformation that strike a good balance in promoting these objectives simultaneously (O'Connor, 2007).

One of the main problems is that the catching-up process could stagnate due to the middle-income trap. Several aspects have to be better understood in order to avoid this trap: (1) the impact of different patterns and paths of technological and structural change on productivity; (2) its impact on the quantity as well as on the types and quality of jobs; and (3) learning effects generated in different sectors and by different technolo-

Source: Based on World Bank, International Comparison Program database.

Figure 7.5 Catching-up process and middle-income trap, 1990 to 2017 (GDP per capita, PPP constant at 2011 international $)

gies. In this process, industrial policy will be key, as it will help to develop those competences that require entering more advanced knowledge communities and related activities. Some countries have been able to redesign their industrial policy to a more dynamic system. South Korea is an example, where government institutions have been redesigned in order to foster transformation. For example, the Ministry of Science, ICT and Future Planning was created in 2013 for this purpose.

Within that perspective, governments have a key role to play in promoting, directing and accelerating the learning process. Policies to promote the development of productive capabilities relate to different areas and require a comprehensive and coordinated strategy. Education, training, trade, investment, R&D, technology, exchange rate and migration policies can all play an important role in this learning strategy as they contribute to transforming and enriching knowledge structures in the labor force and support the evolution of routines and institutions. Again, synergies and trade-offs may arise when setting these policies to address multiple development objectives. Finally, "meta" institutions trigger, accelerate and sustain learning processes as they support the development of high-performing learning procedures in the labor force, in enterprises or in economies. An institutional framework reflecting high competences to support rapid and sustained processes of learning and capability development generates incentives and pressure to learn, encourages experimentation and learning from it, rewards critical thinking and creativity, and provides direct support measures for such activities. Such competences are themselves built up in a learning process. Societies develop learning procedures (institutions) as they gain experience in learning and build up high competences to learn. These competences are at the heart of learning economies and learning societies (Nübler, 2014).

One of the main challenges will be how to bring this dynamic to low-income countries, which have not been able to move into a transformation process and are stagnating. World Development Indicators show that at least 43 countries have an income that is less than 10% of US per capita income. There is a need to redesign the whole policy spectrum to bring them into the transformation process that it has been possible to set up in middle-income countries.

THE MOBILITY REVOLUTION

In the last 100 years, the auto industry has transformed the world economy, but its success has endangered the whole planet; industrial policy will have to address the problem of mobility. Energy transition has been claimed for different types of vehicles, such as hybrid and electric vehicles, and different uses of the product, such as car sharing and ride pooling. But neither of these solutions have solved the problem: large cities have traffic jams, which are translated into millions of hours lost and high pollution. Population and economic growth alongside continued urbanization are the root causes of congestion. By 2050, there will be 9.7 billion people in the world, 70% of whom will live in cities. Over the same period, the global economy is expected to triple in size, leading to more than a doubling in road and rail travel and more than a threefold increase in the amount of road and rail freight.

In our estimation, the share of private cars will continue to increase strongly in developing regions, and to fall only slightly in developed economies. As a result, vehicle-miles traveled (VMT) – that is, the amount people drive – will likely grow at a slower pace in developed countries, while per-capita VMT may stagnate or fall slightly. Freight VMT will also continue to rise as urban populations grow along with demand for goods and services. The challenges faced by households, private companies and transportation officials, and all levels of government, cannot be understated. Left unchecked, congestion will continue to rise. Good data is the first step in tackling this problem. For most cities, applying big data to create intelligent transportation systems will be key to solving urban mobility problems, as adding transportation capacity becomes more expensive and budgets remain constrained. INRIX data and analytics on traffic, parking and population movement help city planners and engineers make data-based decisions to prioritize spending in order to maximize benefits and reduce costs now and for the future (INRIX, 2018). The key findings of the INRIX 2016 Traffic Scorecard provide a quantifiable benchmark for governments and cities across the world to measure progress in improving urban mobility and to track the impact of spending on smart city initiatives.

Industrial policy will have to address the problem, setting a roadmap to solve mobility problems. There has to be a guide for the transformation: markets by themselves will not solve it, and large disruptions will take place. There are 55 countries involved in building transport equipment, and production has substantially increased, from 58 million vehicles in 2000 to 95 million in 2016. The necessary transformations are proceeding slowly, because transition has to be smooth to avoid conflict. However, the mobility problem involves not only personal vehicles but also merchandise trade. Roads have to be maintained and extended to avoid congestion; the skies and oceans are also facing congestion that could lead the world trade to a collapse. Under this scenario, we will have to address the problem with a mobility agenda for the next 50 years.

FINANCING: THREAT AND OPPORTUNITY

In the twentieth century, there was a clear-cut idea that both the productive transformation and the rebuilding of post-war economies required development banking, that is, the International Bank for Reconstruction and Development (World Bank), and KFW (Reconstruction Credit Institute) in Germany, among others. Today that discussion has disappeared. As stated by Griffith-Jones and Cozzi (2017, p. 131):

> the financial sector should help support the real economy. To achieve this key positive role, the financial sector needs to encourage and mobilize savings, intermediate these savings at low cost, ensure savings are channeled into efficient investment as well as helping manage the risks for individual and enterprises. In the context of industrial policy, it should help to fund new sectors and deepen existing ones and to support national and regional development

strategies. Ideally, the financial sector could help societies acquire and accumulate learning, valuable for increasing productivity, especially a dynamic sense.

Bringing back development banking will be one of the challenges of industrial policy in the future. The role of development banks has been important in all countries, including developing, emerging and developed economies. European Structural Funds have funded infrastructure on a massive scale and have been providing funds to reduce inequalities. They have also been complemented by development banking, for example in Germany and in France. One example of development banking in emerging economies is the Banco Nacional do Desenvolvimento (BNDES) in Brazil, which has been key for their recent innovation initiatives. The China Development Bank (the largest development bank in the world) has supported industrial expansion in all regions, and the India Industrial Development Bank has been key for revamping industrialization. Industrial policy can promote development banking, the role of which might be key in times of high technological innovation inducing a need for investment aimed at technological adoption. Industrial policy will also have to stress bringing in all the "unbanked," who are estimated to be around 2 billion persons. Inclusion will help to expand markets mainly in developing economies.

One last point about financing is that industrial policy will have to develop more stable markets to avoid disruptions such as the 2007–2008 breakdown of the financial system that brought destruction of productive capacities. Clear financial rules that could smooth industrial expansion and avoid the destructive effects of the economic cycle is essential.

BIG DATA, INFORMATION NETWORKS AND INDUSTRY 4.0

The knowledge-based economy relies on the information networks that today allow us to collect large amounts of data (big data) that can be used to improve marketing and R&D, and deliver better processes and products. Information networks allow connectivity, speed, accessibility and anchoring (Blackwell et al., 2017). Companies have to harness the power of data, otherwise they will lose competitiveness (Castellacci, 2008).

In recent years, the digital data generated across manufacturing value chains have grown dramatically in volume and variety (Blackwell et al., 2017). These data come directly from smart products, customers, suppliers, enterprise information technology (IT) systems, connected production equipment, the core manufacturing processes, and a host of external sources. According to Behrendt (2017), the sheer scale of the influx has threatened to overwhelm organizations. Storing, communicating and analyzing all the big data is complex and costly, and many companies are not taking the full advantage of big data analytics as a result.

However, the situation is changing fast. The costs of sensors, network hardware, computing power, data storage and communication bandwidth are falling. The performance of data analysis systems is increasing, thanks to advances such as in-memory databases and artificial intelligence techniques (Behrendt, 2017). Thus, Cloud computing systems and standard interfaces have made powerful applications cheaper and faster to implement at scale. According to Blackwell et al. (2017), no part of the modern manufacturing organization will remain untouched by this flood of data, and digital-manufacturing techniques keep getting better while costing less.

Industrial policy has an important role to play to avoid monopolies of information that could hamper development on an equal basis: it has to break down barriers, inside and outside the company. It will have to set up rules for greater flexibility, to allow production agility, to introduce new manufacturing techniques (3D printing), use big data to avoid missing on disruptive business opportunities. Industrial policy needs to help business understand that today, all around the world, a flood of digital data is reshaping the manufacturing landscape.

The German government set the agenda for this aspect of industrial policy when it published its Industry 4.0 report. It recommended to create a regulatory framework for the digital economy, building up the required infrastructure to allow information technology to flow along the system, creating new rules for the market, enhancing security so that the digital economy could be trusted, empowering the consumer, protecting the generated data, enforcing technology sovereignty and improving Internet governance.

EMPLOYMENT AS A CHALLENGE IN THE ROBOT ERA

At the turn of the twentieth century, the big change in employment was the move from agriculture to manufacturing. That trend changed the pattern of development; it led to the emergence of unions and, much later, of the welfare state. Since then, there has been a major transformation of the economy, which can be characterized by two aspects. First, there is an increasing importance of vertical linkages and intersectorial knowledge between manufacturing and services, that has increased employment in the service sector. Second, automation is increasing substantially, with the use of robots in manufacturing. The puzzle that industrial policy will face is how to create jobs and at the same time as taking advantage of the robot era that has improved the workplace (freeing human workers from dirty, dull or dangerous jobs; improving quality by eliminating errors and reducing variability; and reducing manufacturing costs). Job creation is an important challenge, since the UN population projections expect that the cohort aged 15–65 will increase by 1.3 billion[8] between 2015 and 2050. In the meantime robot production has increased, and their cost has gone down. The average robot price has fallen by half in real terms, and even further relative to labor costs, over the last 30 years. As demand from emerging economies encourages the production of robots to shift to lower-cost regions, their cost is likely to reduce further. Scenarios of the labor market under these conditions seem difficult to build, as jobs will be conditioned by technological patterns such as increasing interactions between human beings and robots, and by the evolution of skills. Artificial intelligence is constantly evolving and will impact jobs in the factory at all levels. The manufacturing transition is slowly inducing the emergence of a new culture in the workplace (Tilley, 2017).

CONCLUSIONS

Policy-makers of the twenty-first century will have a hard road ahead, combining innovation with closing existing gaps. The world is facing important societal challenges, such as population growth, immigration and climate change, that have to be resolved in order to avoid conflicts and socio-economic decline. The numerous technological innovations of Industry 4.0 are, however, offering opportunities to develop new products and new processes, that could help to resolve these challenges. The manufacturing transition represented by Industry 4.0 has to be orientated towards specific paths for this to happen. This means, for instance, addressing ethical issues raised by artificial intelligence; or promoting the development of new technologies in certain sectors to speed the resolution of issues such as that of transport and mobility. Industrial policy therefore has an important role to play in this context of deep structural transformations, using a mix of instruments in order to orientate path development, such as public procurement, support to research and innovation, infrastructure provision and antitrust to ensure fair competition on markets.

---

[8]   United Nations, Department of Economic and Social Affairs, Population Division (2017).

If the economy embarks on appropriate development paths favoring the resolution of societal challenges, the diffused mistrust outlined at the beginning of this chapter is likely to disappear.

REFERENCES

Altenburg, T. and Lütkenhorst, W. (2015). *Industrial Policy in Developing Countries: Failing Markets, Weak State*. Cheltenham, UK and Northampton, MA, USA: Edward Elgar Publishing.

Amsden, A. (2001). *The Rise of "The Rest" Challenges to the West from Late Industrializing Economies*. Oxford, UK and New York, USA: Oxford University Press.

Andreoni, A. (2017). Models, Packages and Transformation Cycles. In Akbar, N. and Stiglitz, J. (eds), *Efficiency, Finance and Varieties of Industrial Policy*. New York: Columbia University Press.

Aoki, M. and Rothwell, G. (2013). A Comparative Institutional Analysis of the Fukushima Nuclear Disaster: Lessons and Policy Implications. *Energy Policy* 53, 240–247.

Asktrakhan, I. (2016). 2 Billion People Worldwide are Unbanked. Here's How to Change This. WEO. Available at: https://www.weforum.org/agenda/2016/05/2-billion-people-worldwide-are-unbanked-heres-how-to-change-this.

Balestro, M.V. (2012). Instituições do Estado desenvolvimentista na América Latina no contexto pós-neoliberal: oscasos do Brasile Argentina em perspectiva comparada. *Revista de Estudos e Pesquisas Sobre as Américas* 6(2).

Behrendt, A. (2017). We are Living in a Digitally Disrupted World. McKinsey & Company. Available at: https://www.mckinsey.com/business-functions/operations/our-insights/we-are-living-in-a-digitally-disrupted-world.

Bianchi, P. and Labory, S. (2011). *Industrial Policy after the Crisis: Seizing the Future*. Cheltenham, UK and Northampton, MA, USA: Edward Elgar Publishing.

Blackwell, E., Gambell, T., Marya, V. and Schmitz, C. (2017). *The Great Re-make: Manufacturing for Modern Times*. McKinsey & Company, June. Available at: https://www.mckinsey.com/~/media/McKinsey/Business%20Functions/Operations/Our%20Insights/The%20great%20remake%20Manufacturing%20for%20modern%20times/The-great-remake-Manufacturing-for-modern-times-full-compendium.ashx.

Block, F. and Keller, M. (2011). Where do Innovations Come From? Transformations in the US Economy, 1970–2006. Technology Governance and Economic Dynamics Working Paper no. 35.

Boschi, R. and Gaitán, F. (2016). Elites, coalizões e Desenvolvimentos. Análise sobre a trajetória recente do Brasil. *Desenvolvimento em debate* 2, 29–61.

Bresser, P. (2010). Macroeconomia estruturalista do desenvolvimento. *Revista de Economia Política* 30(4), 663–86.

Brown, F. and Domínguez, L. (2015). *Los retos de la nueva política industrial*. Mexico City: Facultad de Economía, UNAM.

Bryson, J., Clark, J. and Vanchan, V. (2016). *Manufacturing Industries in the World Economy*. Cheltenham, UK and Northampton, MA, USA: Edward Elgar Publishing.

Burger, P. (2014). Facing the Conundrum: How Useful is the "Developmental State" Concept in South Africa? *South African Journal of Economics* 82(2), 159–180.

Castellacci, F. (2008). Technological Paradigms, Regimes and Trajectories: Manufacturing and Service Industries in a New Taxonomy of Sectoral Patterns of Innovation. *Research Policy* 37(6/7), 978–994. DOI: https://doi.org/10.1016/j. respol.2008.03.011.

Chang, H-J. and Andreoni, A. (2017). Industrial Policy in a Changing World: Basic Principles, Neglected Issues and New Challenges. *Cambridge Journal of Economics 40 Years Conference.*

Choi, C. (2017). Why Hidden "Darknets" are more Resilient to Attacks than the Internet. Available at: https://www.livescience.com/58620-hidden-darknets-more-resilient-to-attacks.html.

Dawson, A. (2017). The Global Calculus of Climate Disaster. *Boston Review.* Available at: http://bostonreview.net/science-nature/ashley-dawson-global-calcu lus-climate-disaster.

Di Liberto, T. (2015). Summer Heat Wave Arrives in Europe. Event Tracker. NOAA. Available at: https://www.climate.gov/news-features/event-tracker/summer-heat-wave-arrives-europe.

European Council (2017). Conclusions on a Future EU Industrial Policy Strategy. Council of the EU. Press Release 283/17, May 29.

European Environmental Agency (EEA) (2015). Freight Transport Demand. European Environment Agency. Available at: https://www.eea.europa.eu/data-and-maps/indicators/freight-transport-demand-version-2/assessment.

Gertler, M.S. (2004). *Manufacturing Culture: The Institutional Geography of Industrial Practice.* Oxford: Oxford University Press.

Gomide, A. and Boschi, R. (2016). *Capacidades Estatais em Países Emergentes: O Brasil em Perspectiva.* Ipea: Rio de Janeiro.

Griffith-Jones, S. and Cozzi, G. (2017). The Roles of Development Banks. In Noman, A. and Stiglitz, J. (eds), *Efficiency, Finance, and Varieties of Industrial Policy: Guiding Resources, Learning, and Technology for Sustained Growth.* New York: Columbia University Press.

Humphrey, J. and Schmitz, H. (2002). How does Insertion in Global Value Chains Affect Upgrading in Industrial Clusters? Institute of Development Studies, University of Sussex.

IMF (2017). *World Economic Outlook: Gaining Momentum?* April. Washington, DC.

INRIX (2018). *Global Traffic Scorecard.* February. Kirkland, WA.

Kanger, L. and Sillak, S. (2018). Exploring the Evolution of Mass Production (1765–2018) from Deep Transitions Perspective. Available at: http://documents. manchester.ac.uk/display.aspx?DocID=37430.

Kenderdine, T. (2017). China's Industrial Policy, Strategic Emerging Industries and Space Law in Asia and the Pacific. *Policy Studies* 4(2), 325–42. DOI: 10.1002/app5.177.

Kimberlain, T., Blake, E.S. and Cangialosi, J.P. (2016). *Hurricane Patricia (EP202015).* National Hurricane Center Tropical Cyclone Report. NOAA. Available at: https://www.nhc.noaa.gov/data/tcr/EP202015_Patricia.pdf.

Kulfas, M. (2015). Perspectivas económicas en Argentina. Elementos de diagnóstico sobre el financiamiento del desarrollo con especial énfasis en las pequeñas y medianas empresas y sus perspectivas. Entidad contrastante, Banco Interamericano de Desarrollo (BID).

Kumar, R. (2014). *Role of State-Owned Enterprises in India's Economic Development*. Paris: OECD.

Mancini, M., Namysl, W., and Ramaswamy, S. (2017). Global Growth, Local Roots: The Shift Toward Emerging Markets. Available at: https://www.mckinsey.com/business-functions/operations/our-insights/global-growth-local-roots-the-shift-toward-emerging-markets.

Milberg, W., Jiang, X., and Gereffi, G. (2014). Industrial Policy in the Era of Vertically Specialized industrialization. In Salazar-Xirinachs, J.M., Nübler, I. and Kozul-Wright, R. (eds), *Transforming Economies: Making Industrial Policy Work for Growth, Jobs and Development*. Geneva: ILO.

Mukherji, R. (2016). Is India a Developmental State? In Chu, Y. (ed.), *The Asian Developmental State*. New York: Palgrave Macmillan.

Mutimer, D. (2000). *The Weapons State: Proliferation and the Framing of Security*. Boulder, CO, USA and London, UK: Lynne Rienner Publishers.

Nübler, I. (2014). A Theory of Capabilities for Productive Transformation: Learning to Catch Up. International Labour Organization. Available at: https://www.ilo.org/wcmsp5/groups/public/---dgreports/---inst/documents/publication/wcms_315669.pdf.

O'Connor, D. and Kjöllerstörm, M. (eds) (2008). *Industrial Development for the 21st Century*. New York: Orient Longman, Zed Books.

Pingle, V. (1999). *Rethinking the Developmental State: India's Industry in Comparative Perspective*. New York: St Martin's Press.

Salazar-Xirinachs, Nübler, I., and Kozul-Wright, R. (2017). *Transforming Economies: Making Industrial Policy Work for Growth, Jobs and Development*. UNCTAD/ ILO. Geneva: International Labour Office.

Tilley, J. (2017). *Automation, Robotics, and the Factory of the Future*. McKinsey & Company. Available at: https://www.mckinsey.com/business-functions/operations/our-insights/automation-robotics-and-the-factory-of-the-future (accessed January 2, 2018).

Veugelers, R. (ed.) (2017). Remaking Europe: The New Manufacturing as an Engine for Growth. Blueprint Series 26. Brussels: Bruegel.

Weiss, J. (2011). Industrial Policy in the Twenty First Century Challenges for the Future. UNU –WIDER Working Paper No. 2011/55.

Williams, J. (2017). How Many People Still Live in Poverty? Available at: https://makewealthhistory.org/2017/02/02/how-many-people-still-live-in-poverty/.

Zimmermann, K. and Emspak, J. (2017). Internet History Timeline: ARPANET to the World Wide Web. Available at: https://www.livescience.com/20727-internet-history.html.

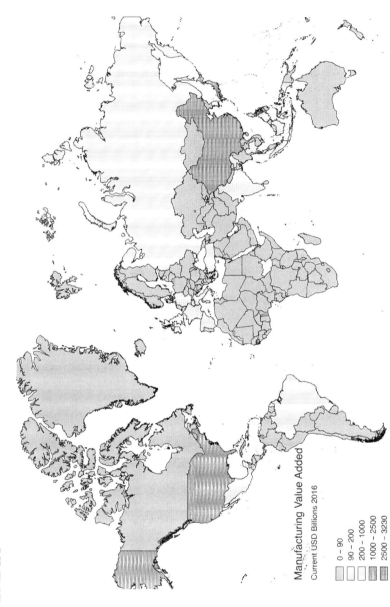

Manufacturing Value Added
Current USD Billions 2016

0 – 90
90 – 200
200 – 1000
1000 – 2500
2500 – 3230

Source: Based on data from World Bank (2017).

Manufacturing Exports
Current USD Billions 2016

- 0 – 50
- 50 – 200
- 200 – 300
- 300 – 610
- 610 – 2100

Source: Based on data from World Bank (2017).

Figure 7A.2 Exports of manufacturing cultures

PART III

Uneven development in times of industrial revolution and need for territorial industrial policy

8. Industry 4.0+ challenges to local productive systems and place-based integrated industrial policies

Marco Bellandi, Lisa De Propris and Erica Santini

INTRODUCTION

Since 1970s, a post-Fordism model of flexible production has replaced models of mass production (Salais and Storper, 1992). Competitiveness, economic growth and development of industrialised countries have been linked to local models of industrial organisation. Territories and communities all over the world have shown patterns of agglomeration and specialisation in a variety of industries, including advanced sectors as well as more traditional, labour-intensive ones (see Pyke et al., 1990). There are places in Europe well known for their industrial specialisation characterised by constellations of independent small and medium-sized enterprises (SMEs) specialised in specific phases of complex manufacturing value chains: these include Watch Valley in Switzerland, Baden-Wurttemberg in Germany, Småland in Sweden, and areas of Central and North-East Italy (see Becattini et al., 2009; Porter, 1998). These manufacturing value chains largely dominated the economic structure of the respective local productive systems, so much so that in many cases such territories stood out and became known worldwide thanks to their main industry, for example, in the United Kingdom (UK), 'Steel City' in the case of Sheffield, 'Cottonopolis' for Manchester, and 'The Potteries' for the area of Stoke-on-Trent (Popp and Wilson, 2009).

However, in advanced economies, local productive systems specialised in manufacturing sectors have experienced persistent jobs losses and declining value-added over the last two decades, driven especially by off-shoring pressures and the globalisation of markets (Castellani et al., 2015; Mayer and Gereffi, 2010). The decoupling of manufacturing from services was indeed justified by the perceived high value creation of services. The scholarly and policy debate flagged up particular business services and creative industries (Florida, 2002) as key sectors able to drive long-term development strategies in territories characterised by manufacturing specialisations. In this regard, it seemed inevitable for manufacturing systems in advanced economies to replace blue- with white-collar jobs, and to move from local manufacturing specialisations such as in industrial districts, to local specialisation of services such as in cultural and/or tourist districts, and creative cities (Cooke and Lazzeretti, 2008). Neither the emergence of the knowledge economy nor the hype of the creative economy delivered the renewal power both advocated. Manufacturing systems failed to experience the complete transformation they required, and evidence points to a continuous loss of skills and competences, loss of control over the value chain and, ultimately, a loss of identity for places.

The nature of competition is changing again. Less predictable consumer demand (Lester and Piore, 2009) and the introduction of new disruptive technologies are significantly impacting on the vitality of local productive systems. Consensus is emerging around the transformative force of the current wave of technological change, or 'the Fourth Industrial Revolution' (Schwab, 2016) shaping a new production model often referred to as Industry 4.0 (Hermann et al., 2016). It presents renewed opportunities as well as threats (World Bank, 2017). Specifically, the production transformation that is characterised by the complementarity between digital, physical and biological technologies and manufacturing competences is triggering an extensive reconfiguration of global and local economies, affecting production organisations, business models and consumption models (Bianchi and Labory, 2018).

According to some researchers, windows of opportunity for a 'manufacturing renaissance' will open up (Andreoni and Gregory, 2013). Some signals in this direction come from reshoring and near-shoring phenomena (Bailey and De Propris, 2014). On the other hand, the disruptive and global nature of this transformation poses new threats related to labour markets and the future of work, income inequality, social value systems, and so on (World Bank, 2017). In this chapter, we draw on the definition of Industry 4.0 proposed by De Propris et al. (2018) and outline four challenges (opportunities and threats) emerging from the possible relations between technological change and the manufacturing renaissance of local productive systems in advanced regions, especially in Europe.

After some general remarks on the meaning of the so-called fourth industrial revolution, we discuss four opportunities and threats related to the renewed models of value creation and redistribution. We then discuss policy recommendations and introduce the idea of place-based integrated industrial policies; we present possible scenarios of manufacturing renaissance in local productive systems characterised by specialised SMEs.

SMEs AND LOCAL PRODUCTIVE SYSTEMS BETWEEN THE THIRD AND FOURTH INDUSTRIAL REVOLUTIONS

This is not the first time that the disruptive introduction of new technologies has strongly modified the world where we live and produce value (Allen, 2017). Innovations related to steam power, cotton, steel, and railways were coupled with mechanisation contributed to the 'first' industrial revolution. Standardised demand was satisfied by mass production thanks to scale and scope economies that become the main way to generate value. The 'second' industrial revolution was triggered by the introduction of electricity, heavy and mechanical engineering and synthetic chemistry. New sectors emerged, and we saw the consolidation of the large-scale production model. The 'third' industrial revolution was triggered by innovations in electronics and computers, petrochemicals and aerospace. Large-scale production also became multi-plant, multi-product and multi-located because of the volatility of demand, marking the expansion of complex organisational forms such as multinational firms and manufacturing clusters.

There is some consensus that a fourth industrial revolution can be somewhat associated with the new technological wave (De Propris, 2016). The current wave is indeed characterised by a broad range of technologies, related to telecommunications, bioscience, electronics, green and renewable technologies, artificial intelligence, robotics, sensor and space tech, and so on. They are reconfiguring or even creating new production and business landscapes around the world. Such transformation is identified not only with a particular set of emerging technologies, but crucially with the introduction of an infrastructure of digitally enabled technologies, that is driving the transition to new organisations of production and business models.

The most emphasised components in those fields include cyber-physical systems (CPS), the Internet of Things (IoT), the smart factory, and the Internet of Services (IoS). They intersect various design principles, such as interoperability, virtualisation, decentralisation, real-time capability, services orientation and modularity (see Hermann et al., 2016). For instance, the IoS (with Cloud computing and big data) allows enhanced optimisation of complex distribution processes, logistics and production networks, at a local and global level. The smart factory implements the automation of modular manufacturing production and, combined with IoT, allows interoperability and real-time capabilities. After the rise in the past decade of digital technologies, including artificial intelligence (AI), Cloud computing and mobile communications, the variety and the adoption of those technologies will expand, contribute to transform every industry together with the nature of work, and combine with changes in consumption, social habits and life practices (Anthes, 2017; World Bank, 2017).

In reality, the fourth industrial revolution should have – and can have – a much more disruptive impact than a pure 'technicist' approach would advocate for. We draw on De Propris et al. (2018) and define Industry 4.0+ as the deployment of all the technologies of the fourth industrial revolution that will trigger a transformational shift in the techno-socio-economic paradigm attuned to a green economy and society. Industry 4.0+ can deliver an inclusive socio-economic growth.

The broad range of transformations related to digital technologies will redefine the forces that shape industry competition (Porter and Heppelmann, 2014; Mitchell and Brynjolfsson, 2017) and, as highlighted by many studies, will affect not only routine and codified activities, but also those that require tacit knowledge and experience. The way we produce, consume, communicate, travel, generate energy and interact with one another will change forever (OECD, 2016).

One of the main issues is the emergence of renewed models of value creation and value redistribution. New pathways of value creation have indeed been activated at a local and global level (OECD, 2016). Digital technologies foster closer interaction between innovators, manufacturers and customers which may translate into a more participative model of value creation and value distribution. However, how territories adjust their structures to participate in these processes is still unclear (Anthes, 2017; Harari, 2017). The ways socio-economic actors interpret and embed such new technologies within their cumulative and embedded know-how will define different models of value creation and redistribution. Such models in turn will present different ways to seize the technological opportunities as well as minimise the related threats. Opportunities and threats are moderated by the multi-tier institutional infrastructure and the design and implementation of policies that the former delivers locally.

OPPORTUNITIES AND THREATS OF A NEW CENTRALITY OF MANUFACTURING IN LOCAL PRODUCTIVE SYSTEMS

Industry 4.0+ solutions enter the models of value creation and redistribution of territories, opening opportunities for a new centrality of manufacturing specialisations, in old or post-industrialised regions and countries. Such opportunities depend on how public, collective and private strategies

Table 8.1   Challenges for territories and Industry 4.0+

	Value creation	Value redistribution
Economic actors	Smart factory	Global oligopolies
	Interdependencies around smart micro-manufacturing	Digital participation and distributed service provision
Societal actors	Digital divides	Skill polarisation
	Quadruple helix	Makers and smart skills

at different levels coordinate change and provide for the management of the related risks. Looking at how societal and economic actors create value and experiment with new models of value redistribution, we can identify four main challenges (Table 8.1).

We look at each challenge in more depth below, starting from the exploration of the economic actors' answers to the challenges posed by Industry 4.0+ in terms of value creation and distribution. We will process clockwise around the table.

Challenge 1: New Interdependencies Around Smart Micro-manufacturing

We have already suggested how the smart factory shapes new interdependencies inside and between factories and firms. Intelligent machines enhance the productivity and flexibility of productions that deliver 'mass customised' products. The use of sensors, actuators and data communication technology built into physical objects can also enable the tracking, coordination or controlling of machines within networks (World Bank, 2017).

In parallel, the greater adoption of digital technologies throughout production processes will also shape new interdependencies within and across value chains. Indeed, a range of new technologies allows for a 'micro-manufacturing' model to emerge, whereby the efficient scale of production is low and small specialised firms can leverage international networks of designers, customers and suppliers. This would favour the creation and expansion of market niches for personalised, customised and innovative products. This latter model requires the integration of manufacturing functions with advanced digitally enabled services that allow for a continuum of co-innovation solutions between firms and customers and the sharing of information between machines and people. For example, design or innovation-related data may be digitally delivered to a producer located near the point of consumption in a third country where it is physically produced. The manufacturing sector is changing even more fundamentally by adopting a business model that is typical of the service sector. An emergent literature on servitisation suggests that manufacturing systems are moving away from just selling products to offering the intrinsic service that products embody. As the line between manufacturing and services is blurring, manufacturing systems evolve in product–service systems. As pointed out by Lafuente et al. (2017, p. 25): 'Territorial Servitization can contribute to local competitiveness and employment creation through the virtuous cycle generated when a resilient local manufacturing base attracts or stimulates the creation of complementary knowledge intensive business services businesses, which in turn facilitates the creation of new manufacturers.'

This implies the spawning of new nuclei of know-how within the local system and an appropriate governance of new classes of local transaction costs related to the increasing density of sharable, ambiguous and immaterial characteristics in product–service exchanges. However, without targeted support in terms of institutional solutions and entrepreneurial drive, the advantages of such new interdependencies around smart micro-manufacturing remains weak and underdeveloped.[1] Equally, the lack of a critical mass of innovative and motivated 'new makers', or poor digital communication infrastructures, again will quash such opportunities.[2]

Challenge 2: Between New Global Oligopolies and Digital Participation

Following the models of value creation, new models of value redistribution are indeed emerging, in particular in information and communication technologies (ICTs), like those expressed by global monopolies that exploit, at a global scale, the private information gathered through the free release of apps servicing the digital social networks (Kurz, 2017). Some policy-makers have started to fear the consequences of regulatory shortcomings in those fields (OECD, 2016). On the other side, new technologies can improve public institutions by means of more inclusive and transparent governmental models. For example, a not-for-profit social enterprise,

---

[1]   Bellandi and Santini (2019) present research on trajectories of territorial servitisation in industrial districts, under the MAKERS project (see the Acknowledgements).
[2]   Bellandi et al. (2019) go deeper on the study of local dynamics and the spawning of new nuclei of productive know-how, under the MAKERS project (see the Acknowledgements).

www.mysociety.org, based in the UK, builds and shares digital technologies to empower citizens to get things changed, across the three areas of Democracy, Freedom of Information, and Better Cities. However, a lack of public understanding or social acceptance of technological advances might hold back potentially beneficial effects.

Such relations affect local productive systems from two sides. One concerns problems of fiscal sustainability, social welfare and inclusivity, participation and governance in the local society. The other concerns problems of market power in the vertical relations between local SMEs and large oligopolistic national and international platforms of digital-based services of trade, finance, advertising, labour selection and training, enterprise resource planning and relationship management, collaborative knowledge and innovation networks, and so on (De Maggio et al., 2009).

When the value creation processes based on a distributed service provision such as territorial servitisation (Lafuente et al., 2017) is not strong enough, the risks of oligopolistic exploitation increase. The returns of local SMEs may be squeezed further by the standardised quality of digital services provided by large platforms neither able nor willing to customise services to the very specific and differentiated needs of SMEs. An even more important and real source of squeeze emerges when digital platforms are internalised by large manufacturing or trading companies that are big players in the SMEs' product or raw material markets. Consider a big player demanding small manufacturing suppliers/customers, as a compulsory requisite for trading, to insert in a proprietary digital platform that manages, for example, resource planning, quality and ethical standards, cost controls and budgeting. This is perhaps an opportunity for the small suppliers/customers to upgrade and learn about digital solutions. The dark side is that crucial business information is acquired by the big player, via the platform, and is easily used to reduce partners' margins of profits and independent decision-making. Turning our attention to the societal actors, we focus on the other two challenges emerging from Industry 4.0+.

Challenge 3: Landscapes of Labour between Displacement and New Makers

In the debate over the interplay between new technology and development, there is a palpable concern about the combined effect of digitalisation and robotisation on the balance between labour and capital input in production processes. Breemersch et al. (2016) find that the adoption of digitally enabled technology in the production process is associated with job and income polarisation in manufacturing industries between operative functions and knowledge-intensive directive functions (see Rifkin, 2013; OECD, 2015). 'Digital technologies are upending the workforce'

(Anthes, 2017, p. 315), though modalities are still unclear. Workers may move beyond their local labour markets and this can reduce the bargaining power of employers, but at the same time many employers can easily practise 'labour arbitrage'.

As stressed above, the key terms of the current transformation seem to be flexibility, variety, short-term and long-distance. Such changes in the labour market are calling for new training models that go beyond upgrading curricula in primary and secondary education, and also include job retraining and life-long learning, to ensure constant upskilling (Harari, 2017). Moreover, they also require an alternative to the dominant models of Industry 4.0 and smart factories that place the decisive source of progress and organisation in the analytical and codified knowledge developed and/or controlled by restricted elites of scientists, technologists and top managers.

The alternative is expressed by productive systems where new 'makers' (Anderson, 2012) take the role of entrepreneur, innovator, artisan and manufacturer as they reconcile innovation with production. They bring together particular capabilities that allow the command of specific production processes and products, as well as an appropriate selection and organisation of components and solutions related to new technologies (Bettiol and Micelli, 2013). The new makers represent a worker-centred and sustainable alternative to the challenges of Industry 4.0+ in the labour market. Production activities that require experience-based competences accrued on the job will still be needed in some key phases, such as the choice of materials of variable quality, the judgement on the appropriate use of multi-purpose tools (4.0 as well) in non-parameterised work contexts, or quality control of highly customised products, and so on. More generally, it is increasingly believed that the introduction of robots and automation in the workplace cannot replace the human contribution, especially in relation to experience-based competences, creativity, innovativeness, improvisation and unpredicted problem-solving. This calls for an understanding of the future of work that sees a complementarity between the analytical and codified knowledge, and the synthetic, tacit and experience-based knowledge that is cumulated and embodied in tasks and roles (Barzotto and De Propris, 2018).

Therefore, if the alternative to technicist models of Industry 4.0 finds receptive fields of application, technologies will not replace all valuable operative and manual skills. Instead, they are complementary to a professional and creative process that meets the customer-specific demand in complex ways. The organisation of production must adapt at firm and system levels, together with consistent technological and scientific solutions, which Bianchi (2018, pp. 104–107) calls 'techno-science for human and sustainable development'.

Challenge 4: Quadruple-helix Approaches

Contemporary disruptive dynamics in technological, societal and environmental spheres make for even more complex interrelations between state and market governance, and between local and regional, and national, international and global innovation systems. These same phenomena make it difficult to understand the identity and the nature of the agencies of beneficial processes. Linear top-down models for organising research, innovation, technological transfer, and so on are not adequate. Triple-helix approaches of university–industry–government relations emerged in the mid-1990s precisely to understand and drive impending governance problems in knowledge-based regions (Etzkowitz and Leydesdorff, 2000). Although even these approaches easily reflect technocratic self-confidence and elitism.

Neither technological innovation nor economic growth have, per se, necessarily long-run positive effects on human, social and environmental capital (Lundvall, 2017). On the contrary, technological or digital divides can emerge within societies polarising social as well as economic opportunities and well-being. The access to and use of digitally enabled technology can create segments of exclusion from engagement in civic society, urban living or basic public service provision. For instance, technocratic approaches to digital adoption might leave the increasing needs and opportunities related to smart city and smart land solutions unexplored and underexploited (Bonomi and Masiero, 2014; Morozov and Bria, 2018). In contrast, the innovations and applications brought in by new technologies deliver societal benefit if they relate to new interpretations of local traditions and heritage, or if they tackle societal challenges such as environmental and migration crises, ageing, new poverties, shortages of food and water, or concentrated pressure of mass urbanisation or mass tourism. These solutions may support the development of smart productive systems of 'residential economy' that, starting from specific local needs, are also able to provide successful solutions for adaptation and application in broad sets of life contexts (Segessemann and Crevoisier, 2016). Similar potentialities appear, even if with different contents and requisites, in places and in production and innovation systems of either advanced or emerging economies (OECD, 2012; Arocena and Sutz, 2017).

Therefore, in recent years, the necessity to consider a fourth helix has become more and more evident. It is the collective sphere of local civic societies and larger social networks, adding to the three initial ones (Leydesdorff and Deakin, 2011). Quadruple-helix (QH) initiatives more easily and explicitly connect to the purpose, or just the effect, of contributing to inclusive, smart and sustainable paths of local and regional growth (McCann and Ortega-Argilés, 2015), open to global networks of production and knowledge (Barnard and Chaminade, 2017). They also extend to 'hybrid' forms of governance of projects of social and cultural development of territories (Aoyama and Parthasarathy, 2016). However, the local society still risks being locked into either a regressive status quo of oligarchies concerned by the extent of change, or a domination by the marketing and cultural strategies of external agents which do not always give undemanding support to participatory actions at local level. Collaborative and reflective schemes are needed, but they can be based neither on records of past success of single stakeholders and traditional governance solutions, nor on optimistic declamations of 'nice' common targets in public–private partnerships.

Within such dynamics, policy-makers and public organisations represent the helix devoted to take public resources, non-repayable funding and legal control. More than this, they should also protect and share the view of the general objectives of productive development and manufacturing renaissance, helping coordination at the different scales where local strategies and possible QH projects insert. Conversely, political struggles and government failures explain how many places and productive systems get trapped in slow or poor transition paths.

PLACE-BASED INTEGRATED INDUSTRIAL POLICIES

As stressed in a recent World Bank report, 'change is coming, bringing with it uncertainty and likely disruptions in manufacturing-led development strategies ... Countries do need to address the costs of change. However, they also need to better position themselves to take advantage of opportunities' (World Bank, 2017, p. 169). Technological transformations will indeed require adjustments to the governance system and the institutional infrastructure (Geels, 2002).

As transformative challenges will deeply reshape the European industrial landscape, it becomes fundamentally important to explore the windows of opportunities and possible threats for local production systems. This calls for the design of a new industrial policy that can enable change, empower decision-making and share risk-taking. Scholars and policy-makers have already started to conceive new industrial policies aimed at promoting a technological shift in the private and public sectors, to ultimately deliver a sustainable and inclusive growth in such territories.

A deep understanding of how new technologies are likely to impact on the organisation of production at a local level, such as in industrial districts or clusters, is crucial to design and implement truly transformative industrial policies. Some contributions on new policies for productive development argue that they are 'augmented' industrial policies.[3] We propose to collect a set of lines of initiative under the concept of 'place-based integrated industrial policies', aimed precisely at the development of production capabilities. They include horizontal and vertical initiatives that are place-based and systemic, albeit having a multi-scale approach.

In terms of policy design, we maintain that their elaboration, implementation and control should be understood as step-wise processes, developing around 'place-based projects' characterised by value creation processes and driven by models with a quadruple-helix nature (see Challenge 4 above). They feature evolving balances of public and private agency (Rodrik, 2004), leadership and participation (Sotarauta et al., 2017), and social and business targets (Bianchi and Labory, 2018). Learning by interacting, learning by monitoring and evaluating, should be practiced deliberately along such evolving equilibria, in order to align stakeholders' interests on common development and experimental projects for sustainable growth (Sabel and Zeitlin, 2012). Evidence-based tools exploiting various types of digital technologies could help to design and implement projects. Such place-based industrial policies integrated to address the challenges of Industry 4.0+ can be conceptualised as Industrial Policies 4.0 (Challenge 2).

We propose place-based integrated industrial policies that have a clear systemic focus, which is represented by the provision of public goods specific to the development of value creation systems underpinned by an extended division of labour among different manufacturing and service firms as well as institutional stakeholders. One main issue is how technological change will impact on the organisation of the systemic production, and what support is needed to allow the combination of new knowledge with that cumulated in embedded pools of local knowledge.

Success activates further differentiation thanks to the spawning of new nuclei of productive know-how across manufacturing, services, and other fields of natural and social life (Challenge 1). However, new forms of asymmetries of information and competence divides might emerge with the absorption of radically new technologies leading to transaction costs and possible market barriers. We argue that the presence of strong professional and entrepreneurial drivers and the creation of platforms and infrastructures to promote innovation and training can reduce barriers to adoption and foster a critical mass of experimental solutions (Challenge

---

[3] For example, Amison and Bailey (2014), Andreoni and Chang (2016), Barca et al. (2012), Bianchi and Labory (2018), Caloffi (2017) and Crespi et al. (2014).

3). Training and normative structures that give such drivers appropriate multi-disciplinary and 'new makers' capabilities, as well as open platforms for intermediating and implementing projects that develop from such capabilities (Asheim et al., 2011), are at the core of public goods specific to the transition.

Therefore, such public goods should be characterised by:

- Multi-disciplinarity that helps when technological shifts and organisational changes erupt; indeed, multi-disciplinarity is needed because of the transverse nature of Industry 4.0 technologies and their intersection with the current societal and environmental challenges (Challenge 3 above).
- Openness of technological platforms that helps in reducing local rents built on obsolete techno-organisational equilibria (where manufacturing and trade are separate business functions), as well as sheltering the local system from new large-scale oligopolistic power (Challenge 2).
- Networking business culture among SMEs, together with good practices in innovative public funds, that targets and supports both product-service network projects and innovative start-ups/academic spin-offs in new specialisations as a basis for developing a larger variety of related sectors (Challenge 1).

The third aspect of the place-based integrated industrial policies we are proposing is their multi-organisational engagement. Policy-makers should consider the complexity and the changing forms of local productive systems with their specialised and heterogeneous population of production organisations and competences.[4] They include:

- Path-breaking SMEs, adopting smart micro-manufacturing, developing smart connectivity services, and integrating them within business models characterised by high intensity of qualified professionals, creative people and cross-sectoral interdependencies (Challenge 1).
- Medium-sized and large firms, supporting the constitution of open innovation platforms that, in partnership with SMEs and

---

[4] A paper published by Bellandi and De Propris (2017), again reflecting results of the MAKERS project (see Acknowledgments), discusses new forms taken by industrial districts under the current wave of technological and societal challenges. It also touches upon some of the concepts presented in this chapter and illustrates the relation with new classes of economies of specialisation and Marshallian external economies.

universities, include new education curricula, the design of firm-driven training or placement activities; and favouring an active role of the local system within national competence networks, international value chains or even global social networks (Challenge 2).

- Utilities, co-working spaces and social enterprises, involved under quadruple-helix constellations in the provision of local public services, to address emerging needs in cities, healthcare and social innovation, sustainable tourism, restoration of historical buildings and conservation of the architectural heritage, cultural enhancement of products, and greening of manufacturing processes (Challenge 4).
- Agencies for knowledge transfer and social innovation, helping political and business leaderships in the stepwise negotiation of progressive equilibria characterised by the three above-mentioned features and outlining models of society, innovation and labour for human and sustainable development (Challenge 3).

Finally, we argue for a multi-territorial scale of policy. The local level of industrial economies and of their related policies is fundamental, but also dependent on dynamics that take place on larger territorial scales of interaction across different local systems (large cities, industrial districts and smaller cities, rural systems, and so on), favoured by a sub-network of bridging actors, and multi-scalar institutional actors. Localism should be avoided; 'place-blind' interpretations as well, as they look only at the higher urban nodes of global networks (Barca et al., 2012). This multi-territoriality is not a novelty when considering policies of local industrial development (Caloffi, 2017). However, some specific qualifications apply in the face of current transitions:

- The higher urban nodes have specific roles within multi-disciplinary, cross-sectoral and fluid spaces of innovation. 'Place-sensitive distributed development policies' (Iammarino et al., 2018) should both acknowledge such specificity and use it as a lever of the development of wider and plural territories, without waiting for the effects of implausible trickle-down mechanisms (Challenges 1 and 4 above).
- A variation on this theme concerns relations between regional and national innovation systems (Cooke and Morgan, 1998), which are crucial to give robustness to smart specialisation strategies (McCann and Ortega-Argilés, 2015), and to find new coordinated regulations on both international trade and investments (Amison and Bailey, 2014) and digital-based oligopolies (Bianchi, 2018, pp. 99–104) (Challenges 2 and 3 above).

- Structures and skills for international mobility and digital communication should help to bridge across local productive systems for international collaborations and within wide cognitive networks, through which places assert their identity and experiment with novelties for wider adoption (Challenges 3 and 4 above).

CONCLUSIONS

The challenges of Industry 4.0+ may trigger solutions that renew the bases of local manufacturing specialisations, cross over sectoral boundaries, and address societal and environmental problems (OCSE, 2016). Specifically, for SMEs' local productive systems, digitalisation empowers 'micro-manufacturing' models, where versatility is coupled with industrial efficiency, while producers co-develop personalised and innovative products with customers, according to various social, economic and environmental sustainability needs. A source of effectiveness of this model is that it is potentially the basic unit of an organisation of labour and knowledge between firms, inside territories and between territories, as an alternative to top-down technocratic models. Decentralised bases of operative (also manual and artisanal) skills can combine with synthetic and analytical knowledge (Asheim et al., 2011) as a non-casual source of exploration and exploitation of opportunities opened by digitalisation and Industry 4.0.

The place-based integrated industrial policies we advocate are inspired by Giacomo Becattini's vision of local development. Such policies should be both light and complex, reflecting a system-based view of trans-local and upper-level relations, though not pretending to deterministically shape the profound factors of local socio-economic dynamics (Caloffi, 2017). According to Becattini (2015), the decisive factor for the resilience of local productive and reproductive systems – such as industrial districts – is the confidence of their people, enterprises and institutions. If able to individually and collectively maintain such self-confidence, they can constantly innovate and change, while remaining faithful to local evolving but authentic productive cores, cultural heritages and social identities.

ACKNOWLEDGEMENTS

The research referred in this chapter has been supported by the European Union Horizon 2020 project MAKERS, which is a Research and Innovation Staff Exchange under the Marie Sklodowska-Curie Actions, grant agreement number 691192 Conferences. Versions of this chapter have been presented, firstly, at the international conference on 'Globalisation, Human Capital, Regional Growth and the 4th Industrial Revolution' (Bologna, 19–20 October 2017) and, secondly, at the international Eurolics workshop on 'Industry 4.0: Sustainable Development, Growing Inequality and/or Reindustrialization' (Aalborg, 31 May 2018).

REFERENCES

Allen, R.C. (2017). Lessons from history for the future of work. *Nature*, 550, 321–327.

Amison, P., and Bailey, D. (2014). Phoenix industries and open innovation? The Midlands advanced automotive manufacturing and engineering industry. *Cambridge Journal of Regions, Economy and Society*, 7(3), 397–411.

Anderson, C. (2012). *Makers: The New Industrial Revolution*. New York: Crown Business.

Andreoni, A., and Chang, H.J. (2016). Industrial policy and the future of manufacturing. *Economia e Politica Industriale*, 43(4), 491–502.

Andreoni, M., and Gregory, M. (2013). Why and how does manufacturing still matter: old rationales, new realities. *Revue d'Économie Industrielle*, 144(4), 21–57.

Anthes, E. (2017). The shape of work to come. *Nature*, 550, 316–319.

Aoyama, Y., and Parthasarathy, B. (2016). *The Rise of the Hybrid Domain: Collaborative Governance for Social Innovation*. Cheltenham, UK and Northampton, MA, USA: Edward Elgar Publishing.

Arocena, R., and Sutz, J. (2017). Inclusive knowledge policies when ladders for development are gone: some considerations on the potential role of universities. In B. Göransson and C. Brundenius (eds), *Universities, Inclusive Development and Social Innovation* (pp. 49–69). Springer International Publishing.

Asheim, B., Boschma, R., and Cooke, P. (2011). Constructing regional advantage: platform policies based on related variety and differentiated knowledge bases. *Regional Studies*, 45(7), 893–904.

Bailey, D., and De Propris, L. (2014). Manufacturing reshoring and its limits: the UK automotive case. *Cambridge Journal of Regions, Economy and Society*, 7(3), 379–395.

Barca, F., McCann, P., and Rodriguez-Pose, A. (2012). The case for regional development intervention: place-based versus place-neutral approaches. *Journal of Regional Science*, 52(1), 134–152.

Barnard, H., and Chaminade, C. (2017). Openness of innovation systems through global innovation networks: a comparative analysis of firms in developed and emerging economies. *International Journal of Technological Learning, Innovation and Development*, 9(3), 269–292.

Barzotto, M., and De Propris, L. (2018). Skill up: smart work, occupational mix and regional productivity. Mimeo. University of Birmingham.

Becattini, G. (2015). Beyond geo-sectoriality: the productive chorality of places. *Investigaciones Regionales – Journal of Regional Research*, 32, 31–41.

Becattini, G., Bellandi, M., and De Propris, L. (eds) (2009). *A Handbook of Industrial Districts*. Cheltenham, UK and Northampton, MA, USA: Edward Elgar Publishing.

Bellandi, M., and De Propris, L. (2017). New forms of industrial districts. *Economia e Politica Industriale*, 44(4), 411–427.

Bellandi, M., De Propris, L., and Santini, E. (2019). An evolutionary analysis of industrial districts: the changing multiplicity of production know-how nuclei. *Cambridge Journal of Economics*, 43(1), 187–204.

Bellandi, M., and Santini, E. (2019). Territorial servitization and new local productive configurations: the case of the textile industrial district of Prato. *Regional Studies*, 53(3), 356–365.

Bettiol, M., and Micelli, S. (2013). The hidden side of design: the relevance of artisanship. *Design/Issues*, 30(1), 7–18.

Bianchi, P. (2018). *4.0 La nuova rivoluzione industriale*. Bologna: Il Mulino.

Bianchi, P., and Labory, S. (2018). *Policy for the Manufacturing Revolution: Perspectives on Digital Globalisation*. Cheltenham, UK and Northampton, MA, USA: Edward Elgar Publishing.

Bonomi, A., and Masiero, R. (2014). *Dalla smart city alla smart land*. Venezia: Marsilio.

Breemersch, K., Damijan, J.P., and Konings, J. (2016). Labor market polarization in advanced countries: impact of global value chains, technology, import competition from China and labor market institutions. Working chapter prepared for the OECD.

Caloffi, A. (2017). System-based, light and complex: industrial and local development policies in the thought of Giacomo Becattini. *Economia e Politica Industriale*, 44(4), 473–480.

Castellani, D., Mancusi, M.L., Santangelo, G.D., and Zanfei, A. (2015). Special Issue: Offshoring, immigration and the labour market: a micro-level perspective. *Economia e Politica Industriale*, 42 (2).

Cooke, P., and Lazzeretti, L. (eds) (2008). *Creative Cities, Cultural Clusters and Local Economic Development*. Cheltenham, UK and Northampton, MA, USA: Edward Elgar Publishing.

Cooke, P., and Morgan, K. (1998). *The Associational Economy: Firms, Regions, and Innovation*. New York: Oxford University Press.

Crespi, G., Fernández-Arias, E., and Stein, E.H. (eds) (2014). *Rethinking Productive Development: Sound Policies and Institutions for Economic Transformation*. Inter-American Development Bank (IDB) series. New York: Palgrave Macmillan.

De Maggio, M., Gloor, P.A., and Passiante, G. (2009). Collaborative innovation networks, virtual communities and geographical clustering. *International Journal of Innovation and Regional Development*, 1(4), 387–404.

De Propris, L. (2016). How the Fourth Industrial revolution is powering the rise of Smart Manufacturing. https://www.weforum.org/agenda/2016/06/how-the-fourth-industrial-revolution-is-powering-the-rise-of-smart-manufacturing (accessed 1 June 2017).

De Propris, L., Bailey, D., and Bellandi, M. (2018). Disruptive Industry 4.0+. Background paper for OECD, mimeo.

Etzkowitz, H., and Leydesdorff, L. (2000). The dynamics of innovation: from National Systems and 'Mode 2' to a Triple Helix of university–industry–government relations. *Research Policy*, 29(2), 109–123.

Florida, R. (2002). *The Rise of the Creative Class: And How It's Transforming Work, Leisure, Community and Everyday Life*. New York: Perseus Book Group.

Geels, F.W. (2002). Technological transitions as evolutionary reconfiguration processes: a multi-level perspective and a case-study. *Research Policy*, 31(8), 1257–1274.

Harari, Y.N. (2017). Reboot for the AI revolution. *Nature*, 550, 324–327.

Hermann, M., Pentek, T., and Otto, B. (2016). Design principles for Industrie 4.0 scenarios. In *2016 49th Hawaii International Conference on System Sciences (HICSS)*, 3928–3937.

Kurz, M. (2017). On the formation of capital and wealth. Stanford University working chapter.

Iammarino, S., Rodriguez-Pose, A., and Storper, M. (2018). Regional inequality in Europe: evidence, theory and policy implications. *Journal of Economic Geography*. doi: 10.1093/jeg/lby021.

Lafuente, E., Vaillant, Y., and Vendrell-Herrero, F. (2017). Territorial servitization: exploring the virtuous circle connecting knowledge-intensive services and new manufacturing businesses. *International Journal of Production Economics*, 192, 19–28.

Lester, R.K., and Piore, M.J. (2009). *Innovation: The Missing Dimension*. Cambridge, MA: Harvard University Press.

Leydesdorff, L., and Deakin, M. (2011). The triple-helix model of smart cities: a neo-evolutionary perspective. *Journal of Urban Technology*, 18(2), 53–63.

Lundvall, B-A. (2017). Is there a technological fix for the current global stagnation? A response to Daniele Archibugi, Blade Runner economics: Will innovation lead the economic recovery? *Research Policy*, 46(3), 544–549.

Mayer, F., and Gereffi, G. (2010). Regulation and economic globalization: prospects and limits of private governance. *Business and Politics*, 12(3), 1–25

McCann, P., and Ortega-Argilés, R. (2015). Smart specialization, regional growth and applications to European Union cohesion policy. *Regional Studies*, 49(8), 1291–1302.

Mitchell, T., and Brynjolfsson, E. (2017). Track how technology is transforming work. *Nature*, 544(7650), 290–292.

Morozov, E., and Bria, F. (2018). *Rethinking the Smart City: Democratizing Urban Technology*. New York: Rosa Luxemburg Stiftung.

OECD (2012). *Innovation for Development*. Paris: OECD Publishing.

OECD (2015). ICTs and jobs: complements or substitutes? The effects of ICT investment on labour market demand by skills and by industry in selected countries. OECD Digital Economy Working Chapters, No. 259. Paris: OECD Publishing.

OECD (2016). *Science, Technology and Innovation Outlook 2016: Megatrends Affecting Science, Technology and Innovation*. Paris: OECD Publishing.

Popp, A., and Wilson, J. (2009). The emergence and development of industrial districts in industrialising England, 1750–1914. In G. Becattini, M. Bellandi, and L. De Propris (eds), *A Handbook of Industrial Districts* (pp. 43–57). Cheltenham, UK and Northampton, MA, USA: Edward Elgar Publishing.

Porter, M.E. (1998). Clusters and the new economics of competition. *Harvard Business Review*, 76(6), 77–90.

Porter, M.E., and Heppelmann, J.E. (2014). How smart, connected products are transforming competition. *Harvard Business Review*, 92(11), 64–88.

Pyke, F., Becattini, G., and Sengenberger, W. (eds) (1990). Industrial districts and inter-firm co-operation in Italy. Geneva: International Institute for Labour Studies.

Rifkin, J. (2013). *The Third Industrial Revolution: How Lateral Power Is*

Transforming Energy, the Economy, and the World. Basingstoke: Palgrave Macmillan.

Rodrik, D. (2004). Industrial policy for the twenty-first century. KSG Working Chapter No. RWP04–047.

Sabel, C.H., and Zeitlin, J. (2012). Experimentalist governance. In D. Levi-Faur (ed.), *The Oxford Handbook of Governance* (pp. 169–183). Oxford: Oxford University Press.

Salais, R., and Storper, M. (1992). The four 'worlds' of contemporary industry. *Cambridge Journal of Economics*, 16(2), 169–193.

Schwab, K. (2016). *The Fourth Industrial Revolution*. Geneva: World Economic Forum.

Segessemann, A., and Crevoisier, O. (2016). Beyond economic base theory: the role of the residential economy in attracting income to Swiss regions. *Regional Studies*, 50(8), 1388–1403.

Sotarauta, M., Beer, A., and Gibney, J. (2017). Making sense of leadership in urban and regional development. *Regional Studies*, 51(2), 187–193.

World Bank (2017). *Trouble in the Making? The Future of Manufacturing-Led Development*. Washington, DC: World Bank Publications.

9. Economic policy in the time of reactionary populism[1]

Michael J. Piore and David W. Skinner

This chapter is an attempt to address some of the problems which have surfaced in the political reaction which produced Brexit in Europe and Donald Trump's surprise victory in the 2016 presidential elections in the United States (US). It argues that the prevailing policy has been conceived and understood in terms of a series of policy paradigms which are in many ways limited and misleading. Those policies include the Silicon Valley consensus, the Washington consensus and globalization. These paradigms have promoted major structural changes in the US economy, the costs of which have been concentrated in the old industrial heartland of the Midwest and undermined the employment opportunities which sustain the communities in which the identities and self-conception of the people who lived there were embedded. The chapter argues that the paradigms offered a limited and incomplete view of the nature of productive knowledge, the way it is acquired and the way it evolves over time. They have also led to a focus on the potential welfare gains of the processes of technological changes and of globalization, while ignoring the processes through which we adjust to these changes and the way in which the costs of adjustment are distributed across different groups and communities. The chapter does not offer a fully developed alternative set of public policies. But it does identify a series of ways which public policy might moderate the pace of change and promote a more even distribution of the costs and benefits.

As I sat down to write this chapter, I realized that I could not escape a set of fundamental questions about how to think about the economy and public policy. These questions are of course always in the background of any analytical endeavor, but usually we start from a developed framework of thought which we proceed to apply to the problem at hand, without reflecting on where that framework comes from and whether it is indeed relevant to the problem we are attempting to solve. Recent political

---

[1] An earlier version of this chapter was presented as a paper at X Congresso Asociación Mexicana de Estudios del Trabajo (AMET) 2017 in Hermosillo, Mexico, in October 2017.

developments – nobly the 2016 electoral campaign in the US, and Brexit in the United Kingdom – have forced me, at least, to go back to first premises. It has, at least in the United States, become increasingly clear that though these campaigns may have centered on economic problems, they have revealed a depth of anxiety and resentment that go well beyond the economic environment and probably cannot be addressed by economic policy alone. Nonetheless, the economy appears to have been the key to the political upheaval though which we are now living, and while solutions to these problems may no longer be enough to stabilize the political and social environment it is difficult to imagine how we can restore a sense of order without addressing the economic concerns.

Those concerns, I would submit, are the product of the pressures for structural change and adjustment which have battered the economy over the course of at least the last 30 years. Pressures for structural change and adjustment are of course inherent in any dynamic economy; indeed they are the engines of economic growth and development. One can argue about whether the recent pressures have been greater than those which the economy has absorbed in the past, but in the US there is no question that whatever their absolute magnitude, their costs have been very concentrated in the old industrial heartland of the Midwest, where they have undermined the communities in which people's identities were embedded and the terms in which they understood themselves. These communities were a key constituency of the Democratic Party, and their desertion of the party was the determining factor in the electoral victory of Donald Trump.

The principal forces producing the structural changes against which the Midwest electorate was reacting were globalization and technological change. But they have been aggravated, I would argue, by institutional changes in corporate governance associated with financialization. Most importantly for the discussion I would like to engage in here, the country has been guided in its response to these pressures by a framework of economic analysis which has made the forces producing these changes seem beyond the control of politics and policy, and is crippling our ability to anticipate the problems which they have engendered and to conceive of alternative solutions.

That analytical framework can be understood in terms of what might be called policy paradigms, the broad frameworks through which policy-makers tend to think about the economy, judge its performance and attempt to influence its direction (Hall, 1993). In the post-World War II period, policy has been guided by four such paradigms: a Keynesian paradigm in the immediate post-war decades; the so-called Washington consensus, emerging in the late 1970s and continuing through the 1990s and into the new millennium; and more recently what might be called the Silicon Valley consensus encapsulated by the mantra "innovation and entrepreneurship in the knowledge economy." The Silicon Valley and Washington consensuses have been linked to globalization in a way which constitutes almost a fourth paradigm, but in ways that are differently understood in each case. In the Silicon Valley consensus, globalization is seen as the product of innovations in communication and transportation. In the old Washington consensus, it is promoted by trade treaties and innovations in regional and international governance conceived as an expression of the efficiency of a market economy as understood in terms of standard economic theory.

That such paradigms exist and that they vary over time is difficult to deny. Where they come from and what role they actually play in the evolution of the economy, on the other hand, is unclear: do they reflect social and economic reality or do they actually influence and direct its evolution? Are they, in other words, a camera or an engine – to borrow a phrase from the academic researchers who are most concerned with this problem (see MacKenzie, 2006)?

The difficulties which the conservatives in the United Kingdom and the Republicans in the US are having in translating the political reaction which brought them to power into a coherent program brings this question to the fore, and suggests the intellectual vacuum in which the political reaction is taking place. These are ominous developments, given the way in which communism, fascism and two world wars grew out of the collapse of what my colleague Suzanne Berger calls the "first globalization" in the early twentieth century (Berger, 2013). And the parallels and the dangers were reinforced in the summer of 2017, at least in the US, in Charlottesville, Virginia, by the marching of youths shouting Nazi slogans seemingly encouraged by President Trump. But a major difference between this and the earlier period is that the reaction against globalization today is occurring without the kind of alternative paradigm which Communism and fascism offered in the earlier period, creating an opportunity to meet the challenge with a new series of ideas.

It is evidently premature to say what an alternative policy paradigm might look like, and I certainly do not have an alternative to propose here. But at least with respect to issues surrounding the income distribution and human resource policy, one can, I think, identify some of the limits of the prevailing paradigm which any alternative would have to take into account.

First, putting aside the question of entrepreneurship (largely because of the limitations of space here), the two pillars of the Silicon Valley consensus are innovation and the knowledge economy. For labor, they imply the evolution of the job structure toward sophisticated technology which requires highly skilled workers to create and manage it. Combined with globalization, this implies the increasing dependence in legacy industries on low-skilled, uneducated labor in the developing world, which the part of the US labor force that cannot be absorbed into the high-tech sectors is basically unable to compete with. Implicit here is a view of technological change and a view of knowledge, both of which are highly suspect.

The view of technological change is particularly suspect, given that it is not attached to any real theory about the direction of technological change but is promulgated in a world in which there is a belief (which the Silicon Valley consensus promotes and reinforces) that knowing the direction and pursuing it successfully is the key to economic prosperity, both for individual actors in the economy and for cities, regions and nation-states. And hence it is bound to play a role in determining what projects inventors work on and which ideas entrepreneurs and financiers choose to develop. Its role in this respect seems to have been enhanced by the changes in corporate governance associated with financialization. As business has become increasingly dependent on outside financing, outsiders have become increasingly influential in business decisions. And management is called upon to justify decisions which depart from "fad and fashion" to people who are not in a position to form an independent judgment about what the business is doing.

But the commitment to the development of Silicon Valley technology goes well beyond a diffuse consensus which influences private decision-making. In the US, the federal government plays a pivotal role in the evolution of technology. The government finances more than half of national expenditures on research and development (R&D), and has been responsible for the key innovations in communications and bio-medical technologies. It has been financing and promoting robotics technology as well, most prominently through the Defense Advanced Research Projects Agency (DARPA) robotics challenge. And most recently, as the loss of manufacturing jobs has become a major concern of public policy, the government has launched a program to promote advanced technology in a way which, ironically, seeks to preserve manufacturing by reducing the employment requirements and increasing the educational requirements of the jobs which remain. To the extent that the concern is with the gap between worker qualifications and job requirements, the focus is on raising worker qualifications, rather than technological developments which could lower the job requirements and hence bridge the distance between the existing labor force and the employment requirements.

At the same time, the consensus about the direction in which technology is evolving leads policy-makers to tilt investments in education and training toward the formation of engineers and scientists or, more broadly, toward institutions of higher education rather than, for example, primary and secondary education or vocational training or – a point to which I return below – training on the job. It makes it easier to staff the new technologies which these beliefs foster and to expand the R&D facilities which generate those technologies. And it does not only have these kinds of effects in advanced developed economies: it also leads developing economies such as China and India, and the country which is actually a model of this pattern of development, the Philippines (see Ruiz, 2014), to overinvest in higher education and then export the educated labor force to North America and Europe where they facilitate the movement of technology in that direction. The belief in the inevitability of this kind of technological change has led to a virtual panic about the availability of skilled and highly trained manpower. This, despite the fact that half of the science, technology, engineering and mathematics (STEM) graduates trained in the United States are working in non-STEM jobs and occupations. Thus, there is an interaction between the policies of the US and those of India and China which is leading to increasing immigration of highly educated workers from abroad, as opposed to the adjustments in job design and recruitment practices in which business might otherwise be forced to engage.

The second problem with the Silicon Valley consensus is that the "knowledge" around which it is built is exclusively formal knowledge acquired through classroom learning in distinct educational institutions, and carried into the productive sector by students who graduate from these institutions and by their professors working as consultants and entrepreneurs. It does not recognize at all tacit or clinical knowledge, acquired on the job in the process of production. Clinical knowledge, moreover, appears to evolve informally through practice as less-educated workers working alongside formally trained engineers and managers gradually take over many of their tasks, actually inventing other ways of doing the job and understanding the work (Doeringer and Piore, 1971; Iskander and Lowe, 2010). The relationship between formal and clinical knowledge is unclear in large part because clinical knowledge is seldom explicitly recognized; and because it goes unrecognized, it is understudied. Recognition is complicated by the fact that tacit knowledge is by definition immeasurable and its nature, even existence, draws on anecdotal evidence which is easily dismissed as atypical or anachronistic and which is destined to be replaced by the kind of formal "scientific" analysis[2] which we think of as characteristic of modernity.

---

[2]   But see Polanyi (1944).

It therefore seems particularly relevant to underscore the role of tacit knowledge in the development of software, since we think of information technology (IT) as emblematic of contemporary modernity. Efforts to standardize and formalize software development have proven particularly frustrating, and instead rapid, efficient development depends on the tacit understanding embedded in a community of practice which grows up through direct, personal interaction among a team of developers and the architects and designers of the programs which they are attempting to write. Thus, for example, GE, when it began offshore development in India, found that it was difficult to limit the number of people from the Indian team in the US at any moment of time to 30% of the total work-force assigned to the project. And Fred Brooks in his famous treatise on software development, *The Mythical Man-Month* (Brooks, 1975), argues that adding new people to a development project as it falls behind schedule actually slows down the development process still further, because the newcomers do not share the tacit understanding of the architecture, an understanding which can only be developed through interaction with experienced members of the team on the job. This suggests – to underscore the point – that for certain processes clinical knowledge is indispensable. Even where it is not over a range – possibly a very wide range – clinical and formal knowledge are substitutes for each other. But clinical knowledge provides opportunities for upward mobility to workers for whom a lack of resources or educational preparation bars access to formal education. But clinical knowledge goes largely unrecognized, and certainly undeveloped, when employers are able to recruit formally trained labor abroad and public policy reinforces this bias.

The third problem with both the Silicon Valley consensus and with globalization is widely recognized and almost universally ignored. Both technology and trade policies in recent years imply fundamental structural changes in the economy. As we are quick to point out in elementary economics courses, such changes typically generate both gains and losses. The structural changes are desirable and the public policies which encourage them are justifiable if the gains outweigh the losses; in other words, if there are net social gains. Where this is the case, the gainers can compensate the losers. But in fact net gains are not enough to justify such policies. In the conventional theoretical framework, the structural changes are only justi-fied if the compensation is actually paid. And in practice compensation is almost never actually paid. This, moreover, is not surprising: There is no institutional mechanism to ensure that compensation will be paid. Indeed, there is no institutional mechanism for systematically weighing the gains against the losses to determine whether there is a net social benefit. The people who make the critical decisions and reap the gains are not generally linked to the people who experience the losses. In fact, it is not usually possible to trace worker displacement to particular causal factors, and certainly not the displacement of a particular worker. And if the problem is, as argued above, that the high cost of displacement in recent years is the way that technological change and globalization have been imposed together on the same communities, so that alternative employment opportunities have been limited and ancillary economic activities in these communities destroyed, then you cannot really argue that the costs are directly related to any identifiable gain.

The major exceptions here are programs designed to provide training (or rather, retraining) to workers displaced by globalization. Such programs exist in virtually all advanced developed countries. And in the trade debate ignited by the US presidential campaign, the only policy which has been proposed in support of trade has been adjustment assistance of this kind for displaced workers. But such programs are everywhere also very limited in scope, and their success has been limited as well, even for those displaced workers who actually get to participate. Studies suggest that the returns to participation in such programs, relative to control groups of similarly displaced workers who do not participate, are barely enough to yield a positive return on the investment, let alone actually compensate the workers for the loss of their previous jobs.

I do not have space here to discuss the reasons for those failures in depth, but the basic problem is the institutional difference between the schools which run the programs and the businesses who first "create" the displaced workers which the programs are supposed to aid, but which eventually would have to hire the graduates of the programs if the issue of compensation for those workers were to be addressed in this way. Schools and productive enterprises have different missions and face different constraints and different incentives. To take one example, schools face a hard budget constraint which leads them to minimize the wear and tear on the equipment and wastage of material used in the teaching process; whereas businesses are willing to tolerate equipment damage and material scrap in order to meet tight delivery schedules. Thus schools train workers to be, from a business perspective, overly solicitous of equipment and material consumption, and in the eyes of business, graduates from school training need to be retrained; often it is easier to hire untrained workers than to break what business views as the bad habits cultivated by the schools. Unless the enterprises take an active interest in the schools and intervene to mold the programs to their needs, the schools do not produce graduates who are useful to employers.

That enterprise participation is important is now widely recognized particularly in the literature on vocational education and community colleges. What is not recognized is that getting the enterprise to take an interest in the schools is itself an institutional problem: the firms have no incentive to do so if they can find trained workers more easily in other enterprises by poaching, or in other countries by recruiting immigrants.[3] Most programs try to recruit business participation by appealing to civic responsibility. But without the pressure of labor shortages and a tight labor market, they must compete in their appeal to businesses with the Boy Scouts, breast cancer and the homeless, and it is unclear why business should care more about displaced workers than these other civic ventures, particularly workers displaced from other enterprises.

But the more serious problem is that in failing to focus on the adjustment costs, policy analysts fail to examine the adjustment process analytically. They do not consider the way in which that process is affected by the timing of trade treaties, or the way in which they overlap in their impacts with other treaties or with technological change. Ideally, the pace of employment displacement should be held to the rate of natural employee attrition; this, of course, for a variety of reasons would be very costly and difficult institutionally to achieve (although government restrictions upon lay-off and discharge do work in this direction), but policy-makers do not even know how the impact of the different treaties and technical innovations they have promoted in recent years relate to each other. In retrospect, it seems crazy that in the waning years of the Obama administration, when the political reactions in the form of the Trump candidacy and that of Bernie Sanders on the Democratic side were already setting in, policy-makers were promoting two new major trade treaties, one with the countries of the Pacific Rim and the other with Europe. What could have been presented as a question of the pace and timing of globalization was instead made an issue of globalization itself. (The "fast track" process through which trade treaties are reviewed by Congress encourages the negotiation of multiple treaties at the same time.) Moderation in the pace of change could, in fact, have been built into the treaties themselves, and their impacts spread out over time, but this was not considered either.

Indeed, the analytical framework though which trade was viewed did not lead these considerations. In this sense, the failure to consider time and geographic dimensions of trade are basically symptoms of the general problem with the paradigms in which policy has been conceived in recent years, as well as with the Washington consensus which dominated thinking before them, in their treatment of structural change. They all imply major changes in the structure of the economy; they promote and celebrate such

---

[3]   See Cavaco et al. (2013), Jacobson et al. (1993, 2005) and Kletzer and Koch (2004).

changes, viewing them generally as producing desirable increases in social welfare, at times arguing that such changes are inevitable. But they are focused on the end point of the changes which they advocate, and have very little to say about the process of change, about alternative paths of adjustment. They foresee an increase in overall social welfare, but offer no insight into the costs as well as the benefits, nor as to how those costs and benefits will be distributed. Thus the whole debate around NAFTA, arguably the pivotal point in the US turn toward globalization, was conducted in terms of computable general equilibrium models, focused as the name implies on a comparison of equilibria under the new and old trading regimes. Much more recently, and tragically, the sudden end of the Multi-Fibre Arrangement, which distributed the production of garment exports to the industrial world across developing countries, led to an abrupt concentration of production in Bangladesh, which the real estate market did not have time to anticipate. Production facilities moved into hazardous buildings, one of which collapsed, causing thousands of fatalities. Other tenants moved out of the building when it was condemned, but the garment manufacturer remained, fearing that if it moved they it miss the tight production deadlines imposed by the international brands and be blacklisted as a result, denied any contracts in the future.

This discussion leads to several distinct points. First, the foregoing argument implies that the Silicon Valley consensus has had the effect of divorcing the process of adjusting workers to jobs and to new technologies from the productive process itself. The result is that forms of learning and understanding which would facilitate worker adjustment are neglected. Most importantly, the key decisions which affect structural change – in technologies and in trade – are made by institutional actors who reap the benefits of these changes but escape the social cost. As a result, the costs are not only uncompensated, they easily go unrecognized as well and are not taken into account in the key decisions that determine the direction in which the economy evolves. This is true not only in the Silicon Valley consensus, but it was also true in the Washington consensus which preceded it. It was not true of institutional structures which emerged out of the first of the post-war policy paradigms, the "Keynesian consensus." In the early post-war decades, businesses were not free to lay off workers when they introduced new technologies or developed new patterns of trade. The restrictions on their ability to do so varied from country to country, but for the most part lay-offs required the consent of government or of worker representatives or both, and typically compensation was required as well. Nor were companies free to adjust wages so as to attract better-trained substitutes and thereby avoid providing training themselves or adjusting new technologies so that jobs were accessible to the existing labor force.

The institutional structures which the policy paradigm sustained forced adjustment to take place within the productive sector, closely linked to the production process. This was true not only in Western Europe and Latin America, where the Washington consensus has brought those institutions under particular scrutiny, but it was also true in the US, despite the efforts in the last several decades to paint the country as the paragon of a liberal market economy.

In the US of the early decades of the post-World War II period, union seniority rules imposed restrictions that made lay-off and discharge costly, and adjustments in the wage structure virtually impossible. The threat of union organization imposed these restraints even on non-union firms. Wage adjustments were further inhibited by federal government incomes policy: the policy involved statutory wage controls during the World War II and the Korean War periods which left a legacy that persisted in the 1950s. After formal controls were lifted, in the 1960s, the wage-price guidelines were promulgated by the President and enforced by, among other things, public shaming and regulatory and tax harassment which had a similar effect. Statutory controls were reinstituted once again in 1971 and only finally eliminated at the end of the decade (at which point, incidentally, the income shares at the top of the distribution began to diverge sharply and progressively from those which had prevailed in the earlier post-war decades).

Restrictions of this kind are not an ideal way to force companies to take into account the social costs of structural adjustment. Where individual firms compete with new companies which do not have any institutional obligations to the legacy of older forms of production, restrictions which force the enterprise to absorb the costs of structural adjustment jeopardize the efficiency and competiveness of the economy. Obviously this problem is more serious in an open, global economy than in the relatively closed economies in which the Keynesian paradigm was conceived. But, as argued by Piore and Schrank (2016), the general systems of labor inspection in Southern Europe and Latin America have the administrative flexibility to adjust the regulations to accommodate competitive pressures of this kind. And a similar flexibility was introduced into the US system by the collective bargaining which generated the restrictions in the first place.

The point here, however, is not to promote a revival of the Keynesian paradigm nor of the particular institutions which it gave rise to and sustained; it is to use the contrast between Keynesian and the prevailing policy paradigms to overcome the limits of the frameworks in which policy is currently conceived, and to widen the range of approaches with which we can respond to the political pressures to which existing policy are giving rise. The institutions of the Keynesian period are not irrelevant here, but the world has changed so that they cannot be uncritically recreated. What is more relevant is the critical spirit which Keynes brought to the policy process.

This endeavor would, I submit, be worthwhile at any time. But as noted earlier, it seems particularly important at the current moment, which in so many ways resembles the inter-war period where public policy was caught by surprise, unprepared and ill-equipped to respond to the political reaction against globalization. In that earlier period, economic policy was paralyzed by an intellectual impasse between market liberalism and Marxist historical materialism, diametrically opposed to each other, but each deterministic in a way which left little room for policy innovations to address the crisis. What is most unsettling is the way in which this dichotomy is reproduced in the contrast between the Silicon Valley consensus, which is after all technologically deterministic in the way that Marxism was – however different the technological trajectory which it thinks we are forced to accommodate – and the Washington consensus, which is basically a revival of the deterministic market liberalism of the earlier period. In this context, the great contribution of the Keynesian paradigm is the notion that there is room for action. And it is that aspect of Keynes that we need to recover today.

A second point which emerges from our analysis is also captured by Keynes, in his famous dictum: "In the long run, we are all dead." The point in this context is that the dominant policy paradigms, particularly that of globalization, have focused on the far horizon, where we reach a new, long-run equilibrium without recognizing the process through which we get there or the path which we follow in doing so. They do not recognize the possibility that there may be alternative adjustment trajectories or, indeed, that the end point might not be independent of the adjustment process. Nor do they recognize that the process may be more or less rapid, more or less spread out over time, in ways that are critical to the welfare impact of change and, not incidentally given the present moment, to the political tolerance for the policies which promote it.

Finally, more broadly and more fundamentally, we have failed to recognize and take responsibility for the role which public policy has paid in putting us where we now are. We have subscribed to a kind of technological determinism and ignored the role of the federal government through its financing of research and development that contributes to the upskilling of jobs, and then facilitating an institutional environment which dampens pressures to prepare the labor force to do the jobs which public policy has promoted.

REFERENCES

Berger, Suzanne (2013). "Puzzles from the First Globalization," in Miles Kahler and David Lake (eds), *Politics in New Hard Times*. Ithaca, NY, USA and London, UK: Cornell University Press, pp. 150–168.

Brooks, Frederick (1975). *The Mythical Man-Month*. Reading, MA: Addison-Wesley.

Cavaco, Sandra, Denis Fougère and Julien Pouget (2013). "Estimating the Effect of a Retraining Program on the Re-employment Rate of Displaced Workers," *Empirical Economics*, 44 (1): 261–287.

Doeringer, Peter and Michael Piore (1971). *Internal Labor Markets and Manpower Analysis*. Lexington, MA: Heath.

Hall, Peter (1993). "Policy Paradigms, Social Learning, and the State: The Case of Economic Policymaking in Britain," *Comparative Politics*, 25 (3): 275–296.

Iskander, Natasha and Nichola Lowe (2010). "Hidden Talent: Tacit Skill Formation and Labor Market Incorporation of Mexican Immigrant Workers in the United States," *Journal of Planning Education and Research*, 30 (2): 132–146.

Jacobson, Louis, Robert J. LaLonde and Daniel G. Sullivan (1993). "Earnings Losses of Displaced Workers," *American Economic Review*, 83 (4): 685–709.

Jacobson, Louis, Robert J. LaLonde and Daniel G. Sullivan (2005). "Is Retraining Displaced Workers a Good Investment?," *Economic Perspectives*, 29 (2): 47–66.

Kletzer, Lori G. and William L. Koch (2004). "International Experience with Job Training: Lessons for the United States," in Christopher J. O'Leary, Robert A. Straits, and Stephen A. Wandner (eds), *Job Training Policy in the United States*. Kalamazoo, MI: Upjohn Institute, pp. 245–287.

MacKenzie, Donald A. (2006). *An Engine, Not a Camera: How Financial Models Shape Markets*. Cambridge, MA: MIT Press.

Piore, Michael J. and Andrew Schrank (2016). "Root Cause Regulation," Unpublished manuscript.

Polanyi, Karl (1944). *The Great Transformation*. Boston, MA: Beacon Press.

Ruiz, Neil G. (2014). "The Philippine Emigration State: Facilitating Labor Export as Economic Development Policy," Working Paper, prepared for APSA 2014 Annual Meetings.

Index